MALE ON MALE RAPE

The Hidden Toll of Stigma and Shame

MALE ON MALE RAPE

The Hidden Toll of Stigma and Shame

MICHAEL SCARCE

FOREWORD BY
WILLIAM B. RUBENSTEIN, J.D.

 **INSIGHT BOOKS**

PLENUM PRESS • NEW YORK AND LONDON

Library of Congress Cataloging in Publication Data

Scarce, Michael.
   Male on male rape: the hidden toll of stigma and shame / Michael Scarce; foreword by
William B. Rubenstein.
      p.   cm.
   Includes bibliographical references and index.
   ISBN 0-306-45627-3
   1. Male rape—United States. 2. Male rape—United States—Psychological aspects. 3.
Male rape victims—United States. 4. Sex crimes—United States. I. Title.
HV6561.S32   1997
362.88′3′0810973—dc21   97-25772
                                                                                          CIP

ISBN 0-306-45627-3

© 1997 Michael Scarce
Insight Books is a Division of Plenum Publishing Corporation
233 Spring Street, New York, N.Y. 10013-1578
http://www.plenum.com

An Insight Book

10 9 8 7 6 5 4 3 2 1

Printed in the United States of America

To the memory of Clyde Franklin
and
for Willa Young—my trusted friend and colleague

FOREWORD

Although my focus is on the rape of women, I do not mean to suggest that men are not raped. The general invisibility of the problem of male rape, at least outside the prison context, may reflect the intensity of stigma attached to the crime and the homophobic reactions against its gay victims. In some respects the situation facing male rape victims today is not so different from that which faced female victims about two centuries ago.

Susan Estrich, *Real Rape* (1986)

*I*n 1984, a classmate of mine at Harvard Law School took a seminar from Professor Susan Estrich on gender and the criminal law. Professor Estrich was in the midst of writing her pathbreaking study *Real Rape*. The seminar served as a forum for the discussion of a variety of rape-related issues, many of which later found voice in Estrich's book. My friend proposed to write his seminar paper on adult male rape and set out to find the legal materials to complete the paper. Weeks transpired, and though I knew him to be working diligently, little developed. Although my friend wrote the paper, his primary conclusion was that little or no attention had been paid to this problem by society, much less by the legal system.

The following year, 1985, I signed up for Professor Estrich's course and myself took up the gauntlet. I began to dig further and wrote a seminar paper expanding on my friend's earlier research and conclusions. Since then—for the succeeding 12 years—I have thought about bringing this initial research to fruition by publishing a paper on the legal aspects of male rape. Though distracted repeatedly by other projects during these years, I have always maintained a box in my office labeled "Male Rape." Each year I toss dozens of newspaper clippings, legal cases, magazine articles, and other materials into the box. With each passing year, the box becomes heavier, and the thought of tackling the project more daunting. Nonetheless, I have been amazed that in these many years, no one else has attempted a comprehensive survey of this subject—and thus I hesitate to throw my box away. The subject of male rape has long been something like a stack of disparate snapshots desperately in need of someone to sit down and arrange them into a photo album.

With this wonderful book, Michael Scarce now gives us that album. And with remarkable results. This volume accomplishes a whole series of initial milestones in the study of adult male rape. A central and critical aspect of the book is that it grows out of the actual experiences of rape survivors; the book incorporates the voices of these survivors—including the author himself—discussing what they endured. But importantly, the book does not stop there. It brings together and analyzes a set of statistical data concerning the phenomenon. It analyzes the obstacles to better understanding of adult male rape: individuals frightened to report the crime lest they be considered unmanly; social services providers not trained or equipped to handle male survivors; a legal system—from police and court personnel to the rape laws themselves—unfamiliar with male rape and unsure of how to deal with it. And Scarce offers concrete recommendations concerning how these barriers ought to be addressed. Scarce is also notably sensitive that his study of male rape supplement, and in no way detract from, the study of the rape of women; Scarce's book builds on the pioneering work of feminist scholars like Susan Brownmiller, Catherine McKinnon, and Susan Estrich. With this volume, Scarce has begun to provide a paradigm for the study of male rape. This important overview will, one hopes, be the beginning of a wide new discourse in the whole variety of fields with which the subject of male rape intersects.

In my own field—law—three issues seem most salient. First, and perhaps most importantly to the male rape survivor, personnel throughout the entire legal system must be trained to respond sensitively to incidents of male rape. We cannot expect the survivor of such a crime to report it if he anticipates ridicule or a lack of respect or response. Individuals ranging from 911 operators through judges themselves must be trained to appreciate the fact that men are raped and to deal appropriately with such crimes when confronted by them. Second, criminal laws must provide appropriate and significant sanctions for those who sexually assault adult males. Traditionally, rape law only understood female victims and male perpetrators and defined rape narrowly with reference to penetration of the vagina. Obviously, such a crime could not encompass forced sexual assault of men. Throughout the 1970s, many states adopted gender-neutral criminal laws; in so doing, most redefined rape as criminal sexual assault, thus recognizing, at least at the level of language, that men might be sexually assaulted. Nonetheless, many state criminal laws still define forcible sexual intercourse and forcible anal sex as different crimes. Sometimes the sentences vary. This raises the question of whether these acts should be different crimes, and if so, according to what rationale. Moreover, some laws that provide ancillary protections for "rape" survivors—such as rape shield statutes (which prohibit a survivor from being questioned about her prior sexual activity on the witness stand) and name protection laws (which prohibit publication of rape survivors' names)—remain gender specific in that they might literally apply only to the crime of rape or forcible sexual intercourse. Without adequate formal legal protection, it is unlikely male survivors will turn to this system for protection. What's worse, when male survivors do summon the courage to turn to the legal system, formal legal rules make consensual homosexual sex a crime in nearly 20 states; with fear that his allegations of force might not be believed, the male rape survivor faces the additional burden of fearing that he himself will be charged with sodomy!

Beyond the formal law, though, the legal system's background assumptions about male rape must be addressed. Traditionally, women who asserted that they had been raped—particularly those who accused men known to them—were disbelieved by the legal system. The attitudes of male judges and jurors often suggested that the women "must have wanted it." Convictions were therefore difficult and prosecutions few. Only through careful scholarship and persistent advocacy have feminists (in particular) brought to the understanding of rape a more appropriate response to the assertions of female survivors. It is interesting to consider how society generally, and legal actors in particular, will respond to the growing claims of male rape. In cases of "date rape," male complainants may well encounter responses similar to the traditional response to women—a sense that the gay man "must have wanted it." This response will be exacerbated by society's stereotypes concerning gay male promiscuity. And the legal system's response will be aggravated by a lack of sympathy for the sexual orientation of the male survivor. If the couple met in a bar and proceeded home to have oral sex, will a jury be willing to convict the man accused of forcing his partner into anal sex? Is the legal system prepared to handle a complaint from a gay man who had agreed to anal sex with a condom, but was forced to receive anal sex without a condom? Is that "rape"? In "stranger rape" situations, male survivors will not be assumed, like their female counterparts, to "have wanted it." Yet they might be met with wonderment that they could allow such a thing to happen to them since, after all, they are "men." Moreover, the line between these prototypes—between stranger and date rape—may be blurry; if, for example, two men are caught having sex in a public place, one may have an incentive to allege that he was forced into the sexual activity lest he be thought to be gay. How will legal actors assess such claims? Untangling the strands of homophobia, misogyny, and masculinity in these complicated reactions will prove a daunting task. This field is clearly one in need of increased attention and analysis.

Michael Scarce's volume is the initial foray into the field and sets forth a sound agenda for the future. It should be studied by everyone interested in rape and will be an important guidepost for future endeavors in the field. Most importantly, by having the courage to tell his and others' stories, Scarce couples his scholarly achievement with narrative power and commences the task of diminishing the human suffering that is brought about by forcible sex. Applause applause.

William B. Rubenstein
UCLA School of Law

PREFACE

*I*n the autumn of 1989, my friend Tom and I returned from summer break to begin our sophomore year at Ohio State University. We unpacked our belongings and settled into room 332 on the third floor of Bradley Hall, an undergraduate residence hall in the south area of campus. Each of the four floors of Bradley Hall was divided into two wings—one for women and one for men. Every wing had its own bathroom shared by the thirty-some residents living there. The rooms were not air conditioned and the dining hall food was less than stellar, but we were glad to be back on campus. The majority of the 32 men sharing our wing were first-year students, and they were equally as excited to be out on their own for the first time in their lives.

The return of students to campus ushered in a flurry of activity as Welcome Week programs and parties abounded around us. Tom and I had been elected president and vice president, respectively, of the Gay and Lesbian Alliance, our campus gay and

lesbian student organization. We held weekly meetings and organized events while striving to increase membership and politicize
the organization's activities. As GALA became more visible
throughout autumn quarter, the organization and its officers frequently appeared in the local media, promoting GALA and challenging homophobia on campus. As our visibility increased, so
did our Bradley Hall floormates' recognition that their two neighbors in room 332 were gay.

The stares and sneers from our 30 floormates began early in
the academic year and slowly escalated to verbal abuse, menac-
ing, and death threats. Messages were left on our answering machine, death threat notes were mailed to us, signs saying "Die
Faggots" were posted on our door, and as the intensity of the
intimidation increased, so did the frequency. Eventually the third
floor men's wing became so dangerous for Tom and I that the
university was forced to evacuate everyone, relocating the male
students and splitting them up across campus before someone
was bashed or killed.

Tom and I were moved to a nearby Ramada hotel, where we
lived in adjoining rooms for the last few weeks of spring quarter.
Both of us were escorted around campus by an armed security
guard hired by the university to protect us in the midst of hostility.
A protest of over 300 students erupted on campus soon thereafter.
Some students applauded the university's relocation decision
while others criticized campus officials for "pandering" to gay
activists. Still others blamed the university administration for allowing the situation to escalate to a level that necessitated such
drastic action. The third floor men's wing of Bradley Hall remained vacant, sealed and empty for the remainder of the academic year. A media frenzy ensued, with coverage from CNN to
the *New York Times*. This year was devastating for me as I struggled to survive in such an environment of hostility, humiliation,
and degradation. I lived in constant fear and frustration while the
weight of the events took its toll on my academic performance, my
relationships with family and friends, and my health.

The pain and violation I experienced during those months
before the relocation exceeded the incidents of homophobic ha-

rassment, however. During winter quarter of that academic year, Tom went home for a weekend visit and I was left alone. I was nervous about what could happen to me, what those men could do to hurt and punish me. It was a weekend in February and I decided to go dancing at a gay bar downtown to get out from under the suffocating weight of it all. I went alone, expecting to meet up with friends. The music was great, the bar was hopping, and I was having a wonderful time. As I danced I noticed a handsome man standing at the edge of the dance floor. He watched me for the duration of several songs, and smiled when I returned his stares. Later we talked and I learned he was from out of town, visiting Columbus on business. After an hour of conversation and heavy flirting, I invited him to return with me to my residence hall to escape the loud music, crowd, and cigarette smoke.

On returning to my room and continuing our conversation, we grew more physically intimate with each other. We were on my bed and began to kiss. Slowly he attempted to unzip my pants, and when I resisted, he became surprisingly rough. The more I pushed his hands away, the more aggressive he became until finally he used force. I asked him to stop, but was too embarrassed to raise my voice for fear that others next door or outside in the hallway would hear what was happening. I was afraid the men who hated me for being gay would use this situation as one more excuse to bash me. After several attempts to unfasten my jeans, he finally succeeded and yanked down my pants and underwear. What happened next is somewhat of a blur. I remember he forced me to lie on my stomach and climbed on top of me. He shoved his penis into me, without lubricant and without a condom. He held me down as I squirmed and fought, suppressing the urge to vomit. The physical pain of the anal penetration worsened as he continued and I began to cry. Soon thereafter I stopped moving in hopes he would just finish and get off me. Eventually he did stop, pulled up his pants, and left without saying a word.

The walls in Bradley Hall were very thin. The air vents in the doors were so large you could hear practically everything through those wide cracks, and many of my neighbors were home that night. One yell, one shout would have attracted the attention I needed to stop what was happening, but I could not bring myself to cry out. What would my floormates think? They already hated me for being queer, so how might they react if they responded to my cries for help and burst in on that lovely scene—a man on top of me, penetrating me? There was nothing I could do except lay there and go numb.

After he left I took a long shower, standing under the water and crying. The smell of him was on my body, his semen was between my legs, and I washed with soap over and over—lathering and rinsing continuously. I endured some minor rectal bleeding for the next day, and remained sore for many more. I did not contact the police or visit the hospital emergency room. I did not seek counseling or formal support, nor did I confide in any of my friends for several years. I was ashamed and embarrassed by what had happened, identifying the experience as a form of bad, regretted sex.

It was not until a year later that I began to make more sense of my experience. Through my academic coursework in OSU's Department of Women's Studies, I took an internship with the university's Rape Education and Prevention Program, where I conducted library research on rape and sexual violence. Gradually I came to terms with the fact that I had physically and mentally resisted that night a year ago in Bradley Hall and that I had been, in fact, raped. I now blame those 30 floormates for my rape as much as I blame the man who assaulted me. They created and shaped a space, both actively and through negligence, in which I was gagged, effectively silenced and unable to resist. Their intimidation weakened my spirit, lowered my self-worth, and forced me to appropriate a victim mentality that impeded me from regaining control of my life.

So very little has been published on the rape of adult males. As I began to search for documentation that resonated with my own assault, I was dismayed at being unable to locate many scholarly articles or even popular, first-person accounts of this form of sexual violence. Slowly, over the last few years, I have collected what scarce writing and research has been published about men raping men. Although I was raped by a gay male acquaintance, I discovered multiple other forms of same-sex rape between men—rape in prison institutions, assault by strangers, gang rape, familial rape, and more.

As my knowledge and understanding of the subject has grown, so has my interest in speaking and educating others about this form of sexual violence. When I speak publicly and conduct sensitivity trainings on male rape, I relate to others the story of my own assault, for it serves as a highly useful illumination of the ways in which homophobia and other forms of oppression create climates that foster and perpetuate rape behavior. My rape in Bradley Hall was simply a microcosm of the broader rape culture we all live in, a culture that encourages and condones sexual violence wielded as a tool for the subordination and control of those with less power in our society. Scores of male survivors have approached me after speaking engagements or contacted me later to share their own rape stories with me.

As I gradually became more involved in antirape work on campus, I began facilitating sexual assault workshops for the Rape Education and Prevention Program in classrooms, residence halls, student organizations, fraternities, and sororities. My involvement continued through graduate school, and after receiving my master's degree I was hired as the full-time coordinator of the program. My transformation from helpless victim to empowered survivor has refashioned my sense of self and purpose in life. The atrocities I have experienced provide a lens through which I am better able to see the complexity of injustices around me, and I have learned to harness the resulting anger in positive and productive ways that fuel my drive for social change. I wonder if the man who raped me realizes what he has created.

ACKNOWLEDGMENTS

I wish to thank a number of individuals for their support in the formulation and writing of this book. For their patience and editorial expertise: Frank K. Darmstadt and Charlie Cates; for their personal and professional encouragement of this project: Willa Young, T. J. Ghose, Dottie Painter, Verta Taylor, Clyde Franklin, Matthew Brown, Marc Conte, Randi Love, Maureen McCarthy, Jan Fonarow, Thomas Fletcher, Amy Rizor, Don Cook, John Stoltenberg, Andrea Dworkin, Doug Ferguson, Kate Husband, Jill Hornick, Kevin Simpson, Laura Campise and The Ohio State University Hospitals' Sexual Assault and Domestic Violence Advocate Program, the Ohio Coalition on Sexual Assault, Gloria McCauley and the Buckeye Region Anti-Violence Project, Peggy Reeves Sanday, Brian Oleksak, Hart Roussell, Staci

Swenson, and my family; for their written contributions: Christopher B. Smith, Robert E. Penn, and Rus Ervin Funk; and the incredibly courageous rape survivors who allowed me to ask them difficult and painful questions, trusted me with their words and experiences, and inspired me to believe in our ability to survive.

CONTENTS

ONE

INTRODUCTION

The following items are a sampling of male rape accounts from articles that have appeared in major newspapers in the last several years:

- ✓ In 1990 the *New York Times* reported that ethnic tensions among the soldiers of the crumbling Soviet army had resulted in male troops raping, hazing, and even murdering one another.
- ✓ Also in 1990, the *Washington Times* documented the rape of Kuwaiti men by Iraqi soldiers as part of the horrifying crimes suffered by the Kuwaitis during the encroaching Iraqi invasion.
- ✓ In October 1991, the *Houston Chronicle* reported on the trend of reported rapes of men in Philadelphia. Two assaults were highlighted in detail: a man raped by an acquaintance giving him a ride home from a bar, and a

man who was abducted and raped by three men while walking down the street to meet his spouse. The article also reported that 26 male rape survivors had been treated at a Boston hospital's counseling center within the previous year.

✓ The *Chicago Tribune* reported that in 1992 there were 320 victims of male rape in Britain. The article profiled the rape of one of these men, whom they call Ben. When Ben entered a London subway restroom, he was attacked by three men. One of the men wielded a knife and raped him in a toilet stall.

✓ On two occasions in July 1993, men were kidnapped outside of gay bars in Salt Lake City and gang-raped. One man was abducted and repeatedly raped for 3 days. Local gay and lesbian community leaders identified the gang rapes to be hate crimes.

✓ In July 1994, five African immigrant men, all delivery van drivers, stepped forward to accuse a police officer in Queens, New York, of raping them. The resulting court case drew national attention.

✓ In August 1995, 146 Chinese men and boys attempted to illegally immigrate to the United States aboard a smuggling ship. After being intercepted by the U.S. Coast Guard south of Hawaii, the smuggled passengers reported they had been repeatedly sexually assaulted by the smugglers. At least 35 of the passengers had contemplated killing themselves on board the ship.

✓ In December 1995, Baton Rouge police arrested a 58-year-old apartment complex security guard for allegedly raping an 18-year-old man after offering him a ride home from a local laundry. The guard drove the man to a parking lot and raped him at knife point. A police officer publicly commended the rape survivor for stepping forward and reporting the crime, and stated that adult male rape is probably the most underreported violent crime.

✓ A 19-year-old prisoner escaped from the Missouri Training Center after he had been raped repeatedly. On his

capture, the Missouri Supreme Court affirmed his conviction for the escape charge and concluded that conditions
of confinement do not justify escape.

As clearly demonstrated here, the practice of men raping men
occurs around the world in practically every environment, from
prisons and military organizations to small-town neighborhoods
and college campuses. Why, then, has so little attention been paid
to this form of sexual violence? This book aims to answer that
question and, in doing so, generate solutions to the invisibility and
silence surrounding the rape of adult males.

Presented here is the culmination of over 6 years of research,
personal experience, and professional work concerning the topic
of men raping men. In an attempt to explore the many facets of
this form of sexual violence, I have taken a decidedly interdisciplinary approach to a topic that is so rarely discussed. The
few book-length texts published in the last 20 years that include
the same-sex rape of men have focused primarily on psycho-
therapeutic treatment of adult male rape survivors. A more thorough analysis of the complex underpinnings of this violence
necessitates a broader examination of the social and cultural forces
embedded in science, politics, medicine, law, and history of sexual violence between men. The purpose of this book is to breach
a number of silences, to open a dialogue that must be set into
perpetual motion, for the more we speak of the violence that sur-
rounds us, the better we are prepared to tackle it.

After speaking at conferences, giving presentations in professional settings, and providing referrals to rape survivors and their
support people, numerous individuals have asked me for a reading list of materials on the topic of male rape that would be
accessible to a general audience, something appropriate for anyone seeking an introduction and overview of sexual violence
between men. Although I continually update a research bibliography of male rape literature that has predominantly been published in academic journals, there has been very little I could offer
in the way of accessible reading. Unfortunately, many of the more
popular articles that have appeared in magazines and newspapers

in recent years have been incredibly insensitive, overly sensational, homophobic, or written in a blame-the-victim tone.

In part, this book ambitiously attempts to begin to fill that void, with an intended audience consisting of anyone who possesses a personal or professional interest in learning more about the rape of men, including mental health professionals; law enforcement officials; academics in a variety of fields and disciplines; sexual assault crisis, intervention, treatment, or prevention organizations; health educators and public health professionals; and perhaps most importantly, male rape survivors and their support people.

The scope of this work on sexual violence, however, is not as inclusive. Just as no single book could possibly cover every aspect of men raping women, this book is by no means exhaustive in its examination of men raping men. The sexual assault of boys and teenage males is unfortunately not within the scope of this book. The topic of women raping men is also not included in this volume, although the rape of men by women is certainly possible and does occur with more frequency than previously believed. Only one chapter is specifically devoted to the rape of men in single-sex, institutional environments such as prisons and military organizations. Although same-sex rape in these environments may very well constitute the majority of male rape incidents, this book also addresses rape in noninstitutional settings. Again, this is in the interest of filling gaps in the existing body of literature, as much more research has been conducted on prison rape than the rape of men in other communities.

The method of research for the book consists of personal interviews with men who have been raped by men; case studies of male rape; reviews of medical and other scientific publications; examination of legal statutes and public policies related to sexual violence; analyses of film, television, and other media representations of the rape of men; and a collection of male rape reports from scores of newspapers and other periodicals from around the world. Analyses of these texts offer insight into the dense meanings and intricate complexities of sexuality, gender, and violence.

The 24 adult male rape survivors I have interviewed were

recruited through friends, service providers, professional conferences, and the Internet. Whenever possible, I conducted face-to-face interviews. I interviewed a number of survivors, especially those I met across the Internet, anonymously. Some telephoned my home at a predetermined time to be tape-recorded. Others responded directly through interactive, typed question–answer sessions on Internet relay chats and commercial services such as America Online. These men range in age from 20 to 42 years old. I was able to interview self-identified gay, bisexual, and heterosexual men, and men from a variety of racial and ethnic backgrounds. Two of the men were HIV positive; the remainder were either HIV negative or unsure of their status. All but three of the men were U.S. citizens, with one from Australia, one from England, and the other from India.

Although not all of the survivors are quoted or mentioned in this book, all of them contributed significantly to my understanding of sexual violence. They were incredibly brave and unconditionally frank in their willingness to answer uncomfortable questions and share their stories. Their names have been changed to protect their anonymity, and I refer to them throughout the book by fictional first names. The results of these interviews cannot be generalized to a large population, as they are not a random sample. They do, however, serve as useful case studies and demonstrate the diversity of meanings and reactions men have after being raped.

A methodology of comparison is utilized throughout the chapters, with an emphasis on similarity and difference between the ways in which various cultures, professions, and disciplines address, or fail to address, the rape of men. The purpose of this approach is not to determine whether or not, for example, certain forms of sexual violence are more devastating than others, or to suggest that one particular population is more prone to rape behavior than another. Rather, the process of comparison should map territories where new collaborations, solutions, and understandings can be reached for the benefit of everyone.

This book is structured into 14 chapters that critically examine same-sex rape from a number of standpoints. With this in mind I turn to an examination of the treatment of male rape in several fields. Chapter Two reviews the existing body of research that has been conducted on male rape in the last 15 years in an attempt to identify broad themes and recent trends. Chapter Three examines male rape in single-sex institutions such as prisons and military organizations, noting how these environments set the stage for an increased prevalence of male on male sexual violence and the politics that currently impede effective intervention efforts.

The tenuous dichotomy of "rape is not sex" makes sexual orientation an issue of primary concern in male rape, especially given the level of societal homophobia and complexity of sexual identities. Chapter Four explores how sexual orientation manifests as a power dynamic between men. Comparisons are conducted between the rape of gay men by gay men, straight men by straight men, straight men by gay men, and gay men by straight men. Chapter Six identifies and critically analyzes male rape content in several films, television programs, nonfiction texts, journalism reports, and other mass media. Analyses of these depictions and discussions of male rape reveal the popular fears and anxieties surrounding same-sex rape and male homosexuality, rape mythology, an intense level of social denial, and the interconnectedness of male rape, sexism, homophobia, classism, and racism.

The growing number of HIV infections in the United States and other countries underscores the concern of viral transmission during sexual assault. The ways in which male rape can be a vehicle for infection are outlined in Chapter Eight, coupled with guidelines for the assessment of a male survivor's risk of infection. Beyond the possibility of physical transmission of HIV via same-sex rape, the recent trend of HIV-biased male rape as a hate crime is discussed. Protocols for sensitive HIV test-counseling are offered. The overlapping areas between safer-sex education and rape education movements are identified as an important opportunity for increased collaboration.

Chapter Nine offers a critique of the history of medical insensitivity displayed toward male rape, an analysis of the scarce medical literature that discusses clinical treatment of male rape survivors, and the lack of forensic science procedures and protocols applicable to the rape of men. Turning to policy and law, Chapter Eleven explains how male rape is legally defined in the United States and abroad; the origin and history of their structure and function; and these laws' relationship to sodomy statutes, rape reform legislation, gay rights legislation, policymaking, and more. Chapter Thirteen tackles the positioning of male survivors and same-sex rape within the broader antirape movement. Born out of feminist organizing in the 1970s, the antirape movement has historically defined itself as by women, for women. The growing recognition of male victimization, however, has forced male rape into a hotly contested field of prioritizations, funding concerns, and political philosophies.

The concluding chapter outlines strategies for the creation of initiatives to address adult male rape. These include educational approaches, training of service providers, a call for more research and writing, prevention and risk-reduction work, lobbying and legal reform, approaches to public policy, grass-roots organization, interdisciplinary collaboration, and cultural transformation. Interspersed between appropriate chapters are four short essays (Chapters Five, Seven, Ten, and Twelve) written by male rape survivors to illuminate certain areas and lend validity to the whole of the book. Three appendixes follow the text and consist of a listing of male rape resources such as organizations and crisis hotlines; an extensive bibliography on the topic of adult male rape that includes scholarly articles, books, magazine pieces, and multimedia; and finally a compilation of U.S. legal statutes that define sexual assault. Particular attention is paid to the gender-specific and gender-neutral language of the statutes as they equate or distinguish between the rape of men and the rape of women.

LANGUAGE

My working definition of the word *rape* for this book is any penetration of a person's mouth, anus, or vagina, by a penis or any other object, without that person's consent. Throughout this book I also use the term *male rape* in reference to the act of an adult male raping an adult male. Unless carefully defined, the latter term may be semantically confusing, as many people remain unsure whether the *male* in *male rape* is an indicator of rapist, victim, or both. The use of *homosexual rape* to connote "men raping men" is further problematic in its emphasis on the root word *sex*, implying a more sexual than violent overtone. This (homo)sexual terminology also perpetuates the stereotypical notions that gay men are sexual predators or that only gay men rape other men.

When referring to those people who have experienced sexual violence and successfully escaped with their life, I choose to use the word *survivor* over *victim*. *Victimization* implies powerlessness and a lack of control, whereas *survivor* carries a measure of strength, perseverance, and empowerment. Most legal terminology still uses the word *victim* as a technical term to define a person against whom a crime has been committed. With the exceptions of legal instances and situations where someone who has been raped did not live through the assault, I employ *survivor* as a constructive preference.

THE GENDERING OF RAPE

As social problems emerge and attract increasing attention, the struggle to create a common language that accurately names and defines those problems is inevitable. Such is the case with male rape. Although the rape of men is not a new phenomenon, it certainly has not attracted the same amount or kind of public attention as the rape of women. From this difference we presently find ourselves in the necessary position of using the adjective *male* as a modifier to *rape* so as to communicate "men raping men." In most cases, the stand-alone term of rape is automatically presumed to involve a male perpetrator and a female victim. The gender-specification of *male rape* and other terms such as *male nurse, female judge,* or *women's football* usually occurs when such terms deviate from traditional expectations of male-typical and female-typical associations. The general belief persists that either men cannot be raped, or if they are, so few men are raped that it becomes a freak occurrence, an act so bizarre that it bears no formal similarity to the commonplace rape of women in society.

The more recent gendering of rape as an act of violence against women has occurred for a variety of reasons, not least of which is the fact that approximately 90% of rapes involve female victims. The bulk of political progress and organizational response to rape must be credited to feminist social movement activity since the 1960s, including the understanding that rape is an act of violence and power rather than an expression of sexual passion. But where do the 5 to 10% of rape victims who are male fall in this realm of women-centered knowledge and practice? Very often they slip through the cracks of an already overburdened and underfunded social service network and a culture that believes the rape of men to be a laughable impossibility.

The rape of men in our communities is perhaps the most underreported and unaddressed violent crime. The intense shame and stigma attached to adult male rape arguably exceeds that of the rape of women, which has become a widely acknowledged and public issue only within the last 20 years. Much more has been written, discussed, and documented on the rape of boys, in fact, than adult males. This willingness to address violence against children more easily than that against adults serves a specific function. It feeds into our collective denial, a refusal to recognize that men are not the ultimate providers and protectors of themselves and others. We can easily believe that a child might not be able to defend himself against an adult, but the sexual violation of a man may come as something of a shock, for men have traditionally been expected to defend their own boundaries and limits while maintaining control, especially sexual control, of their own bodies. When this does not occur, when men are raped by other men, society tends to silence and erase them rather than acknowledge the vulnerability of masculinity and manhood.

Quantifications of male rape would indicate no epidemic of men raping men, for few men who are raped report their assault to authorities. When statistics are compiled from law enforcement crime records, male rape is frequently absent or considered statistically insignificant. A vicious circle then ensues: Men who are raped feel isolated and alone, as if they are the only ones to have ever suffered from this violence. Their failure to report reflects their isolation and embarrassment. Police and other authorities receive few reports of male rape, so they believe it is not a problem in their community. The lack of visibility reinforces the male rape survivor's sense of isolation, and the cycle of silence is perpetuated.

In these and many other respects, the rape of men is not altogether unlike the rape of women. Both are frequently downplayed or dismissed. Both are wedded to systems of power, male dominance, and sexual culture. The popular belief that a woman who is raped really wanted it, or participated willingly only to later recant her story, also translates into the ways in which male rape survivors are judged. Through an inability to distinguish sex from rape, our society often treats same-sex rape with the same disgust and hatred as homosexuality. This homophobia plays a key role in the shame and negligence that have surrounded male rape.

Exactly what are the processes that render the rape of men invisible? Why do so few men report their rape experiences? How do the rape of women and the rape of men intersect, if at all? How can we foster an environment that addresses male rape with compassion, respect, and justice? The time for taking an unflinching look at male rape is long overdue, as is the creation of a network to research, treat, and prevent this violence.

TWO

UNCOVERING MALE RAPE

$\mathcal{S}$everal months after I was raped, I felt a strong need to learn more about rape and sexual violence in an attempt to make sense of what had happened to me. In part, this feeling was related to a sense of isolation. At that time I knew of no other men who had been sexually assaulted, but I believed I must not be the only person to have endured the experience of same-sex sexual violence. When I returned to campus my junior year at Ohio State, I headed directly to the library and spent many hours searching for any and all literature related to adult male rape. I found plenty of articles and books written on the subject of childhood assault, but very little on the rape of adult males. What little I did uncover was highly academic and impersonal, articles from scholarly journals that did not resonate with me on an emotional or practical level. Over time I have collected and photocopied every newspaper, magazine, and research article that I have come across in hopes of piecing together a larger picture of men raping men.

While on vacation in Toronto in 1991, I found a small, hard-back book published in England by Gay Men's Press. That book, *Male Rape: Breaking the Silence on the Last Taboo* by Richie Mc-Mullen, provided me with some of the material I had sought—case studies of men who had been raped, social explanations for rape behavior, and concrete discussions of victim aftermath. McMullen was one of the founders of a London-based organization called Survivors, which operates a male rape hotline and support groups for men who have been sexually assaulted. His experiences with Survivors gave his writing a sense of honesty and reality. I found validation within those pages, despite the book's brevity and British focus. Unfortunately, that book is now out of print. Richie McMullen's work scratched the surface of male rape, attempting to make sense of this violence despite the confusion and silence that surround the issue. I hope to continue that work here. Pulling together the sparse literature that has been published on male rape is an exercise in frustration for a number of reasons that will become evident, but my intent here is to summarize what we know and don't know about male rape and translate it from the dusty shelves of academic journals to a broader audience.

A BIT OF HISTORY

Within the broader context of physical assault, men are more likely than women to be victims of violent crimes. Rape and domestic violence are two of the few exceptions to this likelihood, and the popular perception that rape is a form of violence committed only against women has contributed to the lack of writings published on the topic of male rape. Academic research on male rape has been conducted only since the late 1970s with any regularity, first bolstered by feminist social movements that directed attention toward sexual violence. Although the majority of this attention involved men raping women, the development and dissemination of the idea that rape is an exercise in power began to shed light on the rape of men as well, particularly in prisons and other correctional facilities.

In her landmark book published in 1975, *Against Our Will*, feminist scholar Susan Brownmiller included an essay on the same-sex rape of men in prisons, making connections between the differences in power that exist between men and women as parallel to the power imbalance between men in single-sex institutions: "Prison rape is generally seen today for what it is: an acting out of power roles within an all-male, authoritarian environment in which the weaker, younger inmate, usually a first offender, is forced to play the role that in the outside world is assigned to women."[1] Growing attention to the rape of men in prisons created a public acknowledgment that men can, and are, sexually assaulted by other men, opening the door for other men to step forward and report they had been raped outside of prison walls. The resulting recognition that rape in prison may differ in significant ways from rape outside of prison soon attracted the interest of a handful of social scientists.

In his 1979 book *Men Who Rape*, psychologist Nicholas Groth devoted 22 pages of his work to men who raped, or had been raped by, other men, reflecting the growing recognition of male rape among researchers and academics.[2] This section of Groth's book marks a noteworthy departure from the previous research that had been conducted on same-sex rape in that the majority of rape survivors he interviewed were assaulted in such nonprison settings as hitchhiking along highways, outdoors in the woods or at a beach, on the street, in the victim's home, in a parking garage, and at the victim's place of employment. Whereas past work had focused almost entirely on rape and its relationship to homosexuality behind bars, Groth's interviews laid important groundwork for a contemporary understanding of the larger picture of power dynamics and sexual violence between men in noninstitutional community settings through his case study analyses.

Apart from some of the theoretical essays such as Susan Brownmiller's that delve into the social meanings attached to male rape, the majority of published work on men raping men is more quantitative in nature—counting and measuring aspects of the rape of men. The investigators who have studied male rape have been primarily grounded in the fields of psychology, criminology, and epidemiology, and for the most part have been located in the United States and England. Taken as a whole, the approximately 20 studies that have been published in the last three decades often yield conflicting results and draw contradictory conclusions in their quantification of the details of male rape. (See Table One.)

These contradictions are frequently the result of differing methods used to gather information. For example, researchers of male rape have conducted studies in a variety of environments—prisons and other correctional facilities, military organizations, college campuses, emergency rooms, rape crisis centers, recruitment from newspaper ads, outpatient health clinics, mental health facilities, private psychological practices, law enforcement agencies, and random community samples. The environment in which male rape occurs, as well as the location from which male rape survivors are recruited for questioning, strongly influences the results of male rape research. For example, a study conducted by Dr. Arthur Kaufman of the University of New Mexico School of Medicine found that male rape survivors seen at emergency rooms have a much higher incidence of nongenital physical trauma than female rape survivors.[3] Male rape survivors, however, are less likely to seek treatment for their sexual assault because of shame and may only visit an emergency room if serious physical injuries accompany the rape.

Specific information about the rape may also come from a variety of sources—written questionnaires, oral interviews, police reports, medical charts, court records, client service statistics, and clinical psychological files. These representations of the assault will influence the data that are collected during male rape research. In this respect, research has focused on secondary sources of a professional's interpretation of male rape cases rather than information obtained directly from the survivor, described in his own words, defining his own experience.

Table One
Comparison of Male Rape Research Findings

Authors	No. of subjects	Recruited from	Stranger assailant (%)	Multiple assailant (%)	Weapon used (%)
Doan and Levy, 1983	29	Hospital emergency room	5/8 (63%) cases documented	3/8 (38%) cases documented	2/29 (6.9%)
Forman, 1982	12	Law enforcement	8 cases (67%)	2 cases (17%)	3 cases (25%)
Frazier, 1993	74	Hospital rape crisis center	32/62 (52%) of respondents	20/65 (31%) of respondents	15/35 (43%) of respondents
Goyer and Eddleman, 1984	13	Military nonincarcerated	Not reported	11/13 (85%)	Not reported
Groth and Burgess, 1980	6	Outpatient mental	3/6 (50%)	1/6 (17%)	Not reported
Hickson et al., 1994	212	Newspaper and other	54/212 (25%)	24/212 (11.3%)	Not reported
Hillman et al., 1991	28	Rape crisis organization	Not reported	Mean no. was 2.8, range 1–8	13/28 armed (46%)
Huckle, 1995	22	Forensic psychiatric service	12/22 (55%)	6/22 (27%)	Not reported
Kaufman et al., 1980	14	Hospital ER	Not reported	7/14 (50%)	Not reported
Lacey and Roberts, 1991	13	Sexual assault referral center	5/13 (38.5%)	3/13 (23%)	3/13 (23%)
Lipscomb et al., 1992	19	Nonhospital clinic	Not reported	10/19 (52.6%)	11/19 (57.9%)
Mezey and King, 1989	22	Newspaper ads	4/22 (18%)	Not reported	2/22 (9%)
Myers, 1989	14	Private practice	Not reported	4/14 (29%)	Not reported
Sorenson et al., 1987	107	Random community sample	20/107 (18.7%)	Not reported	2/107 (1.9%)

THE LARGER PICTURE

An overview of this body of research reveals certain trends and recurrent themes, and simultaneously draws attention to the weaknesses and omissions of the knowledge that has been generated from such inquiry. Although a great deal of progress has been made in investigating male rape, there are still many voids and unanswered questions. What few generalizations have been formulated about the rape of men offer a glimpse of the breadth and depth this violence bears. The following summaries of male rape characteristics are an extrapolation of this body of research, generating a larger picture of the problem.

Incidence and Prevalence

Incidence can be defined as the number of new rapes that have occurred in a given time period among a certain population, whereas prevalence refers to the number of rapes that have ever occurred among a population. In terms of incidence, studies of male rape in the United States and United Kingdom indicate that somewhere between 5 and 10% of all reported rapes in any given year involve male victims. The number and percentage of rapes involving male victims is presumably much higher than this, however, as this estimate reflects only *reported* rapes. Several researchers, including Arthur Kaufman, mentioned earlier, and Deryck Calderwood, the former director of the Human Sexuality Program at New York University, have indicated that male rape survivors are much less likely to report their rape victimization than are female survivors.[4]

Some of the evidence supporting this estimation of 5 to 10% includes:

✓ In 1982, Dr. Bruce Forman of the University of South Dakota School of Medicine published his research findings on 212 rape victims in South Carolina, 5.7% of whom were male.[5]

✓ In a large-scale study called the Los Angeles Epidemiologic Catchment Area Project conducted in 1987, 7% of the males reported having been sexually assaulted at least once as an adult.[6]

✓ Of the 528 clients seen at the San Francisco Rape Treatment Center in 1990, 9.8% were men.

✓ In 1992, the Sexual Assault Center in Hartford, Connecticut, logged 400 calls from men out of a total of 4058.[7]

✓ In 1993, Margaret Henderson, director of the Orange County Rape Crisis Center in North Carolina, reported that 7% of the 147 victims assisted at her agency were men.[8]

✓ The Ohio Coalition on Sexual Assault, polling rape crisis organizations across their state in 1994, found males to constitute 7% of clients served.[9]

✓ Of the average 250 rape survivors seen each year at Beth Israel Hospital's rape crisis program, about 10% are male.

✓ According to the Bureau of Justice Statistics' National Crime Victimization Survey, of the rapes reported to the survey in 1994, 5% of rape victims aged 12 and older were males (1994 is the most recent year for which these data are available).[10]

✓ In addition to the above findings, this 5 to 10% range has been confirmed by other studies.[11,12]

Rapists

The sexual orientation of men who rape other men tends to be heterosexual (either self-identified or as later identified by the men they assault). The rapists are usually in their early to mid-20s at the time of the assault, and are primarily white. Virtually every study indicates that men rape other men out of anger or an attempt to overpower, humiliate, and degrade their victims rather than out of lust, passion, or sexual desire.

Victims

Men who are raped by other men tend to be in their late teens to late 20s at the time of assault. In terms of race, when noted in research studies, African-American male rape survivors in these studies were overrepresented relative to the percentage of African Americans in the communities in which the studies were conducted. In terms of sexual orientation, when documented in research studies, gay men seem to have been raped at much higher rates than heterosexual men.

Assaults

As for the rapist and victim relationship, research studies draw conflicting conclusions regarding the predominance of stranger or acquaintance rape. At a 1996 conference on male rape at DeMontfort University in England, Michael King, head of psychiatry at the Royal Free School of Medicine, presented his research findings that male rape victims are usually attacked in their homes by someone they know. This correlates with earlier studies indicating that weapons are frequently used in male rape, and at a much higher frequency than in the rape of women. Perhaps rapists feel they need an additional form of power to rape other men, whereas psychological fear and intimidation may be enough to overpower many women. Even if a weapon is not used, some use of force or threat of force is almost invariably employed, except in cases where the victim is asleep or unconscious. Multiple assailants also seem to be more prevalent in the rape of men than women. With regard to anatomical site in male rape cases, virtually every study of male rape survivors found that anal penetration of the victim was the most common form of assault. Oral penetration was the next most common assault of men. In some instances, the assailant took the victim's penis into his own mouth or anus, or masturbated the victim. Several studies and news media stories include reports of an attacker forcing one male victim to penetrate another male victim.

IMPACT

There is no single, typical, emotional response that every man will exhibit after he has been assaulted. Some may appear calm and rational, others may exhibit anger, depression, or hysteria. Still others may socially withdraw and appear nonresponsive. All of these behaviors should be deemed normal, as each individual will react to crisis situations in ways that are related to his own identity, culture, and background. Several of the following reactions overlap and intersect, such as anger and self-blame, for example.

Stigma and Shame

Perhaps the most powerful effect of male rape is the stigma, shame, and embarrassment that follows as survivors begin to cope with what has happened to them. The role of self-blame in this shame is prominent, as many male survivors feel a sense of guilt for their assault and feel embarrassed that they were in some way responsible for their victimization. The involvement of body parts that our culture deems to be "sexual" or "private" may also hamper survivors' ability to speak openly about their experience. The general public's equation of rape with sex may also bring on a shame attached to homosexuality. Nathan, a rape survivor I interviewed, explained, "I'm not sure I'll ever tell any of my family or my friends. They would probably understand, but I'd just be too embarrassed. I'd always be wondering if they thought less of me."

Guilt

Shame is most often accompanied by a sense of guilt. Many rape survivors feel as if some action on their part provoked the rape, or that they did not effectively resist to avoid the rape altogether. Usually the shame and stigma mentioned above stems from some form of this guilt and self-blame. As one survivor I interviewed expressed, "It really upset me that I let him do that to me. I can't believe I didn't find a way to make it stop at some point while it was happening. I should've been able to, I really should have." Male survivors' sense of self-blame is not entirely internal, unfortunately. All too often, the friends, family, and service providers of male rape survivors project their judgment of responsibility on the survivor. Marcus, a man who was raped is his early 20s, told me that his rape "began a period, which continues to the present day, almost 5 years now, of a declining relationship with my mother. She bitterly fought against me and the idea that it had happened. When she did kind of admit it had happened, it suddenly became my fault."

Rape Trauma Syndrome and Posttraumatic Stress Disorder

Rape trauma syndrome, a form of posttraumatic stress disorder, was first described in 1974 as a condition affecting female survivors of sexual assault. Professor of Nursing Ann Burgess and Professor of Sociology Dr. Larry Holmstrom at Boston College, who specialize in the research and treatment of sexual violence, initially coined the term *rape trauma syndrome*.[13] They divided the syndrome into two distinct phases: acute and long term. The acute phase is marked by a period of extreme disorganization and upheaval in the survivor's life following the rape. Some of the impact reactions during the acute phase are: physical trauma, skeletal muscle tension, gastrointestinal irritability, genitourinary disturbance, and a wide gamut of emotional reactions. The long-term phase consists of survivors' attempt to reorganize their lifestyles.

The impacted reactions most noted in this phase are: increased motor activity (such as changing residence or traveling for support), disturbing dreams and nightmares, and "traumatophobia," which includes such responses as fear of indoors if the survivor was raped in bed, fear of outdoors if the survivor was raped outside of his home, fear of being alone, fear of crowds, fear of people walking behind him, and a fear of engaging in or resuming consensual sexual activity. Since the initial identification of rape trauma syndrome in 1974, psychological and legal researchers have extended the condition to male survivors as well. In a 1989 study by Michael Myers, a psychiatrist with the Department of Psychiatry at the University of British Columbia, Vancouver, the most common form of psychiatric diagnoses was posttraumatic stress disorder. Dr. Myers described in detail one of his patients, whom he calls "Mr. B":

> Mr. B had flashbacks of the repeated acts of sodomy, rectal pain, nightmares of suffocation and death, and marked detachment from his family and friends. He suffered weeks of initial insomnia and fears of sleeping alone. Showering became an ordeal for him as he feared someone behind the shower curtain attacking him. In order to sleep, he had to lay on his side—lying prone or supine made him feel vulnerable to another attack.[14]

Andrew, a survivor I interviewed who was raped by multiple assailants, explained similar effects that continue to haunt him:

> I don't think I ever leave my house without feeling some fear. Even if I don't consciously think about it, there's that sense within me that I'm at risk, especially when it's dark. I'm very hypervigilant. Nothing goes on around me that I'm not aware of. I have a hard time even paying attention. I get distracted very easily because I'm always watching. At night when I go out I am very careful about where I go. Everywhere I go I have plotted out in my mind very quickly an escape route. That if I feel threatened, I know I've already calculated it's only this many steps to here where I know it would be safe, or there are people over here and if I holler loud enough they'll hear me. I had a security system put in my house and the minute I come home I turn it on. I still wake up in the middle of the night, terrified. I wake up with that taste in my mouth. I can taste it again,

that smell again. Sometimes at night I wake up and—the pain, anally—it feels like a knife going through me to where I almost jump straight up. When that happens, the nights are still pretty hard. I usually don't go back to sleep.

A study of 22 male rape survivors conducted by researcher P. L. Huckle at the South Wales Forensic Psychiatric Service found similar patterns of posttraumatic stress disorder.[15] The effects of rape trauma syndrome can last a lifetime, especially in the absence of therapeutic treatment and a strong social support system from family or loved ones.

Amnesia

When the trauma of rape becomes more than a man can psychologically bear, amnesia may provide a defensive wall by protecting the survivor from his own memory of the assault. One case study of this form of amnesia has been observed and extensively documented by psychologists Alfred Kaszniak and colleagues of the University of Arizona. They described a 27-year-old white male who had been brought to a hospital emergency room after he was found lying in the street. He could not recall where he was from, his name, or any details of his recent or past history. After a series of hypnosis sessions, the man gradually regained his memories, including details of his recent rape. He had been offered work by two men who then drove him to a remote location where they all smoked marijuana. Once impaired, the man was raped at gunpoint. Kaszniak and colleagues deduced that their patient had been faced with such extreme psychological stress and turmoil that "the amnesia seemed to be protecting him from the guilt and shame that later surfaced."[16] Their work illustrates the extreme level of emotional turmoil that many men experience as the result of such trauma, and an example of one way in which male survivors dissociate from their pain as a protective mechanism.

This dissociation can also be the function of behaviors that take place outside the survivor's normal consciousness, constituting a kind of blackout. Andrew related his pattern of experiences with dissociation:

> *I know that some of the times that I dissociate, those are some of the times if not all that I usually go out to find a man to hurt me again. I usually have no idea where or with whom. It took me a while to figure out I was doing that. When I dissociate, I'm usually aware that I've lost a period of time. I noticed that after it happened, anally I would be hurting and I couldn't figure out why. I finally put the pieces together with the psychologist I'm seeing. At times, after I dissociated, I would find blood in my underwear. At first I thought it was just a psychosomatic sort of thing. Then I realized those were the times that I go find someone to hurt me that way again. I just can't remember doing it. I ask myself why I do that and I'm not sure. I really feel like it's the only thing that I'm good for. I feel like I deserve it.*

Dissociation can be an emergency coping mechanism, but can also continue long term as a recurrence of behaviors that are self-destructive, providing a vehicle for acting out the rape experience in unhealthy ways.

Hostility and Anger

In one comparative study of male and female rape survivors at the Hennepin County Medical Center in Minneapolis, psychologist Patricia Frazier discovered that male survivors were rated as more depressed and hostile than female survivors immediately following the rape.[17] Other studies have reported similar findings.[18,19] A man who has been raped may feel a great deal of anger toward the rapist, toward those support persons closest to him after the assault, toward a society that does not recognize or validate his experience, toward service providers who are inadequately prepared to meet his needs, or toward himself for not preventing the assault in the first place. Although anger can certainly be a healthy and valid reaction to sexual violence, survivors may need assistance in managing their anger by channeling it into productive action.

Denial

One study conducted at a hospital emergency room in New Mexico found male survivors were more likely than female survivors to use denial and control their reactions to the assault.[20] Similar to the previously mentioned case study of amnesia, denial may serve a male survivor who is incapable of managing the reality of his assault. Denial of male rape may be much easier for men than women, as the rape of men is rarely addressed in highly public ways. If there is a general belief in our society that male rape is either impossible or never happens, there is little challenge or contradiction to a male survivor's attempt to refute his rape experience. Denial becomes an especially easy and effective tool for avoiding the emotional pain and traumatic memory of sexual violation. Marcus, a rape survivor I interviewed, remembered:

> *I pretty rapidly had moved into a state of denial about its effects on my life even though I look back on that period now and see how tense I was all the time, how I started to pull in and really resist involvement in many important parts of my whole life. I kept walking around afraid that everybody could sort of see what had happened. I stayed in that condition for about 9 months and really just feeling, like, I'm fine. So I didn't even talk with too many people about it.*

Even a lack of resources or professionals who specialize in the treatment and recovery of male rape survivors may reinforce a conclusion that because male rape remains hidden, it must not really exist. Survivors may be able to easily self-identify with the invisibility of male rape to the point of not recognizing or acknowledging their experience altogether. Later in my interview with Marcus, he told me that calling the local rape crisis hotline had never entered his mind as an available option:

> *A friend of mine was a rape counselor. It never even occurred to her that I should call a crisis line and it never occurred to me until years later. I think it's because it was Bay Area Women Against Rape. That's probably the main reason—the focus of the crisis line is towards women and a lot of the counselors don't believe the agency serves men even though they are told explicitly that [the agency] does. And it never occurred to me to call, because it's a women's organization. On an intellectual level I knew that this happened to*

other people. On an emotional level I felt like it didn't happen to any other men and that somehow I was unique because of that and therefore there wouldn't be anything set up for me.

Depression

Varying levels of depression from mild to severe are highly common among survivors of sexual violence. Understandably, the impact of sexual violence may leave many men unable to cope with a perceived loss of manhood, sexual dysfunction, shame, or isolation. In association with some forms of depression, many rape survivors "self-medicate" by consuming alcohol or other drugs to relieve their anguish. As one survivor of prison wrote in a letter to the antirape organization Stop Prisoner Rape, "Today, like every day since I 'died' in a pool of my own blood, I am nothing more than a mannequin of flesh and bone, void of normal feelings, and hopelessly obsessed with cocaine in an effort to medicate my simple mind to oblivion." Issues of addiction, increased risk of HIV infection, consideration of suicide, or unintentional injury may become some of the many key areas of concern in treatment of rape-related depression.

T. J., a male rape survivor I interviewed, told me of an experience during his college years in which he stumbled upon a friend, also a male rape survivor, who was seriously contemplating suicide:

> We were living in this dorm. Next door to us was this really good friend of mine who I had met at the campus Gay and Lesbian Alliance meetings, Bob. So one day my roommate and I knocked on Bob's door and then walked into his room. He was sitting there holding a gun. We said, "What's going on?" He said, "I'm trying to decide whether to shoot myself or not." We said, "What?" He said, "Yeah, I'm sick of getting raped all the time. In every relationship I've been in, at some point or another, I've been raped. It started when my dad raped me." He was in agony. He and I became good friends, and we started processing things together.

When I interviewed Andrew, he told me of the night he was raped and his resulting intent to just give up on life:

> I got back home and I was lost. I felt pretty sure I was going to kill
> myself. I was pretty convinced I would do that before the night was
> over. There was something about the fact that I didn't want to see
> morning. I had enough pills at home that I knew I could do it from
> my training, what to take.

Even though Andrew made it through that first night after he was
raped, he continues to consider suicide and told me:

> At times when I'm laying in bed, I wake up and I feel like there's
> someone standing there. I'm so scared I can't even roll over to look. I
> can't move. I try to tell myself, your alarm system's on, if anyone
> came in, you would know it. And none of that matters. I can't move.
> During those times at night I still think about suicide. I have over
> 700 pills here in a lock box, probably enough to commit suicide 10
> to 12 times over. Some nights when that happens I wake up and I
> think "You don't have to go through this anymore."

Unfortunately, the contemplation and act of suicide is fairly common among male rape survivors, especially those who do not feel
they can reach out for the support they so desperately need.

Surprise

The outright surprise and shock of being raped may be dramatically higher for men than women. From the time when
women are very young girls, our society teaches them to antici-
pate the possibility of rape and normalize the sexual violence of
women as an unfortunate fact of life. Women routinely live their
lives on the defense by altering their behavior to avoid assault—
doing everything from not walking alone at night to changing the
way they dress so as not to "invite" violent behavior from men.
Few men are trained to be aware of their vulnerability to sexual
assault, however, which may seem beyond the realm of most
men's reality. After all, male rape is largely ignored by the media,
public health outreach, and other educational endeavors. When a
man realizes he has been sexually assaulted, it is understandable
for him to feel as if he is the only one to ever undergo such an

experience given this widespread invisibility. This is illustrated by the earlier quote from Marcus, who said that he felt like no other men were raped and that he was unique in his victimization.

The following quotes from survivors, reported in various psychological studies, illustrate this disbelief:

> *I don't think a lot of people believe it could happen . . . I'm 6'2 and weigh 220 pounds.*[21]

> *I didn't know what they [the assailants] had in mind. Rape was the furthest thing from my mind. The furthest.*[22]

> *As his hand went to my belt, I was motionless with disbelief. "What's going on?" I thought.*[23]

Conflicting Sense of Sexual Orientation

Some men who have been raped may interpret their experience as an act of sex, concluding they have had a homosexual encounter. This may lead some men to question their sexual identity in an attempt to make sense of their assault experience. If a male rape survivor is treated with homophobia by those he confides in, he may adopt the label of "gay" that others inappropriately impose on him. Some gay male rape survivors may feel they were targeted for sexual violence because of sexual orientation, and may attempt to deny or hide their sexual identity so as to safeguard themselves from future assault.

Body Image and Self-Esteem

In relation to depression and self-blame, survivors may feel as if their bodies are permanently damaged in the eyes of others, less than their former selves as a result of their assault. Often these feelings manifest themselves in the form of low self-esteem and a lack of self-worth, as well as negative changes in perception of body image.

Heightened Sense of Vulnerability

As with any victimization of violent crime, male rape survivors may experience a heightened sense of vulnerability in their everyday lives, hyperconscious and overly aware of the possibility of future attacks. This may occur as a component of the rape trauma syndrome discussed earlier.

Although the above list of survivor reactions to rape is not exhaustive, it gives a strong indication of just how dramatically sexual violence can alter a man's life. As more research is conducted on male rape, especially in the disciplines of psychology and psychiatry, these responses will be more closely studied and, hopefully, better forms of gender-specific treatment will become available to accommodate the immediate and lasting effects of rape.

A PLAN OF ACTION

As research on adult male rape is still very much in a stage of infancy, some strategic planning is in order to maximize the utility of investigation and application of research findings. For example, rather than duplicating incidence and prevalence studies over and over in similar populations, we must expand the ways in which we explore this form of violence. Only the very surface of this phenomenon has been scratched, so there is a great deal of work and opportunity in this area. Some of the following suggestions for future research outline ways in which these studies can be improved, broadened, or implemented for the first time.

Explicitly Define Rape as It Is Measured and Analyzed in the Research

Almost every study of male rape neglects a crucial determinant of analysis, namely, a stated definition of what constitutes rape for the purposes of the study. These definitions could be adapted from state or local legal statutes, medical diagnoses, survivors' self-definitions, more social definitions unbound by professional terminology, systems of cultural meanings produced by the practice of rape, and more. Integral components of a definition of rape might include the body parts involved in the assault, characteristics of perpetrator and victim such as age or sex, social context of the act, features that distinguish the act from other forms of physical assault, and enumeration of the elements of consent (or lack thereof).

Conduct More Qualitative Work to Explore the Breadth of Rape Experiences that Men Endure

Thus far, published research articles on same-sex rape of men have been "surface" studies. They count and measure the rape of men in highly superficial ways, but fail to articulate the vast array of implications this widespread phenomenon bears. Clearly, male rape survivors interpret and respond to sexual assault in a multitude of ways that have only begun to be explored.

Examine Rape Service Providers' Attitudes, Opinions, and Responses to Male Rape and Survivors

Although research on male rape survivors is crucial for the betterment of treatment made available to them, we must also begin to assess the sensitivity and skill of service providers in their provision of services to survivors. The attitudes and opinions of psychologists, psychiatrists, law enforcement, crisis interventionists, medical personnel, and others may determine the level of empathy and quality of care these men receive. Identifying the areas in which these providers lack knowledge or hold harmful biases can yield more targeted plans of action to increase their competence in work with male survivors.

Explore More Fully Perpetrators' Motivation for Sexually Violating Other Men

Dr. Nicholas Groth's body of work that was mentioned earlier in this chapter is also distinctive in that he has concentrated on perpetrators of male rape in addition to victims. Very often these two roles overlap, as many perpetrators of rape were once victimized themselves. Whereas most studies of male rape have relied heavily on the survivors' perceptions of their attacker for demographic information and speculation about the psychological motive behind the assault, Groth's direct work with sex offenders offers suggestive observations about same-sex rape directly from the mouths of the rapists.

Expand the Environments in Which Male Rape is Studied to Encompass War, Mental Institutions, Military Organizations, and More

The physical site of male rape research has largely been confined to general community surveys, psychiatric practices, and prisons. Numerous media reports of male rape in other environments, however, demonstrate the need to investigate this violence elsewhere. Male rape has consistently been reported in areas rife with warfare and military combat, inpatient psychiatric institutions, and military organizations not in combat.

For example, evidence came to light in 1993 that the sexual abuse of men, including rape and castration, was widespread in the Yugoslav civil war. *Boston Globe* reporter Dusko Doder wrote of the sexual violence, committed by all sides in the war, but indicated that few of the male victims were willing to speak about their experiences.[24] According to a 1993 news report published in *USA Today*, between 5000 and 7000 male soldiers were sexually assaulted in the civil and ethnic unrest in Bosnia. This is in addition to the estimated 20,000 to 50,000 women who were raped.[25] A tribunal investigator named Irma Oosterman reported to Reuters newswire that Serb police and paramilitaries had sexually tortured many men in addition to women: " 'Men were forced to perform fellatio on each other—even sons and fathers,' Oosterman said, recounting how one man had to bite off another's penis, while a third victim had to eat it."[26]

In July 1996, British armed forces issued an evening curfew for their soldiers stationed along the Croatian coast after a series of rapes committed by gangs of local men.[27] Amidst the 1990 unrest in the Soviet Army, male rape became a common manifestation of building ethnic tensions in some geographic regions of the non-Russian republics. Many of these stories were recounted in the Soviet press, detailing the horrors of violence between Russian soldiers and those from the Baltic republics.[28] Also in 1990, Kuwaiti government officials and escaped resistance fighters detailed the experiences they suffered at the hands of invading Iraqi soldiers, which included the rape of many young Kuwaiti men.[29]

Reports of male rape in psychiatric institutions have been equally grim. In 1986 a man was indicted in Cleveland, Ohio, for raping mentally retarded men in a state-run institution. The alleged rapist had been living at the facility even though he was not mentally ill or developmentally disabled.[30] In 1991, a male employee was found guilty of sexually abusing two retarded males in a group home in Lemon Grove, California. Both victims identified him as the abuser. In May 1993, two Cincinnati men were indicted for sexually assaulting a mentally retarded patient. The parents of the victim were unaware of the assault until their son began to lose weight and grow ill. On discovering their son was HIV positive, the parents learned their son had been raped. The son later named the two men and claimed they had sexually abused him.[31]

Begin to Investigate the Influences of Race and Sexual Orientation as Potential Key Factors of Power in the Hate Rape of Men

Cases of hate rape motivated by racism and homophobia have been well documented, but no information has been generated by large-scale studies to determine if men of color and gay men are at particular risk for sexual assault in much the same way as women of color and lesbians. For example, in August 1985, police in Iowa City reported a pattern of male rapes committed against gay and black men, motivated by racist and homophobic hatred. Ku Klux Klan involvement was under investigation. At least four of the survivors reported their assaults. All stated they had previously not believed that male rape could happen, especially to them.[32] On two occasions in August 1993, gay men were kidnapped outside of gay bars in Salt Lake City and gang-raped. One man was abducted and repeatedly raped for 3 days. Local community leaders identified the gang rapes to be motivated by an intense hatred of gay and lesbian people.[33] In May 1994, two gay men were assaulted by a group of four men on the streets of San Diego. After repeatedly shouting antigay epithets and severely beating one of the gay men, the attackers pulled down his pants and threatened to rape him. As the attack continued, the gay man asked his attackers to just go ahead and kill him.[34] At a 1995 annual rally organized by agents from the Bureau of Alcohol, Tobacco, and Firearms called the "Good Ol' Boys Roundup," participants reportedly put on a skit in which one man dressed as a Ku Klux Klan member pretended to rape a man in blackface.[35] Scores of other media accounts relate circumstances that are frighteningly similar to the examples given above.

Whereas limited research has been conducted that suggests gay men, or men perceived to be gay, are at greater risk of being sexually assaulted, practically no studies have examined race as a major factor of vulnerability or power dynamic. Just as there has been a historical legacy of white male sexual access to African-American women as part of racial oppression, there has also been a tradition of attempts to strip African-American men of their manhood and masculinity. This has been true in the United States for men of other racial and ethnic minorities as well. The psychological impact of rape may be a function of a person's self-perception of racial identity and culture. Take, for example, the case of Jimi Sweet. A Vietnamese-American college student, Jimi was raped by a stranger at Cleveland State University in 1993. He decided to write about the details of his experience a few weeks later in the form of an opinion column for the university school newspaper, the *Cauldron*. For Jimi, the violation of his body held deeply meaningful connections to his background and ethnic origin.

> He took something from me. Something special. It's weird because I am the product of a rape. In Vietnam, my father was an American soldier who raped my mother. Then she orphaned me at birth. It's weird that she even decided to give birth to me. That must have taken a lot of strength. I've never thought about it like that. She knew there'd be something better for me somewhere. But she orphaned me at the hospital so shortly after my birth that she doesn't even know if I'm a boy or a girl.

Jimi self-identifies as a survivor of rape in two respects: the rape he had recently endured on campus, and surviving his birth to a woman who had been impregnated when raped. The hope he expresses in his column stresses his ability to overcome his assault and the optimism he feels his mother must have had when leaving him.

The survivor I interviewed named T. J. is from India, living in the United States and studying at a large midwestern university. He was raped by a white man on their second date, and clearly described the racialized importance of the assault:

> And also there's race involved here because up until this point I had not had sex with a white man before. When I came here to this country, I was really badly screwed over by a lot of immigration officials. And when I came to college, a lot of similar stuff happened. All these were white men. I had not had much contact with white men before. Psychologically, I was distant from white people generally, but white men in particular, and big white men. That was a big thing. I am small-boned; I am much smaller than most Americans. Most of my interactions were with really aggressive big white men. And this guy was big and white.

For some men of color, rape may transcend the individual and immediate act of violence, underscoring a history of sexual violence that has been implemented as a tool of racist subordination on a massive and historic scale. The following quotes are from African-American prison rape survivors' letters to the organization Stop Prisoner Rape:

I'm greatful [sic] for one thing in all this experience my Brother. It gave me a first hand knowledge and awareness of what my People went through in the old days of slavery (which we all go through in a more subtle form to this very day) and it strengthened my ties with my own People. The actual contest for me was to avoid letting the feelings turn to hatred which would destroy me and present those who afflicted me with a serious victory; the destruction of my soul. That hasn't happened, thank God.

You isolated the important thing: even though we are constantly subjected to homosexual rape we remain heterosexual. I was able to get my identity straightened out with the help of a Black psychologist who patiently worked with me for three years. I also had some racist problems to deal with. Since I'm light skinned the first dudes that raped me were Blacks who thought I was white. After word got out that I was Black they left me alone but then the whites took me off. After that I was a "Black" punk and passed on to whites.

After being labeled a "nigger punk" and forced into sexual servitude to white men, one African-American prison rape survivor stated, "That was when I realized that my position wasn't too different from my ancestors and that for the rest of the year I wasn't any different from a plantation slave." Both behind bars and out in the community, male rape and racism are strongly linked to larger forces of power and domination that transcend geography and time.

As with the rape of women, scholarly research has frequently preceded popular opinion and paved the way for what might, at the time, seem like outlandish or exaggerated claims. The value and necessity of research on male rape cannot be underscored enough, and particular attention must be paid to ensure that future work is methodologically sound. In addition, we must begin to broaden and deepen the investigations of men raping men to include as many cultures, geographies, and environments as possible. As a more comprehensive body of work begins to develop in this area, solid findings will facilitate better prevention and treatment of the rape of men. These studies will hopefully allow social scientists and public health professionals to translate resulting theory into practice. As male rape becomes extensively documented and analyzed, society will have less and less grounds on which to deny its existence.

THREE

THE SEGREGATION OF MALE RAPE

*T*here is an element of most all-male environments that fosters an encouragement and propensity for men to commit violent acts. Whether it is a sense of macho competition, violence as a rite of passage, an expression of dominant status, or an initiation of hazing, groups of men have traditionally inflicted pain on others at rates much higher than individuals who act independently of such peer influence. Specifically, rape and sexual violence epitomize this exertion of power in single-sex communities of men, be they athletic teams, prison institutions, Greek-letter fraternities, or military organizations. In some of these less confined or isolated settings, fraternities for example, men typically target women as objects of sexual violation. Well-documented trends of individual and gang rape committed by fraternity men and male athletes on college campuses illustrate this form of assault that has become so ingrained in the culture of many exclusively male organizations. Sometimes, however, these men direct their abuse toward members of their own fellowship as a means of establishing an internal hierarchy of authority.

PRISONS

The environments with the highest frequency of same-sex rape are undoubtedly prisons and jails throughout the world. Stephen Donaldson, the former director of an organization called Stop Prisoner Rape, wrote a guest editorial for the *New York Times* in 1993 in which he stated, "The fight against rape in our communities is doomed to failure and will remain an exercise in futility as long as it ignores the network of training grounds for rapists: our prisons, jails and reform schools."[1] This training that Donaldson describes is none other than the brutality of men raping men in prison institutions. Rape is both normalized in these environments and wielded as a tool for aggression, domination, and literal enslavement of others. Donaldson himself experienced this violence when he was arrested at a nonviolent protest in Washington, D.C. During his brief stay in jail, he was orally and anally gang raped by approximately 60 men over the course of 24 hours. On his release, he spent 1 week in a veteran's hospital recovering from rectal surgery. After his discharge he decided not to hide his experience in a protective shroud of fear and shame. Instead he held a press conference to detail the atrocities he had endured and demanded accountability for the negligence that fostered his victimization. For more than 20 years since that day, Donaldson worked as a tireless advocate for prisoner rights, particularly on issues of sexual assault. The psychological impact of all of this trauma set into motion a pattern of behavior that landed Donaldson in jail on several more occasions throughout his life. Raped countless times across the span of his life, he became infected with HIV and eventually died of AIDS-related complications in 1996.

Stop Prisoner Rape conservatively estimates that an average of 360,000 males are sexually assaulted behind bars each year in the United States alone. Of this number, at least two-thirds are repeatedly raped and often gang raped on an almost daily basis, resulting in millions of rapes committed annually. These male rapes in prisons and jails across the United States are not included in the Bureau of Justice Statistics's crime survey or estimates of reported rape. Most other countries do not include prison rape in their national crime reports either, reflecting mostly the fact that only a handful of attempts have been made to seriously investigate the severity of the problem. Michael King, a psychiatrist at the Royal Free Hospital School of Medicine in London, has studied male rape and estimates that the levels of violence in British prisons are significantly less than those in comparable U.S. institutions. Lacking the significance that statistical evidence provides, prison rape is usually disbelieved, ignored, or blamed on the victims themselves. The predominant belief persists that prisoners have no rights whatsoever and that violence inflicted on inmates is an administration of punishment that they deserve. As one prison rape survivor wrote in a letter to Stop Prisoner Rape,

> *No one cares what happens to a prisoner. Everyone has the attitude that prisoners complain too much and have unreal expectations in wanting to live as a human being, that we somehow deserve all that happens to us. I know this attitude well because I used to have this view before my incarceration.*

The logic behind this "eye for an eye" form of justice is faulty, however, because a significant percentage of prisoners are incarcerated for nonviolent crimes. In addition, prisoners who exhibit less violent behavior are usually singled out and raped more often. A process of confinement intended to punish and reform becomes a method of further hardening criminals, having the opposite effect of fostering violence rather than preventing it. There is no reason to believe that a normalization of violence behind bars will not carry over into the behavior of ex-convicts. As a single-sex society isolated from the outside world, sexual violence has become thoroughly ingrained in male prison culture, usually occurring between inmates but also perpetrated by correctional officers against prisoners. Though the dynamics of the violence may vary from prison to prison, male rape is very clearly a central element in the hierarchy of power between inmates—those with more power rape those with less power.

This pecking order is exemplified in the rape-slang used in prison subculture to label men in terms of their status. Psychiatrist Robert Dumond of the Massachusetts Department of Corrections has researched prison rape and the language that inmates use to identify and represent who is in control and who is under control. For example, the terms *jocker* and *pitcher* refer to men who penetrate other men either forcibly or coercively. *Punks* and *kids* are names for men who must submit and provide sexual service to the jockers. Common characteristics of those forced to be punks include men of racial or ethnic minority within their prison population, men of smaller build and physical stature, men who are less masculine in either appearance or behavior, and men who are gay or perceived to be gay. Gay men are usually distinguished from punks and are referred to as *queens*.

Once branded as a punk and sexually assaulted, an inmate cannot shed the imposition of this social role. Unless he "hooks up" with one jocker who will provide him long-term protection in exchange for sexual services, a punk will be vulnerable to any inmates who wish to rape him. Often punks are forced to adopt attributes such as feminine clothing, long hair, shaved body hair, and female names as part of their duties, and are even referred to with pronouns such as *she* and *her*. Amazingly similar social roles of dominance and humiliation can be found in prison environments across cultures and time periods. Robert Dumond notes in his research the multitude of similar subcultures in prison settings in India, Australia, Holland, Canada, and France. A cross-cultural comparison of these prison rape societies could perhaps yield some insight into solutions for prevention and treatment of sexual violence, or at least a better understanding of how these social systems function.

Although on the surface this may seem as if punks are simply substitutes for women in an all-male environment, the punk/jocker relationship is more complex than making do in an environment of limitations. Sometimes punks are prostituted by jockers who serve as pimps within the prison community, and at other times punks are "sold" as more permanent companions to other inmates. Although the sexual activity between jocks and punks is coercive and still falls within the scope of sexual violence, jocks and punks often develop friendships and even intimate relationships with each other. This sense of friendliness or camaraderie does not translate into any degree of equality, however, for jockers are most definitely in power and control over those who are forced to serve them. Frequently this coercive sexual relationship is mistaken for consensual homosexuality. In a lecture on prison sexuality delivered to Columbia University in 1993, Stop Prisoner Rape's Stephen Donaldson explained, "The sexual penetration of another male prisoner by a Man is sanctioned by the subculture, is considered a male rather than a homosexual activity, and is considered to validate the penetrator's masculinity." Donaldson also believed that most punks are, in fact, heterosexual despite their imposed same-sex behavior. He has also attributed the equation of same-sex contact with homosexuality as a middle-class misinterpretation by academics and armchair theorists:

> For the majority of prisoners, penetrative sex with a punk or queen remains a psychologically heterosexual and, in the circumstances of confinement, normal act; the relationships involved are also psychologically heterosexual to them (as well as to most of their partners, willing or not). These prisoners, who are perhaps more focused on the physical and less on the psychological dimensions of sexual activity than members of the middle class, insist that the difference between the experience of entering a female mouth and of entering a male mouth is not significant, that the experiential difference between entering a vagina or female anus and a male anus is not significant.[2]

Unfortunately, this equation of prison rape with homosexuality strengthens the reluctance of prison officials to deal with the problem of sexual violence between inmates. Because same-sex consensual behaviors are considered illegal in almost all prisons, these institutions fear that addressing male rape would be perceived as an acknowledgment of "homosexual" behavior among their inmates. The taboos associated with consensual homosexuality effectively stifle the first necessary step in prison rape prevention and treatment: the very recognition that rape occurs.

Apart from a general recognition of the problem, the amazingly high prevalence of rape behind bars is made worse by the lack of two specific efforts on the part of prison institutions. No comprehensive prevention effort occurs to keep men from being raped; and very few, if any, services exist for those men who have been assaulted—either in the forms of counseling, legal advocacy, or medical treatment. The combination of inadequate resources and collective apathy ensures this continued inaction. As one inmate wrote in a letter to Stop Prisoner Rape, "The psychiatrist here has no time for therapy and has put me on medication . . . and this Band-Aid approach is the best I'll get." Another prisoner stated, "I personally witnessed prison officers ignore inmates cry for help when their cell mates were attacking them. In most cases, the officers actually joked about it." And reports such as the following from 1996 are not uncommon: "I was assaulted in January [1994] and since received neither treatment nor any investigation of a meaningful nature. . . . Department of Corrections has not only suppressed the matter, but threatens my approaching parole date."

In 1989, Professor of Sociology Helen Eigenberg at Old Dominion University in Virginia conducted a study of correctional officers' attitudes toward rape in prison. She reported that "almost half of the officers believe that inmates deserve rape if they have consented to participate in consensual acts with other inmates. This finding indicates that officers believe that some inmates precipitate their victimization."[3] She also determined that correctional officers are less willing to believe black victims of rape than white victims, perhaps because of racism. Existing data reveal that white men are more frequent victims of rape than are black men. This frequency, however, should be viewed with some skepticism, as white victims may be more likely to report their rape because they are more likely to be believed. Also in terms of believability, Eigenberg found that "officers are basically unwilling to believe muscular men."[4] The expectation that physically strong and masculine men will not allow themselves to be assaulted supports the myth that "real men" cannot be raped. There is also some shred of valid logic in this, however, as prisoners who possess more feminine traits are marked as unmistakable targets for sexual assault in prison society and raped with greater frequency.

The continued mismanagement of prisons and jails has extended beyond malicious and negligent behavior of correctional officers, resulting in a broad-scale normalization of rape culture behind bars. Some minor progress has been made in recent years to address prisoner rape, but this has largely consisted of media-directed public attention rather than sweeping policy change or legislative action. Several options that are hardly revolutionary would serve as small first steps if they would only be considered. First and foremost, consensual sexual relations behind bars should be officially decriminalized. Most prison rape survivors will not report their assault to correctional facilities because officers will frequently respond with "You must have wanted it because you allowed it to happen." Once officials redefine prisoners' rape experiences as homosexuality, the rape survivors are punished for confessing to a violation of rules! A decriminalization of consensual behavior would also symbolically diminish a great deal of the disgrace associated with all sexual activity, including sexual violence.

Even the most minimal of training and orientation for both prisoners and correctional officers would be incredibly invaluable. On their entry into prison, inmates could be given training serving to increase their awareness of a number of dangers they will face, including drug use, HIV infection, and violence. Many new prisoners are immediately gang-raped once incarcerated. They are singled out by more experienced inmates who take advantage of their naiveté and seek to immediately establish who is boss behind bars. Early identification and added protection for those inmates who will likely be the most at risk for sexual assault could circumvent this problem to some degree.

Similarly, correctional officers could be given sexual violence sensitivity training and issued strict codes of conduct for rape prevention and intervention when necessary. The establishment of an official mechanism for prisoners to report rape safely and confidentially could help to ensure that rape survivors receive the treatment and protection they deserve. The availability of adequate medical treatment, counseling, and legal services would be ideal, although these would require more economic resources than the previously mentioned recommendations.

A sign of progress in what otherwise looks to be a dismal status quo of neglect came in May 1995 with the publication of the Federal Bureau of Prisons's program statement on Inmate Sexual Assault Prevention/Intervention Programs. The purpose of the document was to "provide specific guidelines to help prevent sexual assault on inmates, to address the needs of inmates who have been sexually assaulted, and to discipline and prosecute inmates who sexually assault others." A first step in national leadership toward a comprehensive prison rape agenda, the document was signed by the Director of the Federal Bureau of Prisons, Mary Hawk. The guidelines are fairly comprehensive and are accompanied by a five-page protocol for responding to a rape crisis behind bars. Although the procedures may be ignored or rejected by many correctional officers in positions of power, the report is symbolic of the government's growing recognition of prison rape.

In addition to the traditional reluctance to admit the existence of prison rape, there is also a vested interest in maintaining the widespread threat of men raping men in correctional facilities. The specter of sexual violence behind bars is often used outside of prison by officials who wish to instill fear in the would-be prisoner. This "scared straight" approach relies on one injustice to prevent another, and assumes that scare tactics work better than internal motivation or true reform of criminal behavior. In March 1996, Sinclairs, a Scottish law firm that specializes in criminal defense, launched a new ad campaign. The television commercial depicts a young man being thrown into a jail cell where he is confronted by a leering convict. The firm was upfront about its use of male rape imagery in capitalizing on the worries of young men who face a possible prison sentence. The voice-over for the commercial ominously says, "In trouble? You could be in a lot more."

The advertisement was approved by Scotland's Law Society and the Broadcast Advertising Clearance Centre.

Tactics of "if you land in jail this is what will happen . . ." also extend to the treatment of juveniles who could possibly be tried as adults or establish a pattern of delinquency that might carry on through their adult years. At an experimental boot camp for juvenile offenders in Florida, simulations of prison rape have been inflicted on adolescents as a method of rehabilitation. A reporter from the *St. Petersburg Times* observed and recounted the following scenario:

> *[Drill Instructor] Venis grabbed a pudgy 14-year-old named Jason for a vivid demonstration of prison rape. The 55-year-old [Drill Instructor] stood directly behind Jason and began gently, rhythmically raising his knee, pressing it into the boy's rump, to simulate an assault. "That's how they do it when you get to prison!" Venis yelled. The fear of homosexual rape quickly became a powerful lever of intimidation. The [Drill Instructors] made sure recruits knew just what happens in prison, subtlety be damned. One told Veysey: "You don't change, they'll be sticking things up your butt, son. Right up your butt!"*[5]

After the article was printed in the newspaper, the commander of the boot camp said he was unaware of the practice, declared it inappropriate, and ordered it discontinued.

In February 1997, Texas corrections officials suspended a sergeant and four prison guards for allegedly inappropriate behavior during a "scared straight" field trip to Eastham prison. The field trip was a tour by prison officials to show 15 teenagers with emotional and substance abuse problems what prison life is like in the hopes that it would be a deterrence to any future criminal behavior. During the visit, the guards allegedly allowed inmates to fondle five of the teenage boys. A spokesperson for the Department of Criminal Justice in Texas told authorities the prisoners had admitted fondling the boys and that their actions were not motivated by sexual gratification but instead were an attempted lesson to show the juveniles what could happen to them in prison.

A different practice was used in a therapy group for prisoners at the Northwest State Correctional Facility in St. Albans, Vermont. The American Civil Liberties Union's National Prison Project filed a lawsuit against the facility in 1996, challenging a behavior modification program for prisoners that involved forcing inmates to undergo a simulated anal rape while a therapist screamed obscenities. Billed as "drama therapy," the simulation was intended to teach male sex offenders empathy for victims of sexual assault by placing them in the role of victim. The program obviously assumed that only men are rapists and only women are raped. Forcing prisoners, many of whom were undoubtedly raped behind bars, to relive a rape experience is nothing more than an infliction of psychological trauma in the form of secondary rape. The ACLU eventually settled the case when the facility agreed to eliminate the program and make improvements in other mental health care and medical services for inmates. The sexual assault of prisoners will never be suitably addressed as long as judges, therapists, and correctional officers continue to capitalize on prison rape as a convenient form of inhumane justice.

MILITARY ORGANIZATIONS

Just as male rape is typically regarded as being more prevalent in prison environments than in noninstitutional settings, at least one study has found that same-sex rape in military organizations is also more common. Military psychiatrists Peter Goyer and Henry Eddleman reviewed cases of Navy and Marine Corps men who reported sexual assault to a military outpatient psychiatric clinic. At least half of those men who had been assaulted expressed a desire to be discharged from their military service, and many of the men described forms of rape trauma syndrome ranging from a fear of living in close quarters with men to severe depression and sleep disturbances. Rape among the ranks of military men produces many of the same results as prison rape, including a great deal of denial, abuse of power over others, and a general lack of recognition of the violence outside the organization.

David Hunter, a writer for the *Knoxville News-Sentinel* in Tennessee, wrote of his knowledge of a same-sex military rape incident that occurred in 1965 at Fort Jackson, and how it was subsequently swept under the rug to protect superior officers. "A drill instructor entered the barracks across from mine one night and tried to sodomize an 18-year-old recruit. Another soldier turned on the lights and literally caught the sergeant with his pants down."[6] The offending sergeant left the barracks in a hurry, but arrived for duty the next morning as if nothing had happened. By the afternoon following the incident, the sergeant had vacated his room and moved to another location.

> That night, after lights out, the entire company was ordered to fall out in front of the four barracks we shared. We stood at attention, all 200 of us, shivering in our underwear, while being questioned about allegations against a drill instructor. We all got the unspoken message. Keep quiet. There was never an official investigation, nothing went on paper.[7]

Some time later, on the evening that the 200 men shipped out of the military base, the same sergeant who had attempted to rape a recruit was seen moving back into his old room as if the whole incident had never happened.

There is a commonality to this cover-up mentality, and it is congruent with the preservation and maintenance of military organizations. This philosophy dictates that the individual must be sacrificed for the greater good and that the reputation of the organization must not be tarnished, even at the cost of individual victimization. Akin to the military science concept of "acceptable loss," the needs of the many are considered to far outweigh the needs of the few. Unfortunately, this constructs a majority rule governance where the minority is not only left unprotected, but stifled in a silence that prevents any challenge to institutional order. The minority victimization extends not only to men who are raped during their term of military service, but also to limitations placed on capable women and gay men who are excluded from traditional male, and heterosexual, establishments of supremacy.

As with prison rape, the confusion between homosexuality and same-sex rape has reinforced misinformation about male rape as well as gay male sexuality. During the debate over whether gays should be permitted to serve openly in the U.S. military, civilian commentators repeatedly expressed their concerns about the possibility of gay men raping their fellow servicemen. Sensationalized media coverage of the "gays in the military debate" has frequently consisted of video footage panning across the cramped barracks and open shower rooms where soldiers live in vulnerable proximity to one another. The underlying message is effectively conveyed that, given the chance, gay men will inevitably become sexual predators and assault their susceptible heterosexual comrades. Bolstering the stereotype of the hypersexual gay man who will seize any opportunity for sexual contact, even without consent, the U.S. military and conservative proponents of the ban have consistently pandered to popular homophobia with confidence that such fears would win their case. The intertwining of irrational distress over homosexuality and the continued belief in popular rape mythology has not single-handedly upheld the ban against gays in the military, but this certainly played a key role in the reluctance to permit gay men and lesbians to serve their country openly. The few remaining armed forces in Europe and North America that continue to discriminate on the basis of sexual preference, chiefly Canada and Great Britain, have also invoked the specter of the homosexual molester to instill similar apprehension in the face of proposed policy changes.

Meanwhile, documented cases of male military officers sexually harassing and sexually assaulting their female colleagues have far outnumbered those of same-sex violations. The notorious Tailhook investigations and the flood of sexual harassment reports from female cadets at U.S. military training camps in late 1996 are but a sample of the double standard to which gay men and lesbian military members are held. Therefore, same-sex rape of men in military settings cannot be equated with gay male sexuality, just as the phenomenon of men raping women is not synonymous with heterosexuality. I argue that military culture, not sexual orientation, is in fact the predominant influence on the same-sex rape behavior of servicemen. What other result should we expect when an organization breaks men down psychologically, systematically trains them in aggressive and violent combat, teaches them to objectify their opponents as nonhuman, and enforces a rigid code of prescribed masculinity that is valued above all else? Similar to life in prison, rape between military men typically results from internal power struggles and the establishment of authority within a broader realm of male superiority.

In 1987 the *New York Times* reported on a culture of brutality within the ranks of the British Army. As part of initiation ceremonies conducted by members of several regiments, multiple beatings and sexual assaults were documented. The initiation rites included forcing naked recruits to perform anal intercourse in public. Four men were accused of assaulting a 20-year-old private by burning his genitals, sexually assaulting him with a broomstick, and forcing him to march in place with string that tied his genitals to his ankles. These acts perpetrated against the younger and more inexperienced members of the group depict a very clear understanding of exactly who wields absolute authority in the organization. Furthermore, the public display of violent initiation serves a much broader function than the impact on individual recruits. The spectacle of the assault and later conversations about it disseminate a more lasting, thorough, and unchallenged adherence to chains of command.

Beyond the establishment of a totem pole, top-down governance, military trainings, and initiations are notorious for "making men out of boys." From a very early age, many boys in our culture are given military toys like GI Joe to play with and are taught that wartime patriotism is equivalent to a respectable manhood. As adults with a firm belief in this equation of masculinity and success, male recruits are systematically instructed how to behave as real men. Men's gender roles become more rigid and narrow, heavily scrutinized for any behavior that might seem the slightest bit feminine, and, therefore, considered weak and unfit for military service. Bonding ceremonies to create group cohesion and interdependence between servicemen fashion a self-policing organization in which peers uphold group norms even in the absence of superiors.

Another example of hazing and violent initiation, though

extreme, appeared in a segment titled "Hell Night" that aired on ABC's news program *Primetime Live* in 1992. As a result of an investigation into military hazing, Sam Donaldson reported on a pattern of sexual abuse in the U.S. Marine Corps. While inducting men into an elite drill team, leaders of the group forced the junior Marines to strip. Once naked, the leaders painted a tarlike, military shoe polish called edge dressing on the men's genitals, resulting in painful chemical burns. The edge dressing contains toluene, a substance that, in heavy doses, has been linked to birth defects and impairment of the central nervous system. In addition to being physically assaulted with fists and rifles, one Marine reported the edge dressing dabber had been shoved into his anus. Two Marines became so distraught after the abuse that they went AWOL (absent without leave) to contact their congressman for assistance.

Sometimes the culture of same-sex military rape is perpetuated under the institutionalized guise of combat training. During the Persian Gulf War, several U.S. military personnel were captured by Iraqis and sexually assaulted. As a result, the U.S. Air Force Academy in Colorado Springs, Colorado, began a "sexual exploitation training program" in 1993, designed to prepare recruits for what could happen to them if they should ever be captured as prisoners of war and subjected to sexual violence. The 17-day classified program consists of resistance and escape techniques for survival as a prisoner, and includes a simulated rape scenario that has sparked complaints from two dozen recruits. Christian Polintan, a 19-year-old cadet who filed one of the complaints, told his story to ABC's investigative news program *20/20* in 1995. In recalling the rape scenario experience, Polintan said he was dressed in women's clothing and paraded around the military camp. A trainer in the program removed the skirt that Polintan was forced to wear and ordered another cadet to mount him. "He told me to bend over the table, I was just in shock of what they were doing. I could not believe it was happening to me." When the scenario was over, Polintan said, "A lot of things were going through my mind. I wanted to kill myself."[8] Although the assault was only a simulation, the training program was designed to toughen cadets, desensitizing them to even the most brutal of personal violations. These dehumanizing experiences may indeed make better soldiers for the purposes of military combat, but not without extreme consequence to the individuals who undergo psychological trauma in the name of patriotic duty. A number of these military trainings in each of the armed forces aim to prepare recruits for the horror and brutality that accompanies engagement in warfare, but a balance must be maintained to prevent this conditioning from becoming a routine submission to unconditional abuse.

ATHLETICS

Like military organizations, sports are a domain where violence is overtly acceptable and even encouraged in society. Athletics are a legitimized outlet for men to express fierce competition in an effort to beat their opponent and engage in violent body contact consisting of tackles and other forms of battery. There are highly structured rules imposed on most sports games and competitions that attempt to limit violent behavior so as to prevent permanent injury or death, but it is not uncommon to witness fistfights and mass brawls break out between individual athletes and entire teams. The all-consuming goals of most sports center around dominance, status, and the acquisition of power that is taken by force from others. These are also the central elements associated with violence, and sometimes the conflict within sports organizations and athletic teams erupts in sexual violence between members of the all-male group.

In 1992 a junior teammate of the Johnson Creek High School wrestling team in Wisconsin filed a lawsuit alleging that his fellow wrestlers had beat him and raped him by shoving a mop handle into his rectum as punishment for missing practice. The athletic director of the high school found the young man stripped naked and sitting on an exercise mat. He was blindfolded and his legs, hands, and head were bound with tape. Another athlete testified during the resulting trial that other team members had also been threatened with "getting the mop." The accused athletes were acquitted of the rape charges, in part because of a lack of evidence. The alleged victim had been blindfolded and could not identify who had assaulted him, although he stated that at least six of his teammates held him down while he was attacked. The assistant wrestling coach for the team testified that "taping" was commonplace among wrestling teams, particularly in college athletics. The alleged victim eventually accepted a $150,000 settlement from the high school and its insurance companies.

Five students at a Waynesville High School in Dayton, Ohio, were suspended in 1988 for allegedly staging a locker room hazing in which freshmen players were forced to masturbate and touch each other's genitals. A blindfolded student was forced to do sit-ups so that his face came into contact with the bare buttocks of another student, while another student was forced to do push-ups in a pool of urine. A similar incident occurred at a 1989 high school football training camp in Pennsylvania when one high school sophomore was allegedly forced to insert his finger into the anus of another sophomore while 20 to 30 teammates watched. All of the school's 85 football players were ordered to undergo mental health counseling.

In 1990 the *Boston Globe* reported on the alleged hazing of eight new members of the local Brockton High School track team:

> According to one anonymous student, the eight new team members were stripped to their underwear and pushed halfway out the back door of the [school] bus. Some of them had their underwear ripped off them, and some were made to choose between eating pubic hair and being beaten up. Some were forced to rub their genitals.[9]

The town of Smithfield, a small Utah farming community, became outraged in 1993 when a member of the local high school football team was taken naked from the shower by 10 of his teammates, bound by his genitals with tape to a towel rack, and put on display for approximately 20 of his male and female schoolmates. High school sports were so popular in the community that when the victim reported the abuse he endured, he began to receive telephone threats. The national media soon picked up the story and the young man later appeared on the television talk show *Phil Donahue* to tell his story. He later told the *Los Angeles Times*, "The humiliation I suffered was tons worse than the physical injury."[10]

In January 1997, Sheldon Kennedy, a hockey player with the Boston Bruins of the National Hockey League, revealed a former coach had sexually assaulted him more than 300 times over the course of 11 years. Beginning when Kennedy was 14 and continuing until he was 26, the assaults included forced oral sex and masturbation. The coach was found guilty on two counts of sexual assault against Kennedy and another unnamed man, who had been assaulted approximately 50 times in 4 years. When the perpetrator was sentenced to 3½ years in jail and the conviction became public, Canada's hockey world reeled in shock. Kennedy reported in a newspaper interview with the *Toronto Star* that the coach had used a variety of tactics to gain control over him, including verbal abuse and even a shotgun. On January 17, Reuters newswire reported that "Mick Mitrovic, president of the eastern region of the Canadian Professional Hockey School, said he was not surprised when he heard about the conviction because there had been cases and rumors about problems with players and coaches before."[11]

Although the preceding reports could be considered isolated incidents, there is no reason to believe that the prevalence of male athletes raping women would stop short of rape and sexual abuse within their own ranks. Athletic organizations, prisons, militaries, and college fraternities are similar in their hierarchies, competitions for power, and heightened masculinities. The commonality of these characteristics demands close attention to possible patterns of same-sex rape in athletic environments.

FRATERNITIES

In her book *Fraternity Gang Rape: Sex, Brotherhood, and Privilege on Campus*, University of Pennsylvania anthropologist Peggy Reeves Sanday discusses the cultural phenomenon of campus fraternity organizations that teach men to debase femininity in all of its forms and claim sexual power as a natural right of privileged manhood. As Professor Sanday focuses on the ritual practice of men gang-raping women as endemic to fraternity life, she lays important groundwork from which we can begin to acknowledge same-sex rape within these organizations as well. As with prisons, there is a remarkable similarity in rape practices between fraternity organizations across the span of time and geography. For example, following prisons and military bases in terms of geographic locality, the U.S. Bureau of Justice claims more alleged rapes occur within the property lines of Greek-letter houses than any other community location. A legacy of sexual violence continues to be transmitted from one generation to the next through a fraternal culture that is comprised of rituals, songs, language, and activities grounded in tradition. Since the early part of this century, this inheritance has maintained an allegiance of rape-supportive belief systems that have only recently been seriously challenged by the institutions of higher education to which they are tethered. The practice of hazing, above all else, has been most severely regulated and punished by campus officials. Scores of cases continue to be documented that involve the serious injury and death of college men who are so desperate to join a brotherhood that they will endure the consequence of any imposed ordeal. The component of total humiliation that accompanies many hazing incidents is often just as damaging as the inflicted physical abuse.

Many fraternity initiation rituals, for example, seek to debase pledges by forcing them into sexually subordinate and feminizing roles. Numerous accounts of sexualized hazing have appeared in the media, representing a trend in fraternity behavior that has come to light in recent years and identified as a growing problem. A University of Minnesota fraternity attempted to appeal a 1982 suspension for allegedly forcing two Kappa Sigma pledges to strip, taping them together while fraternity members photographed them. One of the pledges reported that his genitals were coated with petroleum jelly and cake frosting, and messages were written on his body in lipstick. The pledge who reported the hazing called it "humiliating and hideous." Apart from the obvious component of sexual domination, the use of homophobia becomes a powerful tool for long-term stigmatization, in the previous case complete with photographic documentation of their compromised manhood.

The Delta Kappa Epsilon fraternity at Tulane University was banished from campus in 1984 after a series of hazing incidents. Neighbors of the DKE house said they had seen pledges with cords tied to their genitals and bricks tied to the other end. Two pledges also reported they were ordered to have sex with a goat during one hazing episode. The bounds of cruelty in sexual hazing seem limited only by the expanse of fraternity men's malicious imagination. In 1988 a fraternity pledge at the University of Central Arkansas reported being awakened in his dorm room at 3:30 A.M. during "Hell Week" and taken to a hazing party, where he was forced to get on all fours and bark like a dog. Later in the party, he and another pledge were forced to spread their legs while their drunken fraternity brothers threw darts ever closer to their groins.

In 1990 the Sigma Nu chapter at the University of Texas was expelled from campus for alleged hazing that included sexual abuse. One pledge's mother received an anonymous telephone call that her son was in trouble. She later found him cowering in a closet and reported he had been beaten and trod on by fraternity members who had led him around by a sling encasing his genitals. At the University of Florida, one-fourth of the fraternities faced disciplinary action in 1992 for alcohol abuse and unrepentant hazing. Pledges of Kappa Sigma were forced to ride around campus nude and chained to a pickup truck. A pledge of Delta Tau Delta lost a testicle in a power saw during one episode that consisted of forced labor and sleep deprivation. Alumni and an international fraternity organization later forced the fraternity to disband its 66-year-old chapter. In 1994 the Delta Sigma Phi fraternity at the University of Texas was placed on probation for forcing pledges to eat cat food and applying Ben-Gay to their genitals.

The sexual and genital components of the fraternity men's degradation in these examples underscore the dual purpose of hazing in many single-sex organizations. One's psychological, and sometimes physical, sense of self is broken down and stripped away in highly intimate and personal ways only to be built back up and reconfigured with a new set of ethics, loyalties, and relations of power. The transition of old independent life into newly dependent fellowship is characterized as a one-way street; that is, once a brother, always a brother. Frequently initiation rites involve acts of violence ranging from rape to torture, even branding the fraternity's letters into the pledges' bodies with a hot iron. Once committed, these events cannot be undone. They symbolize crossing the point of no return and ensure a commitment that transcends any challenging principle. After having been broken down (i.e., feminized), the "re-building" of fraternity men's social identity is not simply mapped onto a blank slate, however. The initiates are instructed to regain their virility through the overpowerment of others in a self-demonstration of their newfound privilege and masculine status. As Peggy Reeves Sanday explains,

> The ritual produces anxiety by representing the feminine to the pledge as both dirty and as part of his subjectivity. The ritual then resolves the anxiety by cleansing the pledge of his feminine identification and promising him a lifelong position in a purified male social order. . . . Having resorted to abuse as a means to establish their bond to brotherhood, the newly confirmed brothers resort to abusing others—new generations of pledges and party women—to uphold the original contract and renew their sense of autonomous power of the brotherhood.[12]

Strikingly specific accounts of this process are documented elsewhere. In his book *Stopping Rape: A Challenge for Men*, antirape activist Rus Ervin Funk wrote of his interview with a fraternity man who described the role of same-sex sexual assault in the hazing and initiation process:

> At one fraternity at a large midwestern university, for example, the rush participants were sexually assaulted in a number of ways by gangs of their soon-to-be upper-class "brothers." The attacks included verbal abuse of the victims, referring to them as "little women," "girls," and "wusses," and occurred frequently over a period of a week or so. During this time, they were expected to act out in exaggerated female stereotypes. After the series of attacks, they were told to go "do to women what we did to you to get your manhood back."[13]

The connections between men raping women and men raping men are strongly illustrated by the above quote. The interconnectedness of sexually violent acts, varying in the type of person who is targeted for victimization, remains a largely uncharted territory in rape prevention initiatives. Many psychologists have speculated that a great percentage of men who rape women were themselves sexually violated in the past, as either adults or children. The extent to which opposite-sex rape and same-sex rape propagate or influence one another may hold a great deal of value in our search to understand the complexity of sexual violence in our world.

Another example of this linkage resides in the context of an extensive bibliography on the topic of fraternity men's rape of women, compiled by an anonymous man from Hastings Law College who has mass-posted the collection of citations across the Internet. At the end of the annotated reference list, he explains his motivation for such dissemination:

> *Part of the reason I wrote this is because I was raped myself when pledging ΘX at the University of California, Berkeley in 1977. I am a man, obviously. Obviously women do not bear the pain and horror and embarrassment of Fraternity rape alone; many men do as well, but, like myself, do not report it.*

Although the bibliography contains almost no information on fraternity men's sexual abuse of other men, the author's experience has clearly motivated him to confront a system that produces men who are prone to many forms of sexually violent behaviors. The stigma of the experience is also strongly apparent as he chooses to remain anonymous despite the great deal of work that went into the culmination of his research.

Willa Young, my predecessor as the coordinator of Ohio State University's Rape Education and Prevention Program, shared with me the inability of fraternity men to speak openly about sexual violence within their ranks. She said:

> *Much of this violence is also spoken about in code that suffices to gloss over understood meanings. For instance, one OSU fraternity leader told me recently that hazing among men "remains unspeakable, and the results are new members who will never again speak to the men assigned as their big brothers, whose job it is to mentor*

*them into the organization." This man and I knew we were talking
about sexual assault, but he never spoke of it in an exacting manner.*

Although prisons, athletic teams, military organizations, and
fraternities all differ in degrees of sex segregation, isolation, regu-
lation, and history, they demonstrate in a magnified way the
central roles of authority and masculinity in sexual violence. Just
as the rape of men is not purely random or coincidental in these
organizations, the rape of men in other communities is also not
happenstance. Single-sex environments certainly have unique
characteristics, but they remain a microcosm of a larger world and
embody many of the same qualities of power and control that
people exercise against one another in the form of violence.

I have chosen to discuss only the four institutions of fraternities, prisons, athletic teams, and militaries in this chapter, largely
because of the existing evidence from which to draw some prelim-
inary conclusions and also because of their intensely hierarchical
natures. Other single-sex environments should also be kept in
mind even though they have not been discussed here, such as sex-
segregated mental health institutions, college dormitories, nursing homes, monasteries, boarding schools, and so on. Addressing
rape in these all-male environments is incredibly difficult, mostly
because of these men's unwillingness to either report rape or challenge their peers who commit rape. The code of secrecy and group
allegiance holds the utmost importance, and the fear of retribution
for speaking out serves as an effective enforcement of this silence.
Leaders and officials who oversee the well-being of these single-
sex organizations have even more responsibility to actively monitor the possibility for sexual violence and implement necessary
interventions to prevent same-sex rape among these male ranks.
Until the widespread acknowledgment of this violence occurs, the
rape of men in single-sex environments will continue and, despite
what many people would like to believe, the literal and figurative
walls between these environments and other communities are
neither stable nor impermeable. Sexual violence in any realm will
in some way be a detriment to us all. We simply cannot continue to
ignore or dismiss this crisis any longer.

FOUR

AN ASSAULT ON
SEXUAL IDENTITY

_N_o single factor is more responsible for the stigma attached to male rape than homophobia—the irrational fear and hatred of homosexuality. The cultural confusion of where sex ends and rape begins places sexual preference at the center of insensitivity, injustice, and disbelief directed at survivors of same-sex rape. Every survivor I interviewed for this book expressed some amount of difficulty related to their sexual identity throughout the course of their survival and recovery. The complexity of heterosexuality and how it relates to sexual violence between men and women continues to be explored in depth throughout feminist and other forms of literature. But do these same concepts apply to men raping men, and if not, how can we begin to understand the role that sexual identity plays in same-sex rape? Issues of homophobia and sexual identity are a common thread throughout the chapters of this book, but here I wish to place it in a central focus so as to ask (and possibly answer) such questions as:

✓ Can the rape of a straight man make him gay?
✓ Who are raped more, straight or gay men?
✓ Who are the more common perpetrators of male rape, straight or gay men?
✓ Where do bisexual men fit into discussions of same-sex rape?
✓ Is the definition of rape the same for rape between men and women and that between men?

The fear of same-sex rape has historically been used to justify and enact the oppression of gay and lesbian people. Most of us have at some time in our lives heard the stereotype that all gay men are child molesters, for example, and therefore must be medically institutionalized or banned from professions that involve working closely with youth. Aside from this perception of a child molester, homophobia is also bolstered by the popular characterization of gay men as adult male rapists. This is embodied by everything from the classic "Don't drop the soap" jokes to the increasingly used "homosexual panic defense" in courts of law where the sexual advances of a gay man are used to justify his brutal murder.

In a discussion on same-sex rape, Paul Cameron, head of the American Family Association, a right-wing antigay organization, wrote in his 1991 book *The Gay 90s* that "rape at any age is violent and emotionally devastating. But it can also edge victims toward homosexuality"[1] and that "in line with traditional psychiatric opinion, violence goes hand-in-hand with the gay lifestyle."[2] Similar statements of this nature are not uncommon from such hatemongers. Given that a great deal of homophobia is so firmly rooted in sexual violence mythology, it seems strange that gay and lesbian political movements have thus far appeared to be uninterested in addressing male rape. Even sodomy laws are highly dependent on the notion of sexual consent, which is discussed in greater depth in Chapter Eleven. In terms of equality for gay and lesbian people, the stakes are incredibly high when it comes to perceptions and reactions to same-sex rape.

Male rape is also one of those instances in which heterosexual men greatly suffer from societal homophobia. The fact that a man has had "sexual" contact with another man, even against his will, is more than enough to call into question his manhood and heterosexuality, and these two traits are often considered one and the same. Sometimes these men are left questioning their own sexual identity and wondering if sexual contact with another man constitutes a homosexual experience. As for heterosexual male rapists, stereotypes also prevail, particularly that there are no heterosexual men who rape other men. Without exception, each time I speak to a group of people about male rape and state that the majority of men who rape other men self-identify as heterosexual, I am met with expressions of surprise and confusion. This reaction often comes from individuals working in the field of rape prevention and treatment, people who are well versed in the "rape is violence, not sex" doctrine.

As this chapter will demonstrate, homophobia plays a key role in setting the stage for some men to be raped. However, homophobia actually *protects* the majority of men from being raped by other men. Male socialization dictates that men should be off-limits to each other sexually, even in sexually violent ways. From the time when males are young boys, they are heavily instructed and encouraged to gear their sexualized attention toward women and girls, and most especially their sexually violent conquest of others. Homophobia actually serves as a social deterrent to men raping men in most instances for this reason of compulsory heterosexuality, but the men who are selected as targets of sexual violence are not chosen at random. While homophobia may prevent the majority of men from raping men, it simultaneously and dramatically increases the likelihood that men who do not conform to traditional notions of manhood will be sexually violated.

BODILY RESPONSES

States of intense pain, anxiety, panic, or fear may cause a spontaneous erection and ejaculation in some men. Many rape survivors who ejaculate during their assault may later question whether or not the rape was actually nonconsensual, as ejaculation is commonly associated with orgasm and sexual pleasure. A clear example of equating rape with sex, this may lead heterosexual victims to question their sexual orientation, wondering why they ejaculated in response to "sexual" contact with another man. One male survivor explained, "I always thought a guy couldn't get hard if he was scared, and when this guy took me off [made me ejaculate] it really messed up my mind. I thought maybe something was wrong with me."[3] Spontaneous ejaculation produces a kind of mind/body split for many men, leaving them confused and wondering, "My mind was saying no, but my body seemed to say yes. Why did my body betray me this way?"

Much of this confusion results from a lack of knowledge and education about sexuality in our culture. Most men are not encouraged to learn about their gender-specific health concerns and bodily functions as many women are. The concept of men's health as a field of study and an area deserving of public health attention has only begun to emerge in recent years. Just as knowledge about the rape of women, both popular and scientific, has advanced a great deal in the past 20 years, an understanding of these male rape dynamics will also take considerable time and exploration.

In his book *Men Who Rape*, psychologist Nicholas Groth investigated the motives behind some rapists' attempts to force their male victims to ejaculate:

> *Such efforts may serve several purposes. In misidentifying ejaculation with orgasm, the victim may be bewildered by his psychological response to the offense and thus discouraged from reporting the assault lest his sexuality become suspect. Such reaction may serve to impeach his credibility in trial testimony and discredit his allegation of nonconsent. In the psychology of the offender, such reaction may symbolize his ultimate and complete control over his victim's body and confirm the fantasy that the victim really wanted and enjoyed the rape.[4]*

Others, including medical personnel, family, friends, and other support people, may be reluctant to believe a man who admits rape when he shares that he had an erection or ejaculated. As male rape is widely thought to be impossible anyway, this extra element of doubt may eliminate what few resources male survivors might access.

T. J., a male survivor in his mid-20s was raped by a date in his dorm room while attending college. The man had torn T. J.'s clothing off, turned him around, and was raping him when T. J.'s roommate, Ted, came home and interrupted the assault. T. J. recalled that during the assault, the man raping him "had reached around and was rubbing me. When I'm scared, I'm usually erect too. It's that adrenaline flow. It [the rape] was really hard to deal with after that." Later that evening as T. J. talked with Ted, he wondered aloud if he had done enough to prevent the rape, or if he had really wanted to have sex. "One of the ways my roommate tried to help me was by saying, 'You know you were not to blame. You didn't have an erection.' and I said, 'No, but I did.'" Ted had made the assumption that T. J. did not experience an erection, and attempted to use that information as a strategy for affirming the validity of the rape. Although Ted remained admirably supportive even after learning of the erection, this situation is a prime example of falsely equating an erection with consent, and lack of erection with violence.

Apart from these involuntary responses, male rape survivors sometimes willfully elect to ejaculate in hopes that it will signify an end to the assault, that if the rapist believes the "sexual" experience is over, he will cease the attack. Jonathan, a survivor I interviewed, explained, "I made myself cum very quickly cause I thought that then he would cum and it would be over and I could leave. I consciously decided that if I did cum that maybe it would bring him over the edge and he would cum and then be too tired." As unlikely as it may seem, ejaculation in cases such as this becomes a self-defense strategy to minimize the duration or intensity of the assault. In Jonathan's situation, unfortunately, his ejaculation did not motivate his attacker to stop the rape in progress.

I wish to discuss one more possible connection between the biology of sexuality and male rape, although the issue has not been explicitly raised in the interviews I conducted or the literature I have examined. This connection is the increasingly popular media hype that homosexuality is biologically grounded in the body, and that gay men do not have mental control over what they sexually desire. For almost a century, scientists have searched for the cause of homosexuality. In fact, even the term *homosexual* came from a late 19th-century classification of disease. Since 1990, an abundance of claims have been put forth by scientists who believe they have found anatomical correlates, if not direct causes, of homosexuality in the human body. If we believe that the source of gayness comes from the body (such as a gene, hormone, or brain structure), then how can we refute that a bodily response such as erection or ejaculation to same-sex genital contact (i.e., rape) also indicates homosexuality? As the belief in a biological origin of homosexuality becomes more widespread, so will the confusion between same-sex desire and involuntary physiological responses we label as sexual. This reductive and sensational science—sociobiology—reinforces the mind/body split that many rape survivors experience, declaring that the mind cannot be relied on for the truth, rather that it can only come from the physicality of the body.

Other than these issues related to the penis, penetration of the anus may hold profoundly different cultural meanings for gay men than for heterosexual men. Many gay men consider their anus to be a sexual part of their anatomy, and may feel "sexually" violated if they are anally raped, whereas many heterosexual men may feel that forced penetration of their anus represents participation in an activity that is not necessarily sexual, but "unnatural" or "perverse." (Of course this is a generalization, as some heterosexual men engage in activities that bring them anal pleasure and some gay men find anal sex unappealing.) This leads me to ask the following questions: Are gay men who have previously engaged in consensual, receptive anal intercourse better able to identify forced anal penetration as sexual assault? Overall, are gay men more likely to view forced anal penetration as sexual violence, whereas heterosexual men may view it as some other kind of nonsexual assault? I do not pretend to have answers to these questions, but they do warrant serious consideration if we are to effectively understand the diversity of ways in which men define, or do not define, same-sex rape.

In my interview with T. J., we explored these questions in some detail. But rather than discussing at length the differences between heterosexual and gay male survivors of anal rape, he focused more on a comparison between anal and vaginal rape:

> *To the women who've been raped that I've talked to, they've been raped vaginally. They have not been exposed to anal rape; it's really weird to them. I think it's something they've not actually thought about. This is something that is so rarely talked about. Even when women get raped anally, often I've found that's not something they're willing to talk about the way they are willing to talk about vaginal rape. I think it comes from very ingrained homophobia.*

Despite the lack of consent when women are anally raped, T. J. believes many women are silenced by the taboo of anal penetration that carries the stigma of homophobia. Men also rape women anally in an effort to make the experience of forced penetration as physically painful as possible, and the anal assault may signify a special form of symbolic domination over women that exceeds vaginal rape. Even though heterosexual people engage in anal sex, the act is still very much associated with homosexuality, especially in Western cultures. Having grown up in India, T. J. noted this culturally specific element linking anal sex with gay sex and suggested the taboo is grounded in Judeo-Christian religiosity:

> *In India, when I talk about it [anal rape] I have not had that same reaction. In India, anal sex is very commonly talked about, it doesn't have that religious marginality. In India, gods have anal sex. It's just like any other form of intercourse. But here in the United States, I find that inculcated religious phobia of anal sex which translates into homophobia.*

Building on this devaluation of gay male anal sex, that it is inherently inferior to heterosexual vaginal sex, T. J. theorized that anal rape might be deemed less of a sexual victimization than vaginal rape. With respect to gay men, anal rape may be viewed as even less severe if they have practiced consensual, receptive anal intercourse in the past:

> *I think some people think anal rape of gay men is less of a violation. Especially less of a violation for people who have had anal sex. It's a kind of blame that since you've opened yourself up to violation, you*

somehow deserve it. It's that whole dynamic that if women wear
something sexy and get raped, it's less of a violation because they
chose to open themselves up to it.

T. J. proposed that a history of consensual anal penetration might permanently reduce the innocence, and therefore the tragedy, of the rape of a gay man. A heterosexual analogy to this would be the belief that the rape of a virgin is somehow more of a travesty than the rape of a woman who is sexually experienced—that the context of the act (lack of consent) might be different, but the person has already experienced the physical act, so it's no big deal.

The simultaneous presence of these rationales, that anal rape is both more and less severe than vaginal rape, begins to present something of a self-contradiction. T. J. explained:

On the one hand, it's thought of as really bad, a real invasion
because it's not the right place to insert the penis. I think there is
that general conception. Some women I've talked to have said if they
were to be raped they would prefer it to be vaginal rape. But it's a
paradox, that if you experience anal rape, it's not something to
shout about as much as vaginal rape. That it's somehow worse, but
that you're somehow less of a victim.

The following sections offer some observations and comparisons between the rape of gay men by gay men, straight men by straight men, straight men by gay men, and gay men by straight men. These combinations are only hypothetical illustrations of rape scenarios. In reality, categories of gay and straight relations are somewhat artificial. The ways in which people have sex and think about sex are often less rigid and more fluid than these classifications given that sexual identities and behaviors are not limited to opposites of either heterosexual or homosexual. In fact, some of the men I interviewed and quote here self-identified as bisexual or queer, a more politicized identity with multiple meanings.

As I stated earlier, there is a current consensus among those who research male rape that the majority of men who rape other men are heterosexual. Several published studies demonstrate this belief. Some of these rely on the survivor's perception of his attacker's sexual orientation, such as those conducted by Dr. Richard Hillman of St. Mary's Hospital in London in 1991, P. L.

Huckle's 1995 study at the South Wales Forensic Psychiatric Service, and Richie McMullen's work at Survivors, a London-based male rape agency. Others are based on interviews with the rapists themselves and report these men's self-identified heterosexuality, such as Nicholas Groth and Ann Burgess's 1980 study.

Although it remains uncertain, evidence suggests gay men are more likely to be raped than straight men. Despite the fact that heterosexual men far outnumber gay men in sheer masses, gay men seem to be more at risk, on average, than their heterosexual counterparts. A 1990 study conducted by Dr. David F. Duncan at Southern Illinois University at Carbondale found gay and lesbian college students reported significantly higher lifetime prevalences of sexual victimization than did heterosexual men participating in the same study. He also stated, "It is possible, however, that gay/lesbian students differ from heterosexual students in their openness in reporting experiences of sexual victimization rather than in the frequency with which they have been victimized."[5] In a large-scale study of 930 gay men living in England and Wales, 27.6% reported they had been sexually assaulted at some point in their lives. Sociologists Ford Hickson and his colleagues conducted the survey as part of Project SIGMA, a 6-year nonclinical study of homosexually active men.[6] Gay men's vulnerability to rape is related in part to the fact that they have male sexual partners and are frequently in the company of many men. As with acquaintance rape of women, people are most likely to be raped by members of their own race, class, geographic area, and social relations.

GAY MEN RAPING GAY MEN

Even though same-sex relationships may provide equal footing on grounds of gender, other elements of power may be used by a gay man to rape another gay man (physical, economic, and so on). Rape and domestic violence are frequently not believed to occur within gay and lesbian communities because of these traditional definitions of gender-based violence. Gay men's reluctance to speak openly about violence, especially sexual violence, within their communities is understandable. Drawing any attention to "intracommunity" rape affords numerous opportunities for homophobic critics who would eagerly cry out, "See! We told you they are sexual predators. They even attack each other." Apart from the survivors of this violence, many gay community leaders view highly public discussions of gay men raping gay men as an unnecessary airing of dirty laundry, for this risks a provision of fodder to opportunistic enemies who are anxious for information that demonizes homosexuality when taken out of context. The negative consequence of this protective state of affairs is that gay male survivors feel silenced and predict that if they seek support or provide testimony to their experiences, they will betray their own community. A number of factors play into making this sexual violence both possible and in some situations probable. Some stem from internal aspects of gay culture; others are imposed by outside forces.

Alcohol and Other Drugs

A great deal of gay male interaction has historically centered around bars as social gathering spots, although this is changing over time with the proliferation of opportunities for gay men to meet through emerging organizations and events. Gay bars provide important spaces for gay men to meet, relax, and feel relatively safe with one another, but as important as they are for building and maintaining community, they are still businesses that survive on their patrons' purchase and consumption of alcoholic beverages. Like anyone else, gay men are vulnerable to alcoholism and other forms of substance abuse. This combination of drug-induced impairment and the company of men creates a vulnerability to sexual assault. The use of alcohol and other drugs can create situations where men are unable to effectively define and defend their sexual limits. At the same time, men who are under the influence experience impaired judgments that can lead to misinterpretation or failure to respect another's boundaries.

Domestic Violence

Most discussions of rape between gay men have not addressed these acquaintance rape situations where the men have met in bars, at parties, through friends, or as casual sexual partners; they have focused on sexual violence as a component of domestic violence. In a 1989 study by psychologist Caroline Waterman and her colleagues at the University of Albany, 12% of 34 men in gay relationships "reported being victims of forced sex by their current or most recent partner."[7] David Island and Patrick Letellier, the authors of *Men Who Beat the Men Who Love Them*, estimate that some 500,000 gay men are victims of domestic violence every year.[8] The National Coalition of Anti-Gay Violence Programs released a 1996 report of information compiled from data for San Francisco, Chicago, New York, San Diego, Minneapolis, and Columbus, Ohio. The data indicated domestic violence may be no less common among gay couples than heterosexual couples, but the victims face even more intimidation in seeking the support they need. Gloria McCauley, executive director of the Buckeye Region Anti-Violence Organization in Ohio, told the *Columbus Dispatch*, "I think it's a terrifically high number, particularly because our (gay and bisexual) communities are not recognizing domestic violence. . . . Most of the people who are involved in abusive or violent relationships don't know that they have any resources, don't know what to do. They feel trapped."[9]

As with sexual violence, not everyone sympathizes or recognizes the victimization of same-sex domestic violence. In the December 10, 1996, issue of the *Chicago Tribune*, columnist Mike Royko described his lack of concern for gay men who are battered by their partners because he believes men should have the power and privilege to simply walk away from an abusive relationship, regardless of the circumstances:

> It seems to me that if Bill lives with Joe and Joe makes a practice of pummeling Bill, then Bill would have the good sense to just pack a suitcase and get the heck out of there. It should be easier for a man to walk away from an abusive relationship than for a woman since men don't get pregnant and have babies.[10]

Royko continued by saying that if a battered partner chooses to stay with his partner, for any reason, "that is his choice and I respect it—so long as he is not my neighbor and doesn't scream for help or pound on my door at night."[11] Clearly more work must be done to sensitize the public on domestic violence issues generally and same-sex domestic violence specifically.

The dialogue about gay men raping gay men, although valuable, has been shortsighted in that most of the research and writing within this context involves partners who either live together or are in a serious, long-term romantic relationship. If gay communities do not begin to expand recognition of the varied ways that rape can happen, it could result in gay men's inability to name their experience as rape if it occurs outside such an established relationship. This would be similar to interpretations of heterosexual acquaintance rape where women easily put a name to rape if they are attacked by a stranger, but seem to define rape by an acquaintance as just "regretted sex" or a "bad experience."

Camille's Ideal

Expanding the definition of rape in this way, beyond the scenarios of a battering partner or a deranged stranger leaping out from behind the bushes to sexually attack his unsuspecting victim, has generated controversy and disagreement. For example, some people hold the opinion that if a woman gets drunk and accompanies a man upstairs to his apartment, she is as responsible for her rape as the rapist himself. Cultural critic Camille Paglia puts forth this argument consistently, stating in so many words that women who are stupid enough to be date-raped deserve no sympathy. To support her argument, she holds gay men up as the ideal standard to which heterosexual women should aspire, saying that gay men are "too mature" to whine about a nonconsensual sexual encounter. This takes the form of backlash by depicting feminist definitions of rape to be infantile and childish, not warranting sympathy, attention, or legal action. She paints a worldview where gay men possess a high level of sophistication and maturity whereas heterosexual women who cry rape are hysterical, naive, and overly sensitive. In an interview with Charlie Rose, Paglia elaborated, "I'm using the gay male attitude, okay? Gay men are adults about these things. For thousands of years they have been, okay? . . . gay men don't, in the middle of a sex act, suddenly go, 'I've changed my mind!' "[12] In such a sweeping generalization she positions gay men as unrapeable by their sexual partners with the assumption that gay men do not reserve the right to end a sexual act once in progress.

> *Okay, life is filled with dangers, like I say. Gay men know this. Gay men understand the dangers of the street. They, they're cruising in parks, do you understand? They get beat up, they get killed. Okay, for thousands of years this has been going on. I'm sick and tired of women behaving this overprotective kind of infantilized condition, okay, where sort of like, "That poor middle-class white girl. Look what happened to her." I'm tired of that.*[13]

Paglia makes all gay men out to be hardened, worldly risk-takers who casually accept homicide as an everyday possibility. This serves her purposes by creating a demanding yardstick by which heterosexual women are measured, and the warped reality she imposes on gay men once again serves to silence and invalidate male rape survivors.

Unfortunately, Paglia has had more to say about male rape in her antifeminist tirades. In her book *Vamps and Tramps*, she writes:

> *The dishonesty and speciousness of the feminist rape analysis are demonstrated by its failure to explore, or even mention, man-on-man sex crimes. If rape were really just a process of political intimidation of women by men, why do men rape and kill other males?*[14]

The answer to Ms. Paglia's question, simply put, is that rape is an act of power and control. Such acts of power, or more specifically, overpowerment, often occur in highly gendered ways, as in the case of men raping women. Frequently, however, rape is enacted as part of racist hate crimes, gay and lesbian bashings, assaults on the homeless, and more. Political power manifests itself not only through a lens of gender, but also race, class, age, sexual identity, physical ability, and more. These forms of power do not operate independently, but in a complex and interwoven system that supports a multiplicity of oppression and violence. Rape is but one of the consequences of such power dynamics. Numerous feminist activists and writers, from Andrea Dworkin to Susan Brownmiller, *have* discussed male rape, although it has not been given equal consideration as feminist work has concentrated, understandably, on the rape of women.

Later in *Vamps and Tramps*, Paglia invokes the gay male epitome once again. She recounts a conversation occurring near a New York City pier on the Hudson River where gay men seek out anonymous sex with each other:

> *This is what I'm always saying about the feminist problem with date rape, okay? . . . I've learned so much from gay men. I mean, I love the gay male attitude, which is to go out into the dark, have anonymous sex. . . . You may get beaten up. That's one of the thrills.*[15]

First off, not all gay men have public or anonymous sex. And certainly not all those who participate in anonymous sex do so for the "thrill" of being physically attacked (if there is such a thrill). If gay men are homophobically stereotyped as hypersexual beings always having or wanting to have sex, then theoretically gay men cannot be raped. The old adage, "You can't rape the willing" describes this mentality. In that respect, gay men are culturally designed to be unrapeable, unable to be violated sexually on any level, as it supposedly feeds their self-destructive wish to be brutalized.

The false belief in pleasure derived from violence is sometimes mistakenly equated with sadomasochism—sexual practices involving the infliction of pain. Talking of desire and violence as being one in the same is an oxymoron. If we can agree that desire implies consent, and violence is a lack of consent, then how can one want to be raped? There is quite a difference between rape and sadomasochistic acts, which are typically regulated by a complex system of explicit communication and negotiation of consent. At the same time, violence and pain are not necessarily the same thing. Pain is a physical sensation that most people find unpleasurable, but some individuals find pain to be sexually stimulating and actually enjoy the feeling. A gay male rape survivor I spoke with, Jonathan, engages in consensual sadomasochistic sex. He described how the man who raped him misused this as a venue for violent behavior: "I think he had misrepresented himself and what he was interested in. He wasn't interested in a consensual experience, he was interested in being violent. He wasn't interested in expanding my limits or making me feel something intense. He was mostly interested in beating up on someone."

The Rape Victim Wannabe

The recurring theme that gay men want to be raped recently surfaced in an opinion piece published in the gay literature magazine *Christopher Street*. In his article, "Male Rape: Tragedy, Fantasy, or Badge of Honor?" William Gordon declared the status of rape victim to be trendy among gay men, that they fabricate rape stories to appear desirable in the eyes of others:

> Only women are sexy to men? Okay . . . I'll be like a woman, a really attractive woman, not a real woman, of course, just a 'B' movie type-o-gal, the one who gets manhandled wherever she goes, call me Gina Lollabrigida, call me Marilyn Monroe, call me frail, helpless, call me sex kitten, call me rape victim.[16]

His profile extends to the status of "wannabe," a copycat syndrome of people who imitate trends to an excessive degree, saying, "Just when you think you've met every kind of wannabe in the world, you find a new one: the rape victim wannabe."[17] Once again the claim is made that gay men aspire to some sexual status of "good enough to be raped." In the article, William Gordon describes the night a friend revealed he had been raped, remarking, "I doubt he'd admit it, but I'm sure he told it [his rape experience] to entice me."[18] With the rarity of information and reporting on male rape in the gay press, these insensitive characterizations of sexual violence as meaningless, casual, and seductive can do untold damage as the last word, unchallenged by a body of balanced literature.

The Coming-Out Process

For men who are just beginning the process of "coming-out" as gay or bisexual, rape can be a devastating setback in the development of their sexual identities. Several of the men I interviewed spoke about the disruption of rape as a pivotal moment that influenced their future relationships with both women and men. Marcus recalled:

> It happened in the course of my coming-out and I was just starting to think about my attraction to men as well as my attraction to women and coming-out as a bisexual man. It really made that process so much more difficult for me. I had this huge distrust of men while wanting to be close to them, and a very deep anger toward men.

The attraction and repulsion to men after rape is a common feeling for many gay and bisexual male survivors. Many of these men want to begin exploring their same-sex attraction, but harbor such distrust and anger toward men that it prevents them from building and sustaining healthy relationships.

For T. J., the aftermath of rape became a catalyst for self-reflection as he sought involvement in campus student organizations that addressed issues of sexism and homophobia. Through his growing investment in feminist politics, he slowly developed integrated identities of "rape survivor" and "queer." He told me, "Then I started going to GLA [Gay and Lesbian Alliance] meetings. My rape consciousness began going hand in hand with my queer consciousness." For T. J., the lines between oppressions of race, sexual identity, and gender began to bleed over into each other, and he realized that his rape was grounded in a larger set of power relations that were social forces beyond the scope of his individual circumstance.

The toll of sexual violence on sexual identity development in gay and bisexual men has only begun to be realized by many therapists and counselors who assist these men in their struggle to come to terms with their life's realities. Susan Wachob, a psychotherapist in San Francisco who specializes in working with male survivors of sexual abuse, explains:

The gay survivor, who may have grown up keeping his sexual orientation a secret, is already skilled at hiding important facets of himself. When a sexual assault takes place, he is already primed for how to treat yet another experience of himself that he has been taught is private, shameful, and unacceptable.

The closets in which gay male rape survivors hide, those of rape-related shame and sexual identity, often collapse into one terrifying feat of pretense. Balancing a high degree of internal pain with an outward performance of normative wellness eventually takes a heavy toll on those men who live in the closet.

Some sexually inexperienced men may perceive rape to be the norm of same-sex relations and drive them deep into the closet even if they were already "out," either fearing or denying their desire for men. Others may normalize rape and sexual brutality as if it is an inherent part of gay culture and come to expect violent interactions with other men. The internalization of this violence can also have drastic effects, leaving gay and bisexual men feeling as if they somehow deserved to be raped as a punishment for their same-sex attraction.

Altered Sex Practices

Even for men who have acknowledged their sexual identity and established a firm sense of self with respect to their sexuality, the experience of rape can force a change in the ways that male survivors engage in sexual activity. Marcus commented:

It didn't change my sexuality, although it made the process of coming-out more painful and I still feel the repercussions of that. Most of my sex partners are women and all of my romantic partners have been women. In terms of sex practices, I felt a much stronger need for safety and also a much greater concern for my partner's feeling of safety. Sometimes that causes problems, especially if I'm involved with a survivor. Because then we both sense the other person putting out boundaries and it's made it more difficult sometimes to have sex. For a while I had less sex.

Some survivors may have less sex after their rape, whereas others may have more sex in an attempt to reestablish a normalcy of sexual experience. Rape trauma syndrome also enters the picture here, when even consensual sex can trigger flashbacks, panic attacks, impotence, and other negative effects. The man who raped Jonathan severely beat him in the face while anally penetrating him, and Jonathan vividly described to me the residual impact of this attack:

> I remember talking to people who I was going to have sex with and said, "Don't touch my face. It freaks me out too much." It doesn't bother me anymore, it was for two years afterward. Initially, for a few months afterward, it would have been anytime. For another year and a half, it was just during sex. I would pull away or snap my head back if men touched my face with their hands.

Jonathan's reaction became an involuntary reflex as he was psychologically conditioned to defend himself against a possibly similar assault in the future. This kind of response is normal and to be expected as part of posttraumatic stress disorder in those who suffer from rape trauma syndrome.

In T. J.'s case, this sexual behavior change is especially evident in that he goes to great lengths to monitor his partner's ongoing intentions. T. J. was first raped when he was 12 years old, assaulted from behind while showering in the barracks of his youth military service. He never saw the person who raped him, and was sure that if he had turned around to look, his attacker would have killed him. The man never spoke to him. Ever since he was raped a second time as an adult, he now requires a heightened level of communication with his partner during sex:

> With men, there have been lots of repercussions. For a long time I really, really had a phobia of being entered anally. Primarily because most of the time I couldn't see what was happening. I eventually got over that with lots of techniques. I use mirrors, so I can see their face. That's really, really important to me—that I can see their face and their expression. I also started asking my sexual partners to talk to me more during sex.

T. J. has developed a need for consistent reassurance during sexual activity, which he obtains by assessing his partner's facial expressions, viewing exactly what is happening between his and his partner's bodies, and discerning his partner's temperament. The mirrors provide a literal window for T. J. to view the scene from a distanced perspective, enabling observation from outside the sexual activity to ensure ongoing consent.

The rape that occurs among gay and bisexual male populations can have a myriad of negative effects on both individual and collective well-being. Efforts to prevent and treat sexual violence between gay men must continue to develop with a strong cultural competence that takes into consideration the factors of societal homophobia, individual identity, a diversity of gay culture, and the needs of bisexual men.

GAY MEN RAPING HETEROSEXUAL MEN

Men who rape tend to do so within their own social, cultural, and economic group, or rape those they have power over in society. For these reasons it is not surprising that the incidence of gay men raping heterosexual men is relatively low. This form of violence is possible, however, and does occur, but the fears typically associated with gay on straight rape are greatly exaggerated. As demonstrated throughout this book, many male rape myths are grounded in irrational fears and hatred of homosexuality. The pervasive belief that a gay man will sexually assault a heterosexual man if given the opportunity has been transformed from a possibility into a stereotyped norm. However, one exception to this myth that male rape usually involves gay men assaulting heterosexual men also stems from homophobia. Some people may believe that gay men could not possibly rape straight men because all gay men are supposedly feminine and physically weak, thus unable to overpower a "real man." On a similar note, Ford Hickson and his colleagues at London's Project SIGMA stated, "folk wisdom tells us that it is easy for gay men to find casual sexual partners, so they have no need to force themselves on other men."[19] This folk wisdom is also based on a confusion between rape and sex, assuming that (1) all gay men are promiscuous, (2) rape behavior is driven by one's libido, and (3) sexual violence serves as a suitable substitute in satisfying gay male sexual desire.

If by chance a heterosexual man reports being raped by a gay man, he may be disbelieved or extremely stigmatized for his inability to defend himself against an effeminate person. (Being gay and possessing feminine traits are often stereotypically synonymous.) In one case of military sexual misconduct in 1995, the question of sexual preference became the center of debate during a trial that involved two Army men. After a night of heavy drinking, one man woke up in his bedroom to find another man had broken in, undressed him, and performed oral sex on him. The victim immediately reported the incident to authorities. Army investigators speculated, however, that the sexual contact was consensual and were unsure whether to press forcible sodomy charges against the alleged attacker or consensual sodomy charges against both men. The *National Law Journal* reported on the assault, and in the commentary was a less than subtle argument based on the myth of physical size and masculinity as an inherent self-defense to rape: "[The alleged attacker] could pass for a high school student. He is 5 feet 8 inches tall and slight—perhaps 2 inches shorter and 40 pounds lighter than [the alleged victim]. He admitted in testimony that he was not pinned down or threatened."[20] In the legal determination of consent, the alleged victim's heterosexuality was called into question because of the belief that he should have had no problem fending off the sexual advances of a man who is depicted as young and "slight." As one rape survivor expressed from Drs. Mezey and King's 1989 study at the Institute of Psychiatry in London, "something very dirty has happened to you that nobody believes can happen—if you let it happen you must be queer, if you're not a queer it can't have happened."[21]

HETEROSEXUAL MEN RAPING GAY MEN

Heterosexual men sometimes rape gay men, usually as part of hate-motivated gay bashings. In the book *Hate Crimes: Confronting Violence Against Lesbians and Gay Men*, violence expert Joseph Harry described what might at first seem to be an illogical behavior:

> *Occasionally, gay bashing incidents include forcible rape, either oral or anal. Given the context of coercion, however, such techni-cally homosexual acts seem to imply no homosexuality on the part of the offenders. The victim serves, both physically and symbol-ically, as a vehicle for the sexual status needs of the offenders in the course of recreational violence.[22]*

One might think that if a heterosexual man despises homosex-uality to such a degree that he attacks gay men, he would not engage in sexual contact with them, even for the purpose of violence. Gay men, or even men who are simply perceived to be gay, are commonly viewed by society as traitors to masculinity. They may be raped as a form of punishment for relinquishing their traditional manhood, with a rapist mentality of "You want to act like a woman? Then I'll show you what it means to be one." Gay men might also be perceived by rapists as not only the most deserving of rape, but the least likely to have the strength, either physical or emotional, to effectively resist the assault.

Are Gay Bashers Actually Gay Themselves?

Controversies in psychological literature continue to debate the motivation of heterosexual men to commit acts of violence against gay men. Some recent research speculates that a man's latent, unrealized homosexuality causes internalized hatred that eventually surfaces as aggression directed toward gay men. This is thought to be a lashing out against what one most fears within one's self. The most recent reprisal of this theory comes from research conducted by Henry Adams at the University of Georgia, who suggests that men who bash gay men are often repressed gay men themselves. A 1996 article that appeared in the *Irish Times* newspaper reported:

> *Dr. Art O'Connor, forensic psychiatrist at the Central Mental Hospital in Dublin, believes that some homosexual men only ex-press their homosexuality aggressively, perhaps after drinking. Most likely candidates are those who "in their everyday lives are anti-gay and are trying to cover it up from society."[23]*

Although these research findings may have some merit, we must also consider whether it is simply recycling the same old homophobic myths regarding male rape: that even the heterosexual men who rape gay men are really gay inside, therefore male rape is actually homosexual rape.

HETEROSEXUAL MEN RAPING HETEROSEXUAL MEN

Again, given that men tend to rape others similar to themselves, the practice of heterosexual men raping each other seems sensible and likely. Without a methodical look at male rape on a mass scale, however, we will remain blind to the exact prevalence of each of these above four categories. Same-sex rape between heterosexual men is also largely an exertion of power and control through feminizing the other by forcing a man into the sexually submissive, receptive role of female. This may occur between strangers, male family members (especially as elder abuse), acquaintances, colleagues, and so on. Acquaintance rape is most likely in this situation, meaning the victim has some form of prior relationship, however casual, to the man who raped him. Especially in the case of heterosexual stranger rape, the victim may misperceive the rapist to be gay if he has no other knowledge of the attacker, believing the myth that rape is a sexually motivated crime. Categorizations of same-sex rape can be skewed depending on the victim's own homophobia, belief in popular rape mythology, and degree of prior relationship to the rapist.

In contrast, heterosexual male rape survivors may lack many of the support systems that most gay men are able to access. Gay and lesbian community centers are often a first point of contact for gay male rape survivors who need referrals or other assistance. Additionally, more and more organizations dedicated to gay and lesbian antiviolence work have sprung up across the globe. This infrastructure has been built to counteract the effects of societal homophobia, foster a sense of community, and enable gay and lesbian individuals to lead the productive and healthy lives they deserve. Very few, if any, such services are tailored specifically to the needs of heterosexual men, given their comparative position of status within society. Heterosexual male survivors may be directed to gay community services because these organizations are perhaps the only local ones who address same-sex rape. (This has historically been the case with HIV-positive heterosexual people who depended on gay-specific AIDS organizations, for example.) These men may be further stigmatized for their reliance on the gay community, and this may further provoke one's questioning of sexual identity.

RAPE OF TRANSGENDER PEOPLE

Aside from discussions of same-sex rape based on the model of biological sex (male/female), we should also consider those people who do not fit neatly into traditional or stable categories of the opposite sexes. Around the world, the social movement of people who identify as transgender is gaining strength and influence through their defiance of imposed gender identities based on one's biological sex at the time of birth. Quite literally, the term *transgender* represents a movement along any or all of the gendered spectrums of masculine/feminine, man/woman, or male/female. Transgender identity and practice might also constitute a behavior or identity that is neither masculine nor feminine, neither man nor woman, or neither male nor female.

Because of this lack of compliance to gender roles that society deems to be "normal" and "healthy," transgender people are frequently targets of physical abuse, including sexual abuse. Unfortunately, social and legal systems designed to support survivors of sexual violence are usually less than helpful to transgender people. For example, in June 1996, South Korea's highest court ruled that two men who had sexually assaulted a male-to-female transsexual could not be convicted of rape, as South Korean law only recognizes the rape of women. Supreme Court Justice Chong Kwi-ho explained to the court, "Though the victim in this case behaves as a female, the person cannot be recognized as one because, among other things, his chromosomes remain unchanged and he cannot get pregnant."[24] In South Korea, male on male rape is a legal impossibility, and one's sex at birth remains the determinant of gender despite any changes that may later occur to one's body. Instead of being charged with rape, the two men were found guilty of the lesser charge of "sexual assault" and were each sentenced to a jail term of 2½ years.

In December 1996, firemen in Managua, Nicaragua, rescued a transvestite who had spent 8 days trapped at the bottom of an abandoned well. Two men had brutally raped Shakira, the man dressed in women's clothing, attempted to strangle him with a cord tied around his neck, then threw him into the 100-foot-deep well. Shakira fractured his leg in the fall and was unable to climb out to safety. He was eventually found by friends and family who had launched a search party once they discovered him missing.

In the United States, one of the highest profile cases of sexual assault of a transgender person was the 1993 rape and murder of Teena Brandon, a woman who cross-dressed and lived much of her life as a man, and her three friends in a Nebraska farmhouse. Of the two men who committed the violence, one was convicted on three counts of first-degree murder and sentenced to death. The other was convicted on two counts of second-degree murder and is serving a life sentence. Before Brandon was murdered on New Year's Eve of 1993, she reported to the local sheriff that she had been raped by the two men on Christmas day. They warned her that if she reported the rape, they would silence her. Brandon ignored the warning and went to the police. After her death, a family member filed a lawsuit against local law enforcement claiming they did not take the rape report seriously, in part because she was a cross-dresser, and could have prevented her murder days later.

In October 1996, two prison guards were indicted in Evry, France, after ten transsexual prostitutes who had been prisoners stepped forward to report the guards had raped them. The transvestites had been separated from other prisoners and were forced to engage in sexual activity under the threat of worsened prison conditions, including denial of food. Unfortunately, these cases are not infrequent incidents. As the transgender social movement increases in size and visibility, backlash tactics such as sexual violence will most likely increase as well. The need for adequate and sensitive services for these survivors is necessary in the face of dual stigmatization. Transgender rape will also call into question the gender-specific legal definitions of sexual assault, as in the case of South Korea.

GAY HISTORY OR RAPE HISTORY?

At the heart of confusion between homosexuality and same-sex rape lies the question of consent. The question of exactly what constitutes consent bears a great deal of importance in the distinction between male rape and male homosexuality, simultaneously helping to define and distinguish the two. Beyond our present-day concerns of how sexual identity and sexual assault influence and relate to one another, a critical attempt to tease apart consensual sex from forced sexual activity bears strong implications for a growing field of academic inquiry, namely, gay history. In the last few decades, scholars worldwide have undertaken the monumental project of recovering the history of same-sex sexual behaviors and communities. As homosexuality has long been considered taboo in most Western civilizations, this evidence and documentation is rather rare. What little evidence has survived is often vague or filtered through the perspective of legal and religious organizations that document the punishment of homosexuality.

As a field of study, gay history has been deemed important because explorations of this past can help to fortify modern gay community through the establishment of cultural heritage and an understanding of how antigay oppression has evolved over the centuries. Some anxious and eager researchers, however, have recovered evidence of what they call sexual behavior but in context appears to be rape behavior by our contemporary definitions. Usually this identification of historical same-sex rape as "gay history" goes unchallenged, even by the rigorous process of peer review. Psychiatry professor Ivor Jones at Royal Hobart Hospital Clinical School in Australia notes:

> In historical accounts, problems of definition abound; they arise in
> defining sexual assault as opposed to sexual co-operation and this
> ground can readily be shifted by legislative fiat. Male sexual assault
> is generally regarded as a subset of homosexual behavior, with
> implications and thereby problems of definitions extending beyond
> the genital act to sexual reference.[25]

Even in the interviews that I conducted for this book, a surface
reading or excerpt would imply consent between two men when
in fact there was none. For example, one survivor I spoke with
talked about his communication with the man who raped him
shortly after the assault:

> He called me the next day to thank me and complimented me on my
> performance. I was so confused. He kept telling me how good I was,
> as if I had wanted it to happen. He said he wanted to see me again
> like I would really want for that to happen all over. I wondered if he
> thought I wanted it . . . if I sent him the wrong signals, like I was to
> blame 'cause he misunderstood me somehow.

Marcus recounted a similar experience, only during rather than
after the rape. "He repeated over and over again that he loved me.
He just said, 'I love you. I love you,' over and over again as I was
saying 'No. No.'" This redefinition of reality allows the rapist to
foreclose opportunities for the survivor to identify the experience
as violence, and also affirms the rapist's own denial as he acts out a
fantasy that the experience is in fact consensual. The complexity of
these interpretations can be difficult enough when one has firsthand access to a subject's own words and testimonies, let alone
having to rely on remnant materials that are decades or centuries old.

On the flip side of this, how can we know that records of
same-sex rape are not, in fact, evidence of homosexual behavior?
Because of the severity of punishment and social ostracization
from being discovered to have participated in sex with someone of
the same gender, there is a high likelihood that once one of the
individuals was caught, he might have claimed the act was nonconsensual so as to absolve himself of willing participation in the
deviance. Ranging from public shame to death, punitive measures
for homosexuality could have been (and may still be) a motivation

for one to make a false claim of rape, although I do not wish to assert that this constitutes a significant fraction of male rape reports.

One of the most hotly contested historical elements charged by this debate over rape versus sex has been that of the North American Indian social class known as the "berdache." Although similarities and differences can be found between berdache-like people across the breadth and diversity of native North American nations, they are commonly considered to be a kind of third gender status—neither man nor woman. Some berdache, although biologically male, would adopt pieces of women's attire and women's duties, including sexual activity with males. Because of this gender status and same-sex sexual behavior, gay historians such as anthropologist Will Roscoe and others have closely scrutinized the berdache as a kind of predecessor or counterpart to today's gay, lesbian, and bisexual identities.

There is no consensus, however, regarding the characterization of the berdache in historical context. Ramon Gutierrez, professor of history at the Center for Advanced Study in the Behavior Sciences in Stanford, California, criticizes Roscoe and other gay history scholars for depicting the North American berdache as a social role of pure honor and prestige to serve as a contemporary role model for gay life. He draws distinctions between gender roles that are imposed rather than assumed and differentiates between homosexuality and same-sex rape inflicted for purposes of humiliation and degradation. He believes, "Berdache status was one principally ascribed to defeated enemies. Among the insults and humiliations inflicted on prisoners of war were homosexual rape, castration, the wearing of women's clothes, and performing women's work."[26] In his book *Sex and Conquest: Gendered Violence, Political Order, and the European Conquest of the Americas*, historian Richard Trexler fashions a compelling argument for avoiding the convenient blurring of lines between violence and sex. Similar to Gutierrez, Trexler commented that the berdache, as "important figures are seen more as forerunners of modern liberated gays than as emblems of tribal power and authority, genial artistic types rather than the embodiments of dependence they prove to be in the period of the conquests."[27] His book "argues that, in much of antiquity, males as well as females were born into a world of penetrative penalty. That is, men as well as women were sometimes punished through sexual means."[28]

Although some gay-supportive historians may translate same-sex rape into consensual sexual activity for the purposes of bolstering gay community, a similar slight of hand can be pulled by those who wish to demonize same-sex sexuality. Take, for example, author Scott Lively's book *The Pink Swastika: Homosexuality in the Nazi Party*. In his work, Lively characterizes a number of historical figures as "homosexual sadists" and draws the conclusion that there was a strong and influential homosexual presence within the Nazi party. Much of this "sadism," however, is violent and nonconsensual, and cannot necessarily be equated with consensual relationships between men. Lively puts forth a counterclaim to the belief that gay men were persecuted in Nazi Germany, herded up and exterminated in concentration camps. Instead he purports gay men were a prominent force of fascism, identifiable as gay in part because of their sexually violent behavior:

> Nazi anti-homosexual rhetoric was largely hollow and served to deflect public attention from Hitler's perverted ruling clique. "Gay Holocaust" revisionists exploit the Holocaust to legitimize their "victim" strategy for manipulating public sympathies. The truth exposes these "victims" as perpetrators and thus they must suppress it.[29]

Again, competing realities center around the interpretation of sexual contact with respect to consent. Episodes of same-sex rape can be used just as easily by those who wish to substantiate a tradition of homosexual vilification.

These components of power can no longer be ignored in historical investigations of same-sex sexual behavior and same-sex rape, from "pederasty" relationships between men and boys that appear to have been consensual to male transvestites who served as sexual slaves to men in authority. In some versions of Greek mythology, for example, Zeus abducted Ganymede against his will for sexual purposes. In other versions of the same myth,

Ganymede is simply "seduced" and becomes a willing partner. In every chronicle of earlier sexual events, historians must begin to ask themselves if same-sex rape should be considered homosexual behavior. If so, what are the modern-day implications of using a past of sexual violence to inform and strengthen today's gay male culture and community?

The intertwining of sex and rape has been extensively explored in feminist scholarship, and the need for similar work with same-sex sexuality and same-sex rape is clear. Sexual behavior, psychological wellness, identity formation, social development, historical analysis, and cultural production are but a few of the areas in which sexual identity and rape overlap and affect each other. Dependent on a set of power relations and belief systems that dictate individual realities, the stigma of homophobia is perhaps the strongest element of taboo with respect to male rape. These issues bear strong implications for all men, whatever their sexual identity or history with sexual violence.

FALSE INTENTIONS
by Robert E. Penn

The following essay, contributed by Robert E. Penn and titled "False Intentions," embodies a number of the dynamics discussed in the previous chapter on same-sex rape and sexual identity. The elements of racial power relations, differences in economic class, and a complexity of sexuality transform rape, for many gay men, into an intricate question of subjective interpretation and ethical considera- tion. Robert's work explores the meaning of sexual violence between men with a candidness and depth that is rarely given to male rape.

Laud Humphreys outlines "Rules and Roles" in the third chapter of his groundbreaking, 1970, sociological monograph *Tearoom Trade*. He culled the ground rules from one-on-one interviews he conducted on men who have sex with men. Those samples were from all walks of life and a wide range of ages, some considered themselves heterosexual, others bisexual or ambisexual (a term that has fallen into disuse), and others homosexual; there were hustlers as well as stock brokers. All used public toilets—or tearooms—as venues for "anonymous sex."

For some, anonymous sex may be an intolerable form of sexual socializing. And yet, according to Humphreys's research, there is honor in this silent game of cruising and consummation. The ground rules reveal that anonymous sex, although it may be expeditious, noncommittal, and even exciting for its adherents, does not lead to transgressive acts between the consenting men. The rules are: Avoid the exchange of biographical data (or lie); don't have sex with those who are underage; never force your intentions on anyone; don't bad-mouth a trick; never back down on trade agreements such as paying the amount promised, if a financial transaction is involved; don't kiss above the belt; and silence protects one from being found out.

I am particularly interested in the shared ground rule that stipulates that one may never force one's intentions on anyone. Transgressing on that ground rule is rape. Between a man and a woman, these days, it is often labeled *date rape*. For gay men that term can also apply. In the anonymous world, it could be called *one-night rape* or *anonyrape* or even, in some cases, *gay bashing*. Such violations are often power trips, about dominance and oppression, to which the person who ends up playing the submissive role has not voluntarily subscribed. That's the point. Anything goes as long as the participants agree to the terms. Some people like S&M or master/slave or father/son stuff. It suits them. They negotiate it between them. Neither forces his will on the other.

I was raped. More than once. By more than one person. Why? A couple of times because I was just plain stupid. I agreed with the other guy that he could fuck me first on the condition that I could fuck him thereafter. I remember one white guy, in particular. Let's call him Ardy. He reneged on the "me first" deal after he'd rammed into me as if he were burying all of his anger and hatred along with his ejaculate. When Ardy said he didn't think he could be penetrated after coming, I didn't worry. After all, we had been friends for some time at that point. I knew I would see him again and that we'd be alone together again. However, after two or three subsequent refusals for my turn, I got the picture. Ardy had tricked me. He had manipulated me. Simply put: Ardy lied. He never intended to let me screw him, he had just said what he needed to get what he wanted, when he wanted it. And with his lie, Ardy raped me emotionally. He had penetrated me under false pretenses, which means he had physically abused me, too. I never wanted to be sexual with him again. He had betrayed me sexually once and I wasn't going to risk a repeat with him.

However, I remained friendly with Ardy for several more years because I was lonely. But not just the usual loneliness of one person for the company of another. I unconsciously believed at the time that I needed a white friend to elevate me to a level of equality. I had been bluntly told as much during the junior year of college. A dean suggested that the only thing I lacked was a white wife. That, he insisted, would give me the additional credibility I needed. Implicit was his perspective that being intelligent, witty, and personable was not sufficient for a young black man in 1969.

When I met Ardy in 1975, it was still of utmost importance for me—a black man—to maintain a primary friendship with a white partner. Because I am gay, that meant I gave a huge value to having a white male friend, an age peer of European—"highly valued"—ancestry. I overlooked his faults because he fulfilled my need for a white confidant. I ignored his occasional reliance on racial stereotypes. I was even willing to forget his manipulative and abusive behavior. I thought I perhaps deserved it; black "sissy's" lot. Yes, I was emotionally enslaved long before I was physically abused. The process of that emotional oppression began years before I ever set eyes on Ardy and was perpetrated by every adult—white, black, whatever—I encountered, by the media; and by U.S. society at large.

The racism and heterosexism that I had internalized convinced me that even if Ardy weren't my romantic match; even without sexual reciprocity; and even lacking viable intimacy between us, his presence—unembarrassed and unashamed to have a black friend—enhanced my social life. He was a color advantage when we went to parties. And this BGM (black, gay man) thought he needed any advantage he could get, at just about any price. I was so frightened whenever I was in predominantly white, i.e., most, settings. Each white man represented power, the ultimate potential for benevolence, a.k.a. the good master, and infinite capacity for wrath, as represented in images of a white bearded Christocentric god.

I completely lost interest in socializing with Ardy after I stopped drinking and drugging. This makes me wonder if Ardy had taken advantage of me while I was under the influence. I don't remember exactly, but I was usually high on, coming down from, or recovering from something the year he fucked me. I didn't want to remember. Lots of date rape instances occur when the subjugated party is on substances like alcohol or other depressants. The fact that the rape victim voluntary consumes substances does not make her or him less of a sexual abuse victim. The rapist still takes advantage of the situation, whether or not she or he provided the substances or encouraged their use.

I have to ask myself, would I have played that game with him had I not been drinking? I don't think a similar incident has occurred to me in sobriety. Whenever I'm in doubt about a guy's intentions, I just make sure I get mine first. That hesitancy can reduce spontaneity. Maybe it even had distorted expression of my sexual desires, interests, and attractions. The fear of the "next instant" of emotional harm may render me sexually self-conscious. This condition, I believe, inhibits my self-fulfillment and spiritual alignment. A secret, kept even from myself, precludes intimacy. Closeness and the ability to express and share intimacy is what I consider the substance of life. Rape hinders all that. Rape kills the spirit.

I settled in New York in December 1974. I shared a tiny West Village apartment with a really loony white gay man. Let's call him Bill. Bill "had" a different trick up in his loft bed each night. I felt I had to compete. I found cruising spots and met guys but didn't take them to his place, rather I had sex with them at conveniently located places: dark alleyways, bathhouses, and back rooms of gay bars.

I moved into my own New York apartment in midsummer 1975 when I was 27. It was in the Village near Washington Square. I continued my cruising with greater freedom. My place was close enough to Christopher Street so that men would always accompany me home when I suggested it, but far enough away from the sleaziest spots to make my invitations a little selective.

In those days, cruising Christopher Street usually meant looking at white guys. It was rare that I met another man of color and, though my three prior love affairs at that time had each been with a white man, I was very interested in having sex with other black men. I wanted to discuss Africa and civil rights while being held in their arms. It was a fantasy that I needed to fulfill: physical love combined with self-respect and pride, both racial and gay.

By the summer of 1976, I met such a guy on Christopher, all except for the "in his arms" part. It was clear after our first meeting that the conversation would always be good. I'll refer to him as Hyram. He was bright, funny, well traveled, and highly educated like me. However, Hyram was effeminate (which made me uncomfortable in those days) and I didn't match his taste in men, which included sophisticated white guys and rough black men. (I only learned the latter after I was forcibly raped.)

Hyram and I were out one day and decided that as we weren't going to get it on just the two of us, we might as well pick up a third and share him. That is what we did. We met a third black man who was older, maybe 35 or 40, stockier and very sure of himself. We went back to my place where we learned that he wanted to fuck us both. Hyram and I were both excited. My classism led me to feel as though Hyram and I were in control of this stud. We were more articulate than the boxer-built stranger. We dressed in a more worldly manner than this street-smart brother. And, as far as my mind told me, we were brighter and more powerful than he.

The stranger fucked my friend first. I probably kissed Hyram or participated in some minor way. Hyram seemed to be having a great time, in fact, I remember thinking how much more of a "queen" he was than I had previously admitted. I was sad because I still hoped Hyram would prove "versatile:" the only reason for two men to come together, I had rationalized.

It was my turn and I was very cautious because I hadn't been fucked since 1974 by a bisexual Frenchman (who assured me that my turn was next. Never happened!). In retrospect, I see a pattern: Was I that gullible? Did I want to believe it because I wanted to get fucked and simply couldn't admit it as I was not yet out of the closet? Was I a cock-eyed optimist? It wasn't unreasonable for me to believe him as I had been in two relationships with other European men with whom I had taken turns on top.

Anyway, back in 1976, the stranger put me on the edge of the bed, just as he had done with Hyram and started to penetrate me. It hurt. I told him so and asked him to slow down. He didn't. I tried to get up. He was stronger. Hyram told me to relax even after I told him it hurt and I didn't want to go on, not then anyway. You see, this stranger was endowed with a very large penis that also frightened me. In addition to the pain, which almost always happens at the beginning, I imagined a suffering that would increase as he went deeper rather than decrease then change into pleasure as it had with my former average-sized "tops." I also didn't trust him because he didn't seem to care. He didn't kiss and he didn't waste time on foreplay. "Stop." "Relax. It'll feel good when I'm in there." "He's right. That's what happened for me." "No. Stop!" The stranger ignored my demand. Hyram was so titillated he forgot about our friendship as well as my needs and boundaries. He assured me that the pain would subside.

It didn't happen that way for me. The stranger hurt me. I was bleeding, demoralized, and angry. Yet, I was also "his." By virtue of the fact that I let him fuck me, in my mind, I was "his." I would have to get to know him; have to spend time with him; have to fall in love with him because I had let him penetrate me and cum inside me. He was the black man I was looking for: stocky, like my father, with enough sexual prowess to satisfy two men in a row and still talk about going home to fuck his woman. He would never embarrass me with effeminate antics and at least his muscles felt good next to me if not inside me. I told myself that this stranger would protect me from anyone who might try to harm me in the Big City. He was streetwise, something I had never been and doubted I could learn to be; something I snubbed, saying it would pull me down to the streets rather than uplift me to the art world of white men; something, however, that in an escort, even one-who-remained-a-stranger, confirmed my black authenticity and commitment to the race without sullying me personally.

He was hot! I wanted to be loved by someone as attractive and masculine as this stranger. His masculinity was the medal of honor a black man could provide, just like skin color was the badge a white lover could give me. Some may find this repulsive, taboo. But they are either unconscious of their past and present motives or simply in denial about them.

The stranger stuck around after Hyram left for home. I didn't complain about the pain because I knew he would just tell me it would go away or something like that. We exchanged numbers, at which point he told me to be cool about messages because more than likely his girlfriend would answer but he had her "under control." As long as I was cool, she wouldn't get worried; she only worried when another woman called—hence, his male friends. He told me he liked me and wanted to hang out with me. Then later, you know . . . (Of course I knew. My first boyfriend, my college sweetheart, and I had run the same routine 8 years earlier with our girlfriends: double date, escort the women back to their places, meet up at his dorm, and drink and fuck all night long. I knew . . .). Plus he promised something even easier: His girlfriend hated to go out to the discos but he loved to hear the music, so we could go to clubs where he knew lots of people in The Business who could get us in free, then head back to my place because, of course, he couldn't take me to his.

And I did think, or was it hope, that he would come to his senses, sooner or later, and accept himself as a gay man. Maybe he would even put me ahead of his girlfriend. I would have given up some ass for that because he would have, in my mind, been fucking me with love. I could play any role in bed for love . . . in broad daylight. A desperate need for love, I thought, could excuse rape. I would even allow him to penetrate me emotionally because I believed the deception that special bonds between men are stronger than common-law marriage between husband and wife. They are not stronger, only different, and I can decide when to be deceived, even unconsciously.

Now I ask myself, "Why?" Twenty years later, I ask myself

what I expected to get from this acquaintanceship. A companion, which I desperately wanted at that time? A top, which really didn't sit well with me? And I have to answer that I really expected him to give me "some" at some later date. I saw myself conquering my "top," my straight-acting, beefy "brother," in revenge for a childhood taunted by the athletic boys at my school. And I waited for payback through a few consecutive nights hanging out together—what I would call a "trade date" today.

I will admit that I liked the end to loneliness. I liked his body. I didn't like the pain of him inside me. I'm sure I weighed whether or not the pain was a low enough price to pay if it meant seeing him as often as I needed to see a boyfriend—virtually every minute of the day. But he rarely returned my calls. I entertained letting him fuck me again—after all, I was already "his" emotionally and maybe illicitly, like in the jail of the closet or the prison in Jean Genet's *Thief's Journal*, a reformatory of complicity and silence, of control and fear, of the threat of mutual exposure, dishonor, demonization, and humiliation.

He could tell others, firsthand, that I was a sissy who took it up the ass, and they would believe him because he had a woman and must have given into my superlative seduction techniques (which a lot of people think all gay men have, especially when it comes to "recruiting" straight men). I couldn't risk that. I worked at a commercial bank and was back in college after dropping out/ getting into the trouble the first (and second) time around. My father was a Baptist pastor, my mother a teacher, my sister a psychologist. No one could know. No one would accept it. No one would love me if they knew. I knew they wouldn't because I didn't . . . love me.

In the end, my middle-class attitudes of snobbery, in other words, my classism and moralism, convinced me that I could afford to break it off with him. I turned down a couple of his invites to hang out. It was relatively easy. His friends in The Business could not get us into the hottest spots anyway and he always and only picked places that were very straight. I had already spent time at gay and lesbian discos in Europe and mixed ones in Africa. I was not interested in straight New York even though I still dated a woman from time to time. He couldn't show me the spots I wanted to find: the chic ones where all of the attractive, white and black, gay men hung out in absolute equality. He wouldn't go into the segregated ones where gay, bisexual, and "just fooling around" brothers predominantly went. I wanted to meet the elite brothers and truly liberal, nonracist, white, gay men. That desire saved me. This stranger, in spite of all of his bravura and real connections at the entry level of the music industry, didn't know anyone I could look to; nor, in reality, anyone who could hurt my career. I didn't think any of his connections would try to blacklist me if I "dissed" him because they were probably all getting some booty on the side, too.

Over time, we lost interest in each other. I, because it became increasingly obvious to me that this stranger was not giving any up and he didn't really tell me anything about himself. He, because I persistently refused his advances toward "getting back up there" again. I had decided after the first time that I wouldn't let him fuck me again. I stuck to my guns physically. It took longer to take back my emotions.

Even though I didn't consciously recognize that he had raped me, on a gut level, I knew that I had been abused. Yet I also remembered that at times in my childhood and preadolescent years, I had forced both boys and girls to let me use them for my sexual curiosity and pleasure. I knew I had never questioned the ethics of such activities. I rationalized each time that once they stopped protesting, they were accepting. As I hadn't intimidated them or threatened to report them (which would have been self-exposure), I had never thought they might have been giving in as the path of least resistance as I had done years later. (My youthful partners may have been afraid. I had been ashamed.) Nor did I realize that each time I had given in to men who insisted that I fuck them, I was allowing them to convince me that I really was only rejecting them because of some warped and exaggerated sense of superiority or pride, protesting out of principle. Whether the rapist forces into my mouth or ass, or gets me into him with threats of "outing me," it is still rape.

I suddenly recall now how I first missed, then resented, the stranger. A few months after the last time we hung together, I wanted to run into him again. I practiced what I would tell him:

how furious I was with him and how wrong he had been with me. Then I forgot about him or, at least, suppressed his memory. I even looked for him at a club where he knew the manager. I never located him again and never got to express my rage to that perpetrator or any of the others, like Ardy, or the boy in elementary school who said he had heard that I played with other boys and threatened to tell the coach I was looking at him "funny" if I didn't "lick his thing."

There are lessons I learned that I need to state. First, I know that I had avoided sex with other black men for many years because I was molested by that classmate in the sixth grade. He was not the brightest and had been held back at least one time, so he was at least one year older than I and much taller. In my appropriately childish "I'll-show-them" manner for a 12-year-old, I decided never again to have sex with taller boys. Later, I expanded this exclusion to all other black boys. However, when I got to my 98% nonblack college, I sought out the other black men, hoping to find one gay one. There was none and I settled, happily, on a German-American classmate for double dates and secretive postdate bacchanals. Second, the hulking stranger from my 20s, as well as the boy from my preteen sixth grade year, have inspired characters in at least three pieces of my fiction. Most recently the stranger turned into a black classmate of the black protagonist in a novel. The protagonist catches his classmate in the college library john getting jerked off by a white student. The classmate denies his attraction to men when confronted by the protagonist, though he adds that if he and the protagonist just happen to bump into each other at the right time and place, something might happen between them. Again: skin color and power, sex and power, deception and false coincidence. Third, I avoid receptive anal sex, preferring to arouse myself. I don't even suggest that I would like to fuck a man until I know him pretty well because I expect that once I express my interest in penetrating him, he will reciprocate. Finally, I have set boundaries about what I do on a first encounter with a man, boundaries that may be a little more difficult for me to honor with another black man because of my desperate need to find gay and black in the same person. I was more intent on getting mine first with a brother because I feared none of them was really gay. I feared that my sixth grade perpetrator had been right: I was really the only BGM alive—the only who was wrong, sinful, undeserving, disgraceful, and a traitor to the race.

None of these conclusions solves the problem of rape. Each helps me confront the abject fear that I will be left unsatisfied. The fear set in place in elementary school when Donald (his real name) threatened not only to beat me up but also tell everyone I was a "punk" if I didn't suck him off. The fear was reinforced by moralism, racism, and heterosexism throughout my life. Confronting the fear by coming-out increasingly and in different settings, no matter how late in life, leads me to my sacred self and to feeling truth. One such truth is that a man can be raped by another man.

Recognizing that I was raped, both as a child and as an adult, has made me more sensitive to friends who are also incest and rape survivors. I make room for their pain and respect that they may need time before getting sexual with me, if ever. I am certain that a man can be tricked into sexual activities against his will: The threat of exposure as a gay man is a strong weapon that wields incredible power, far greater than the threat of a pistol barrel.

It is still hard for me to give myself freely and lovingly to another man because of trust issues resulting from the emotional and physical rape, betrayal, and deception that I survive—trust issues that other friends have, too. I try to get an understanding of "where a man is" before spending more than three dates with him. I also struggle to express my concerns and needs before getting physically or emotionally intimate with any prospective close friend or potential lover.

Boundaries must be articulated before getting sexual. Neither force of hand nor threat of shame can ever be acceptable as reasons for denying one's own healthy skepticism of another's intentions. There is no reason for betraying oneself or one's ground rules. Negotiation is necessary, even if it is conducted in silence with the coded gestures catalogued in Humphreys's book, even if the sex is anonymous, tearoom sex with a nameless man who will never be seen again.

SIX

THE SPECTACLE OF MALE RAPE

*T*he popular media in contemporary society wield a great deal of power with the ability to shape public perceptions through depiction of actual and fictional events. The portrayals of male rape in television programs, films, print journalism, and radio have been relatively few and far between. In the absence of frequent attention to the reality of same-sex rape, the select appearances of male rape in mass media often carry a great deal of significance and lasting impact on the minds of viewers, listeners, and readers. With male rape receiving so little news coverage or inclusion in film and television plots, the idea persists that male rape may not be possible and is certainly not a prevalent crime. Sixteen of the twenty-four male rape survivors I interviewed for this book said they could not recall ever seeing or reading anything about male rape in newspapers, movies, or television. Following this answer, many of the survivors expressed anger and frustration about this invisibility. Warren, a rape survivor in his late 20s, said:

> *It pisses me off that we never see this stuff anywhere. How was I supposed to know this could happen to me if no one ever told me? It totally caught me off guard when I was raped. It rocked my world and I can't believe this happens so much without anyone ever talking about it.*

Another survivor I interviewed anonymously on the Internet related his quest to find written materials on male rape after he was assaulted, with no luck from libraries, bookstores, and especially media sources:

> *For years since this happened to me I have always read every word of newspaper stories on rape and not once has there been a man as the victim. Same goes for TV. I keep looking for someone out there like me and I know those guys exist. They're probably totally alone like I am and fumbling around in the dark too.*

I concluded every interview with this question on recalling depictions of male rape, and in almost every case the survivor asked me for any articles or other materials I had found on the topic. It became clear to me that many survivors look to the media in hopes of finding experiences that mirror their own in an attempt to make sense of what has happened to them.

These individual media representations of same-sex sexual violence are both a product of what our society thinks about male rape and a kind of social script that recipients of these messages come to believe as fact. That is to say, the media influence the masses and the masses influence the media. By taking a close look at how male rape is literally and figuratively framed in television, film, radio, and print, we can begin to unveil and understand the popular fears, beliefs, and anxieties that surround the rape of men.

PRINT

Male rape has been documented, discussed, and explored in print journalism (newspapers, magazines, and journals) more than in any other mass media form. The following "media watch" collection is a sampling of but a few reports and discussions surrounding the rape of men that have appeared in major newspapers since 1985. They represent the diversity of male rape incidents as well as the styles and genres that newspapers use to convey information about the assaults:

January 1985

United Press International newswire service detailed a rape in which a disabled man with cerebral palsy accepted a ride home from a man he had met at a local bar in Buffalo, New York:

> *A handicapped man was robbed, sexually assaulted and abandoned in a city parking garage early Thursday in near zero temperatures, police said. Police said the victim, a 25-year-old North Buffalo man with cerebral palsy, was unable to walk and cried for help for nearly an hour early Thursday before he was aided by a passer-by. "This guy was unable to move and could have frozen to death, or certainly suffered frostbite," Lt. Richard Donovan said. "It was a really sick thing to do."[1]*

The article contained the police's detailed description of the attacker and his car, serving the practical function of enlisting assistance in the search for the attacker. The suspect was later arrested after police received a tip from an outraged citizen who had seen the two men together that night.

March 1986

A concerned mother wrote to internationally syndicated advice columnist Abigail Van Buren, better known as "Dear Abby," seeking information and support for her 18-year-old son who was beaten and gang-raped:

> *Dear Abby: Please publish some information about adult male rape. My eighteen-year-old-son . . . was beaten and gang-raped. Going to the police was awful for him. They were not prepared to cope with a*

> *male victim. The criminals who raped [him] are in custody, but they were not charged with rape—only assault and battery, even though the officers know they raped my son. . . . Almost every city has a rape crisis facility where female rape victims can go for counseling, but there's no help in our town for male victims. Please print this. The public needs to know.*[2]

Abby offered a rather vague response to the mother, encouraging male rape survivors to report their victimization and urging rape crisis centers to provide services to men as well as women. Although the attention and empathy devoted to male rape in this column were admirable, no statistics, resources, or referrals were given.

October 1991

The *Houston Chronicle* covered the trend of reported male rapes in Philadelphia. Two assaults were highlighted in detail: a man raped by an acquaintance giving him a ride home from a bar, and a man who was abducted and raped by three men while walking down the street to meet his spouse. The man in the latter case suffered such intense psychological anguish that he hanged himself before the case went to trial. The article also reported that 26 male rape survivors had been treated at a Boston hospital's counseling center within the previous year. The combination of more personalized case studies and citywide statistics is a popular and effective way to disseminate information.

January 1993

The *Chicago Tribune* reported that in 1992 there were 320 victims of male rape in Britain. The article profiled the rape of one of these men, whom they call Ben. When Ben had entered a London subway restroom one evening, he was attacked by three men. One of the men wielded a knife and brutally raped him in a toilet stall. The attack appeared to be random in the selection of the victim, but the violence was noted as part of a larger pattern that generated public distress and concern.

September 1994

A special agent for the Internal Revenue Service testified in a federal court that a Springfield, Illinois, man threatened to have another man raped in a gay bar in Chicago if the informant testified against him. Strangely, this statement appears in the article as a brief aside, but leaves the reader with the sense that there is a great deal more to the story than what has been reported. Obvious questions like, "Was the man who was threatened gay, and if not, why would he be in a gay bar?" and "Why threaten to rape someone in public with so many witnesses rather than in private?" and "Why was the threat of rape used in this case rather than extortion, murder, or nonsexual assault?" Many times, male rape is awkwardly mentioned as part of a larger news story and implicates aspects of the situation that the newspaper chooses not to report, perhaps for reasons of liability, slander, or the public taste of their readership.

December 1995

The *Baton Rouge Advocate* reported that local police arrested a 58-year-old apartment complex security guard for allegedly raping an 18-year-old man after offering him a ride home from a local laundry. The guard drove the man to a parking lot and raped him at knifepoint. A police officer publicly commended the rape survivor for stepping forward and reporting the crime, and stated that adult male rape is probably the most underreported violent crime. The police gave the newspaper a telephone number to print for others who had experienced "similar crimes" and urged other male survivors to seek assistance. The article quoted the district attorney's Rape Crisis Center who said that although they receive few male rape reports, "It is out there. It is happening." An example of quality and sensitive reporting, this article described the rape in nonjudgmental terms, commended the survivor for his bravery in the face of stigma and shame, and communicated the local police department's openness to work with male rape cases.

Language and Gender

When the topic of male rape arises in print journalism, as in some of the previously described articles, the tone of the piece often dwells on male rape as a "new" or recently discovered crime. The treatment of male rape as an emergent form of criminal victimization has been so consistent for more than a decade that one must wonder if male rape will ever be popularly regarded as a violence with a history. Few of the previous articles cite male rape research studies or consult experts other than local police officers and counselors. This creates a "treading water" effect in which every attention paid to male rape reverts back to square one. Although the basic information and facts on male rape are important to reinforce, it is time for journalists to begin tackling the complexity of the issues at hand. At the same time, male rape is frequently viewed within the narrow contexts of legality and pathology. The broader social, cultural, and historical factors, both relevant and interesting, are typically ignored.

In my research I did not, thankfully, come across an instance where a newspaper or magazine had printed an adult male rape survivor's name without his permission, as has been the case with many female survivors. This could be a simple product of timing. As male rape has been discussed with increasing frequency in the media over the last 15 years or so, many newspapers, such as the *Boston Globe*, have developed self-regulating policies stating that they will not print the names of rape survivors in their news coverage. This is not a foolproof safety mechanism, but does provide a much needed structure of ethical guidelines.

Newspaper coverage of male rape incidents also differs markedly from that of the rape of women in the description of certain details of the assault. As compared to female rape survivors, the height and weight of the male victim are often mentioned with both emphasis and specificity, particularly when the man is significantly greater or lesser than average build and height. Comments such as the following are not uncommon: "The 5-foot-6, 110-pound man told the jury how he was forced to the back of the bedroom of his trailer, where he said he was sodomized for 10 to 15 minutes."[3] This description appeared in North Carolina's *Morning Star* newspaper coverage of a 1996 male acquaintance rape. "The man, fair-haired, 6ft tall, slim, and a former school boxer" was used to describe the gang rape survivor in a 1992 *Sunday Times* article in Great Britain.[4] In reporting a series of gang rapes in Iowa City, a United Press International article concluded the lengthy piece with this quote from the director of the local rape advocacy program: "One of the Iowa City victims was taller than 6 feet and weighed more than two hundred pounds."[5]

These are just a few examples of this trend in male rape reporting, and there are several possible reasons for the gendered difference. The reporter may be attempting to dispel the myth that physically strong and masculine men cannot be raped by describing the male victim's stature (taller than 6 feet and more than 200 pounds) or background (a former school boxer). On another level, the description of these men may also tantalize the reader who finds sensationalism in the unlikely rape of "a real man." Despite the debunking of male rape stereotypes in some cases, there is an implied curiosity in this kind of text that begs the question, "If the man is so big and macho, how could he have allowed himself to be raped?"

When specific male rape incidents are reported in these articles, details of the rape that are excessively brutal or bizarre usually become the defining elements of the story, generating a sensationalistic focus on the particular assault. In this respect, articles on the rape of men do not differ significantly from those articles written on the rape of women. Even the basic information that a rape was a same-sex assault is often enough to qualify the event as newsworthy material, prominently featured in the periodical with generic headlines such as "Man Raped" or "Man Raped by Other

Man." In contrast, incidents involving the rape of women are usually headlined with more descriptive information such as "Housekeeper Raped in Hotel Room by Stranger."

In addition, when male rape appears in the news, the accompanying title of the story invariably notes the gender of the victim because male rape is treated as a peculiarity, whereas a story with a title such as "Rape Victim Served Justice With Guilty Verdict of Attacker" is assumed to involve a woman raped by a man. As compared with the rape of women, documentation of male rape court cases and trials are few and far between in newspaper and magazine journalism, perhaps because so few men report their assault, hence precluding the possibility of charges filed against their attackers.

I also noted certain media trends in the language used to describe sexual violence between men. Interestingly, my key word searches in the use of electronic research databases became quite telling. A search under the phrase *homosexual rape* tended to yield approximately 50% more articles than searches under the terms *male rape* and *same-sex rape* combined. This indicates that even the language used to describe and define the same-sex rape of adult men remains varied and unclear, albeit a disturbing preference for the misleading *homosexual* descriptor. Searching under the terms *sodomy*, *buggery*, and *felonious sexual penetration*, also turned up text containing male rape material. Just as there is no strong agreement between researchers about the demographics of male rape, there is not yet a consensus of the everyday language in popular media to even describe the rape of men.

TELEVISION

The impact of television programming as a form of public information is immeasurable, particularly because of its broad viewing audience and the actual combination of video and sound in capturing viewers' attention. Male rape has been largely invisible in television programming, with only a few appearances in talk shows, made-for-television movies, and documentary news stories. When I sent out an announcement calling for male survivors to interview for this book, a Hollywood movie production company that specializes in "movie of the week" television programs contacted me with great interest in creating a movie based on the true story of a man who had been raped. The producer I spoke with asked me for names of male rape survivors, intent on contacting them in hopes of finding someone who would sell their story to the company.

At first he was extremely interested in my personal rape experience, told in the preface of this book, but when I recounted the details of my assault he presented me with two options: either my story would have to be "de-gayed" or he would have to find a different (i.e., heterosexual) male rape story for the screenplay. He explained that the somewhat taboo subject of same-sex rape would make for interesting television viewing, but the incorporation of a gay male acquaintance rape or any issues related to gay men would spell disaster. The reality of current television programming is such that gay and lesbian themes often discourage major advertising sponsors and make network executives uncomfortable with the possibility of lost revenues and public backlash from conservative watchdog groups such as the American Family Association. Although I understand this to be the case, I am also acutely aware that the rampant homophobia in these mass media productions creates an unwillingness to address even same-sex violence if it in any way implicates homosexuality. The following examples of male rape content in television programs serve as noteworthy case studies in their exception to this general silence.

The Oprah Winfrey Show

On February 27, 1995, Oprah Winfrey dedicated her television talk show to highlight Greg Louganis's recently released autobiography, *Breaking the Surface*. The book topped the *New York Times* Bestseller List and revealed, among other things, that Louganis was gay, HIV positive, and that he had been raped by a former live-in boyfriend in 1985. Louganis explained that he had been dating the man for about a year, but the two of them had never discussed monogamy. On discovering Louganis had been sexually involved with another man, his boyfriend reacted violently. In the book, he explained:

> *Tom grabbed me from behind, held the knife to my neck, and forced me facedown onto the bed. With the knife at my throat, he tore off my clothes. To keep control, he grabbed one of my arms and held it behind my back. Then he raped me. . . . I was crying and begging him to stop, but he told me I deserved it and didn't stop until he was finished.*[6]

Louganis recalled that it had never occurred to him to make a police report, seek medical attention, or solicit support from a friend. He told no one about his rape for 5 years. Rather than leave the man who raped him, Greg called the next day to apologize, still believing the rape to be his fault and filled with fear that he would be left alone. He commented, "Rape victims often think they are spoiled forever. I certainly did."

When Louganis told of his decision to continue seeing his boyfriend, even after the rape, Winfrey probed further with what might seem to be judgmental questioning: "How could you—I know how, but—because having read the book. But can you explain to the audience—allow yourself to be raped and live there afterwards?" As a survivor of sexual violence herself, Winfrey paved the way for her guest to explain the state of mind in which victims remain involved with their attackers: "And afterwards, though—I mean, God, it's hard . . . everything inside yourself should say, 'I won't allow myself to be treated this way again.'" Louganis then described the guilt and self-blame that continued his boyfriend's control in the relationship. "I felt like I deserved it. And I—I know now that nobody deserves that, and I really should have, you know, hit the floor running and not looked back."

This interview, in addition to the similar interviews Louganis gave to Barbara Walters and other journalists, marks a pivotal moment in television's attention devoted to male rape. Greg Louganis was the first contemporary, high-profile figure to openly discuss his experience of rape as an adult male. Although a few other male stars, such as Tom Arnold, had previously revealed their childhood victimization, Louganis was the first survivor to bring adult male rape into this kind of popular spotlight in the United States. The revelation of HIV infection might have overshadowed the other hardships discussed in his autobiography, but Louganis's rape experience nonetheless came across as a significant event that shaped his life.

In early 1997, the USA Network on cable television announced a forthcoming movie based on Louganis's autobiography. In what seems a highly contradictory rationale, the movie does not include any scenes of Louganis kissing his lover, but was slated to have a graphic scene in which that same man raped him. USA Network was unwilling to shoot the same-sex kiss out of fear that it would make the movie "unpalatable" for mainstream America. The film's producer, Jim Green, told the *Dallas Morning News*:

> We didn't feel that we needed to get into two men kissing. . . . The television audience is not gonna watch that. They're gonna tune out. And if we turn off the audience, they're not gonna see the messages we want to get out. . . . Tell me a commercial movie in the next ten years that is gonna show two men who kiss. No way.[7]

In this case, an explicit depiction of sexual violence was considered more acceptable and tasteful than a simple, consensual kiss between two men. The portrayal of two men willingly expressing affection was clearly more dangerous than one man raping another at knifepoint. Hollywood's homophobia seems more wary of normalizing same-sex relations than portraying same-sex sexual contact in which the victim "could not help it." In this way they can claim they are not "encouraging" homosexuality through a positive portrayal of gay men, as if the rape was completely unrelated to the circumstances of their relationship as lovers. Louganis had given up most of his creative control over the project, and later expressed concern that "there is hugging and kissing in all intimate relationships. Why can't it be shown on-screen?"[8]

Three years prior to the *Oprah* episode, which was titled "Living With A Secret—Greg Louganis," Winfrey had addressed the topic of male sexual abuse, but focused on the rape of young boys. The June 14, 1993, episode, "Men Who Were Raped," included a guest named Tom. He was raped when he was 19 years old by two older men, one of whom lived along the path he walked to and from school every day. After numerous invitations from the man to come inside the house and visit, Tom agreed one evening:

> He invited me to come in and look at . . . pornographic films. And at
> that time he had a friend over visiting, who was a married man with
> two children. And so they started to show the films and offered me a
> drink. They showed me photographs of [sexual] things they had
> done together. This was their little den of iniquity or whatever. And
> I woke up—I don't know what the time frame was, but they put a
> mickey in my drink and I was raped by both men. I—I left the house
> realizing what had happened.

Tom's story is not uncommon in that alcohol and other drugs played a large role in his vulnerability. Once unable to defend himself, the two men were able to rape Tom before he could effectively react. After Tom left the house, he went to a nearby Lutheran minister's house for help. Eventually Tom received therapeutic assistance from two psychiatrists at Northwestern University, and through counseling began to recover memories of childhood sexual abuse by his father. Again, this revelation is not uncommon among many adult male rape survivors. The experience of being raped as an adult often triggers or heightens some men's memories of having been molested as boys.

Geraldo

More than 3 years prior to Louganis's appearance on *Oprah*, Geraldo Rivera dedicated his hour-long talk show on October 22, 1991, to the topic of male rape, including both the rape of men and boys. The show was dubbed "Male Rape: The Hidden Horror" and, as suggested by the title, reflected the sensationalism for which Rivera's show was well known. His guests who were assaulted as adults included "Bob," who was raped twice at gunpoint; Stephen Donaldson, former president of Stop Prisoner Rape and a survivor of prison gang rape; and J. Ric Rollins who is a local television talk show host in Florida. Rollins was raped by a football player in his late teens, and revealed his assault experience for the first time on national television despite the impact it could have on his professional career as a high-profile media figure.

The bulk of this episode focused on men raping men, but did include some content on childhood sexual abuse of boys. Throughout the show, the guests were fairly adept at providing information to dispel the common myths about male rape. The audience's questions, however, were loaded with accusatory statements and insensitivity. As a forum for male survivors to speak out, a hostile environment impeded the quality of the discussion for the sake of contrived conflict. The opportunity for men who have been raped to tell their stories with honesty also entails a necessarily brutal honesty that sometimes makes the listening audience uncomfortable. Sadly, Rivera himself shut down some of this discussion at the expense of shaming the survivors. At one point, a guest began to describe how he had been raped by his foster brother: ". . . he commenced on using, you know, physical force and I ended up having to do him orally, which—." At this point Rivera interrupted, saying, "All right, that's enough. We get the idea," and then quickly changed the subject.

If male rape is to be fully understood by others for the violation it really is, audiences should not be spared the details of the assault if a survivor is intent on communicating them. Of course the language used need not necessarily be vulgar or even graphic, which in the case of television dialogue is mandatory, but a general description of the assault should not be danced around. This kind of sidestepping sends a very strong message that the rape is, after all, something to be ashamed of, that one should not speak about sexual violence in public beyond euphemisms, and that public audiences should not bear witness to the reality of violence surrounding them. To do so runs the risk of simply restigmatizing the rape of men in a different way rather than strip away the layers of shame imposed by a culture that resists even the most superficial acknowledgment of sexual assault. In the end, Geraldo's "Male Rape: The Hidden Horror" remained just that—hidden.

The Rape of Richard Beck

Richard Crenna starred in this 1985 movie of the week that aired on NBC. His performance as Richard Beck, a veteran cop who is sexually assaulted, later earned him an Emmy. The movie continues to appear on cable television networks, particularly Lifetime, more than 10 years after its original broadcast. The drama centers around Sergeant Beck, who has been an officer on the police force for 23 years. He, his fellow officers, and law enforcement superiors are all insensitive, macho men who lack compassion for violence against women. Midway through the movie, while Beck is off duty and wandering the streets, he is attacked and raped by two male criminals. One of the men tells Beck, "You're gonna love it. Hell, it's better than dying, isn't it?" and as the camera focuses on Beck's belt being unfastened, the other man asks, "You want it, don't you?"

His resulting humiliation from the rape, including a degrading medical examination with witnesses present, raises his consciousness and magically transforms him into the model man of professional and personal sensitivity. The movie's plot, especially the employment of this "walk a mile in another's shoes" philosophy, was inspired by an actual Seattle police officer training. The leader of the training taught male recruits to empathize with female rape survivors by leading them through a guided imagery exercise in which they experience a brutal rape. Once the officers had some idea of what it was like to be raped, they were supposed to be better equipped to interact with rape survivors in the course of their law enforcement work.

Several assumptions are built into this kind of educational model. First, the approach presumes that men are not raped, and, more specifically, that none of the recruits who participate in the training have been sexually assaulted. Second, the exercise relies heavily on the notion that men can only be supportive and empathic in working with female rape survivors if they themselves have had the same experience, even on a superficial level of imagined assault.

A very similar parable appeared in the 1974 book *Rape: How to*

Avoid It and What to Do About It If You Can't by June and Joseph Csida. In a chapter titled "Buggered at High Noon," the writers inquire, "Why are many men unable or unwilling to be seriously concerned about rape? Perhaps they would be, if the following story were true:" They continue by narrating a sordid tale. The time is 1978, and women's organizations have lobbied heavily for a make-believe state's proposed antirape law that will provide harsher penalties for convicted sex offenders. The legislators, all male, either fall asleep or crack sexist jokes throughout the hearings. The Saturday night before the law is to be voted on, the legislators hold a wild party with alcohol and a hired prostitute at the isolated mountain home of a wealthy lobbyist.

That same day, unbeknown to them, eight violent inmates had escaped from a nearby prison and made their way through the mountains to the house where the party was occurring. The story concludes on an instructional, lesson-learned note:

> *All eight escapees had since [incarceration] become confirmed and enthusiastic homosexuals. Seven of them leaped upon a like number of the naked legislators and raped them with obscene abandon, while one of the cons with a gun held the rest of the assembled group at bay. Then another convict held the gun, and the others raped on, exchanging victims, yipping and yelling, laughing and whooping as they raped. . . . The new anti-rape statute was passed on Monday unanimously.[9]*

The title of this fictional piece, "Buggered at High Noon," was taken from Hunter S. Thompson's statement in his book *Hell's Angels* that "any lawyer who says there's no such thing as rape should be hauled out to a public place by three large perverts and buggered at high noon with all his clients watching."[9] The story is clearly dated, and the use of "confirmed and enthusiastic homosexuals" is one more example of the presumption that men who rape men are homosexual with a primary instinct to sexually prey on others. Similarly, it suggests that inmates who are raped will somehow "become" gay. Like *The Rape of Richard Beck*, male rape is viewed as an extremely rare occurrence that, although horrific, serves as a sensitizing tool for sexist men who support or participate in a rape culture. The message that anyone deserves to be raped is atrocious, regardless of how poetic the "justice" might seem within a given context. Again, male rape is invoked here only as a plot device to turn the tables. This "what if?" nature makes male rape an entertaining example and suggests the rape of men only happens in the imaginations of angry feminists to illustrate injustice.

The belief that men could only empathize with women about rape if they are raped themselves also makes a huge statement concerning our faith in men as allies in working to end sexual violence and other forms of oppression. The position that only direct experience can yield empathy suggests an inherent inability of men and women to communicate with each other, as if gender is some kind of natural rift that can never be fully bridged.

FILM

Despite the overabundance of television programming as compared with major motion picture productions, male rape has surfaced with more frequency and intensity in films than on broadcast television. James Limbacher, a scholar who has studied the representation of sexuality in cinema, believes the first male rape scene in a major motion picture was in *Lawrence of Arabia*, released in 1962. Although the rape is implied rather than graphically displayed, and subtle enough to pass by many audiences, the interpretation of the event is unmistakable given Lawrence's autobiography in which he describes being raped while held as a prisoner of war. The scene leading up to the rape was later cut from the video release of the movie, in part because of the suggestiveness of same-sex sexuality, but has since been reinserted with the now available unedited version.

By far the most recognized and remembered male rape scene in any movie came 10 years later in the 1972 film *Deliverance* starring Burt Reynolds and Ned Beatty. *Deliverance* was adapted from the 1970 novel of the same title by James Dickey and garnered much more success as a movie than as an adventure novel.

Dickey wrote the screenplay for the film and even played a bit part as the town sheriff. The movie received critical acclaim and was highly profitable, garnering Oscar nominations for best film and best director. The film chronicles the journey of four men (Bobby, Lewis, Ed, and Drew) who venture off into the Georgia wilderness on a camping and canoeing expedition. During their course of travel, they encounter two uncivilized mountain men. Bobby, played by Ned Beatty, is raped by one of the mountain men, who is killed moments later with a crossbow arrow fired by Burt Reynolds before their other comrade Lewis is sexually assaulted. The rape scene begins with one mountain man forcing Bobby to strip and get down on the ground on all fours. He then mounts Bobby and commands him to squeal like a pig while penetrating him from behind.

The author's description of the rape in the novel concludes with the men's altered perception of Bobby after he has been raped.

> *Bobby got off the log and stood with us, all facing Lewis over the corpse. I moved away from Bobby's red face. None of this was his fault, but he felt tainted to me. I remembered how he looked over the log, how willing to let anything be done to him, and how high his voice was when he screamed.*[10]

His comrades cannot stop thinking of Bobby's "willingness" to be raped, as is common treatment for many male rape survivors. We like to believe that men are capable of defending themselves physically, and if a man is raped, he must have somehow allowed it to happen. This classic blame-the-victim mentality is accompanied by a feminization of Bobby. Having been forced into a sexually submissive role, he is somehow less of a man, signified by the focus on his high-pitched screams. The discomfort and resistance to acknowledge the rape is represented by the narrator's inability to even look Bobby in the face. In the film version, denial and shame take root and the rape is never directly discussed or reflected on for the rest of the movie.

James Dickey died in January 1997 of complications from lung disease. In a 1993 interview with National Public Radio, he explained why the rape scene was so important to the story line of *Deliverance*:

> What I wanted to do was to have a scene which would bring into focus the most abiding and the deepest fear of people in our time, in our century, which is the fear of being set upon by malicious strangers, to be assaulted by people who would just as soon kill you as look at you. . . . That's the fear of our time, and I wanted to use, use that motif as a lead-in to what happens in the rest of the story.

In Burt Reynolds's autobiography *My Life*, he described the intensity of filming the rape scene, which he believes was generated by the blurred line between reality and performance. The actor who played the rapist was Bill McKinney, who was later typecast in portraying a string of mentally unstable and violent characters. Reynolds recalled how strange McKinney was in real life and noted that his method acting went too far at times. As the time for filming the rape scene drew closer, Reynolds noticed that McKinney would stare at Beatty on the set in a very unnerving way. The actual shooting of the rape scene took on an element of reality that no one had planned. Reynolds recalled:

> None of that creepy "Squeal, piggy, piggy" stuff was in the script. But McKinney, I swear to God, really wanted to hump Ned. And I think he was going to. It's the first and only time I have ever seen camera operators turn their heads away. Finally, I couldn't stand it anymore. I ran into the scene, dove on McKinney and pulled him off. [The director], hot on my tracks, helped hold him down. Ned, who was crying from both rage and fear, found a big stick and started beating him on the head. Half a dozen guys grabbed Ned and pulled him away.[11]

Reynolds felt that crossing the boundary from fiction into real life was what made the rape scene so incredibly powerful and frightening for movie audiences. Although the end product may possess the disturbingly realistic qualities the director had desired, the process of reaching that believability is more than questionable.

Apart from this context behind the scenes, the story itself contains elements that have shaped popular beliefs about men who rape men. The "back to nature" theme of the movie is accentuated by the assault, positioning male rape as a kind of savagery that only happens in primitive and uncivilized environments, committed by impoverished hillbilly men. The primitive nature of the act implies not only an animalistic sexual drive that substitutes men as sexual objects in the absence of women (as is commonly believed to be the case in prisons), but also characterizes a form of bestiality. In the case of *Deliverance*, Bobby is violated as both a foreigner and an animal, a civilized man who has strayed so far from nature that he has lost his manhood and the masculine ability to maintain sexual control over his own body. The mountain men prove this to Bobby, and the plot device is powerful in underscoring the weakness of "civilized" males. The trio's journey and ultimate survival (i.e., deliverance) is seen as a rite of passage and testament to their manhood. Even though the characters had led safe, comfortable, suburban lives before the expedition, they proved they were still men by conquering nature in all of its barbaric forms. Despite this success, Ned Beatty's character is left permanently emasculated to some degree as a result of being raped, even though he ultimately survived the experience.

In a guest editorial column published in 1989 in the *New York Times*, actor Ned Beatty described how, for 17 years since *Deliverance* was released, he had been repeatedly taunted by men in public. "'Squeal like a pig.' How many times has that been shouted, said, or whispered to me, since then?" he wrote in anger.[12] Beatty speculated that men feel the need to ridicule him for the role he played as a rape survivor so as to distance themselves from their own vulnerability to sexual violence. *Deliverance*, Beatty's first movie and most commercially successful role, revealed to men just how easily they could be violated, and the backlash against this revelation has carried over into verbal abuse against the actor for more than two decades.

The longevity of the *Deliverance* rape scene has been extended by the varied ways in which other media have capitalized on its notoriety. Take, for example, an advertising promotion that aired in 1996 on WLVQ, a radio station in Columbus, Ohio. In August of that year I received a telephone call from an outraged female student at a nearby college. She had been listening to the radio and heard a piece promoting an upcoming pig race at the Ohio State Fair. The promotion, created by the radio station, announced that a handful of callers would become sponsors of the pigs and receive a gift certificate from a local restaurant. After the race, the lucky caller who was the sponsor of the winning pig would receive $500 worth of Dinner Bell pork products and a trophy from the contest. Callers were instructed to listen to the station as much as possible, and telephone WVLQ when they heard a sound clip from *Deliverance* of Ned Beatty squealing like a pig. The tone of the promotion was obviously humorous.

When a local reporter decided to write a story detailing the inappropriateness of the promotion, she contacted me for my opinion. I responded by stating, "It's sort of like using the clip of Jodie Foster being gang raped in the movie *The Accused* to sell pinball machines. . . . I'm outraged as a sexual assault educator and as a male rape survivor. I think it's completely inappropriate. It trivializes the rape of adult males."[13] Male rape was being parodied to sell pork products and increase radio listener ratings.

The Ohio State Fair, Dinner Bell meat company, and Damon's restaurant chain had all signed off on the script as part of the radio promotion, but had no idea the *Deliverance* audio track would be used. They later indicated they would not have agreed to participate had they known the promotion would be in such poor taste. The station's promotion director rejected the complaints by responding that Ned Beatty's rape-induced screams were "just a sound effect," and reported to a local newspaper that she had considered using a pig sound from the 1995 movie *Babe*, but decided on the 1972 film *Deliverance* instead because she thought it was "the most common pig noise." By the time the controversy erupted in other media, the promotion had ended.

The intended humorous element of the promotion is unfortunately not uncommon as a popular cultural response to the rape of men, as Ned Beatty's *New York Times* editorial indicates. Once again, the reality of male rape invokes a recognition of self-vulnerability and homophobia. All too often these social discomforts are allayed with humor that attempts to dismiss or deny the existence of sexual violence against men. The result, however, is a further shaming of men who have been raped. Survivors who are already stigmatized and silenced are further humiliated in becoming the punchline to the ever-popular "don't drop the soap" jokes.

This malicious humor that mocks male rape survivors is not limited to the public's response to movies, but sometimes blatantly appears in films billed as comedies. Two movies released in 1996 used the threat of prison rape as comedy. The comedies *The Cable Guy* starring Jim Carrey and Matthew Broderick and *Celtic Pride* starring Dan Aykroyd and Damon Wayans both included rape jokes in their "trailers"—the promotional clip used as a commercial movie preview. Their inclusion in the trailer indicates the producers not only think the rape joke is one of the funniest lines in the movie, but something appropriate for all audiences, even those who choose not to see the entire film. Ward W. Triplett, a movie critic for the *Kansas City Star*, wrote in his review of *Celtic Pride* that "the biggest laugh the audience gets in the entire film comes when Jimmy tells his grandma he may have to go to jail and 'be some bad man's boyfriend.' "[14]

Where's Poppa?

One of the first comedy films to employ male rape as a humorous event came in the 1970 movie *Where's Poppa?* The story centers around two brothers, Sidney and Gordon. One night Sidney is walking alone in a city park when he is accosted by a gang of African-American men. They corner him and explain they are searching for a woman to rape. When Sidney reacts with surprise, one of the gang members explains, "We always rape somebody the night of the big dance." Another member adds, "It's tradition." A third says, "Shit, it's part of our heritage," and a fourth declares, "Everybody knows that." The gang attacks a woman, pins her to the ground, and rather than rape her, forces Sidney to rape her. Sidney initially resists, but once he begins to rape the woman his demeanor changes and he increasingly appears to enjoy the experience. The gang members run away as Sidney carries on assaulting her, so enraptured that he does not notice an approaching police officer.

Keeping in mind that this movie is a comedy, the racism is painfully transparent in reinforcing the stereotype that all African-American men rape and that the propensity to commit sexual violence is an inherent element of black culture and history. The scene is also symbolic in that it portrays the gang members as definitive agents of temptation, enticing the white man to give in to his primal urges. The rape humor doesn't stop there, however. Once Sidney is arrested, his brother Gordon arrives at the jail to bail his brother out. Sidney explains to Gordon that the "woman" he raped was in fact a male police officer dressed in women's clothing, roaming the park as a mugging decoy. When Gordon asks Sidney what happened to the officer, Sidney replies, "I don't know. He was all shook up. He had never been raped before." A guard then approaches the jail cell and hands Sidney a bouquet of flowers through the bars. Sidney reads the card, smiling, and tells his brother, "I don't think I need your help anymore. These are from the cop I raped. 'Thanks for a wonderful evening' [reads the message on the card]. He's not going to press charges, wants me to leave my name and phone number with the guard."

The decoy police officer patrolling the park was dressed as a woman, hence his masculinity was already suspect. His sexual submission to another man seems to complete this transformation of emasculation, and he is refashioned into a gay man so completely that not only does he forgive Sidney, but wants future, and presumably romantic, contact with him. Although the plot twist is meant to be one of ironic and morose humor, the formulaic narrative of male rape mirrors popular stereotypes about same-sex rape: Men who are raped are not "real men," men who are raped become gay, and gay men both desire and enjoy being raped. Sidney's prefacing comment that the officer was emotionally distraught because "he had never been raped before" implies that if a man is repeatedly raped, the assault becomes an experience of little consequence or cause for concern.

Pulp Fiction

The rape scene from *Deliverance* inspired a similar scene in Quentin Tarantino's 1994 movie *Pulp Fiction*, starring John Travolta, Bruce Willis, and Samuel Jackson. The re-creation of the rape scene in the movie dates back to Tarantino's childhood when, on his seventh birthday, young Quentin was treated to a double bill of *The Wild Bunch* and *Deliverance* at a local movie theater. In describing his childhood reaction to the graphic depiction of male rape on the big screen, Tarantino told the *Evening Standard* newspaper, "That scared the living shit out of me. Did I understand Ned Beatty being sodomized? No. [But] I knew he wasn't having any fun."[15]

Pulp Fiction is a tale of corruption and organized crime in modern-day Los Angeles, and has attracted controversy through its graphic display of violence and drug use. Two of the main characters include Butch, a professional boxer who has agreed to purposefully lose a match for Marsellus, a crime lord who will win a large sum of money betting on the fixed sporting event. When Butch goes on to fight and win and skips town instead, Marsellus dispatches his goons to look for him. As fate would have it, Marsellus and Butch soon cross paths on the street and begin to fight. Their brawl carries them through the doorway of a nearby pawnshop. Bloodied and bruised, the two men find themselves held at gunpoint by the pawnshop's owner, Maynard. Both Butch and Marsellus are knocked unconscious and when they awake, they find themselves bound and gagged in the basement of the store. Maynard's friend Zed soon arrives, and the two contemplate how they will physically torture Butch and Marsellus.

When Marsellus is chosen first, Maynard and Zed take him into another room where they begin to rape him at gunpoint. Butch loosens his bonds and successfully escapes, but decides to return to the basement and save Marsellus from his cruel fate. Once Butch slices Maynard with a sword, Marsellus picks himself up, grabs a shotgun, and fires it at Zed's crotch. Clutching his bleeding groin, Zed begs for mercy while Butch ask Marsellus,

"You okay?" He responds, "No man, I'm pretty fucking far from okay." While holding the gun on Zed, Marsellus calls a truce with Butch based on the following conditions. "Two things: Don't tell nobody about this. This here's between me, you, and Mr. Soon-to-be-living-the-rest-of-his-shortass-life-in-agonizing-pain rapist here. It ain't nobody else's business."

Some similarities exist between the rape scenes in *Pulp Fiction* and *Deliverance* in the characterization of the rapists. As in *Deliverance*, Maynard and Zed are portrayed as redneck hillbilly men, complete with southern rural accents, poor grammar, and a Confederate flag prominently displayed in the pawn shop. Zed even yells "Yee-hah" several times as he rapes Marsellus. Both men appear to be of a lower economic class. This deep South imagery may be a direct transplant from the rape scene in *Deliverance*, which occurs in the mountains of rural Georgia. *Deliverance* author James Dickey was raised in this area of the United States, and frequently borrowed from those experiences in his fiction and poetry.

Zed wears a police uniform, although he is clearly not a police officer, which in context appears to be some sort of fetish or sexual fantasy. Zed also wears an earring and acts slightly feminine, resulting in a perception that he is gay. These scenes lead audiences to the conclusion that men who rape other men do so out of ignorance and from a position of rural poverty. The two men keep a human sex slave in the basement of the pawn shop. Referring to him as "The Gimp," they keep the man bound in sadomasochistic leather gear from head to toe and caged in a cramped box. The Gimp never speaks, but kneels beside his masters in total subservience. Although the gay implication of Zed and the human slavery of Gimp serve no real purpose in the plot, they are still included in what seems to be another of the many gratuitous oddities that make the film so bizarre and disturbing.

Marsellus's demand that Butch not tell anyone of the rape parallels the pact made by the men at the end of *Deliverance* in which they pledge never to share the gruesome details of their journey. These agreements represent a silently shared understanding that male rape must be kept hidden to protect the male survivor's reputation and manhood at all cost. Although many male survivors choose never to reveal their rape experience in an effort to protect themselves from stigmatization, this silence easily becomes a prescription imposed on all men who have been raped. A general lack of men reporting rape then translates into an expectation that men should not speak about their victimization or seek support as a result of having been assaulted.

In 1995, a thread of discussion about male rape erupted on the Internet "usenet" group named *talk.rape*. In debating the provision of services for male rape survivors, one man from the University of Washington used the rape scene from *Pulp Fiction* to argue the following point:

> I object to some silly counselor telling a GUY how to cope with rape. Seen the movie Pulp Fiction? Well the black guy was raped by a man, yet he didn't cry and just kept going. That is the correct attitude. Guys should not be all whimpery and pansy-like. You get raped, smile and move on, guy. I feel only gals should be crying about rape.

Despite his reference to the rape in *Pulp Fiction*, the man who wrote the above message chose not to acknowledge Marsellus's reaction to having been raped. The statement, "I'm pretty fucking far from okay" can hardly be equated with "smile and move on," even if there was no crying or whimpering. The belief predominates that men who are raped, as opposed to female survivors, should react with stoic callousness and that their assault is no big deal beyond any physical injuries. Men are often denied the ability to experience their emotional pain and recover from the psychological scars that remain long after bodily wounds have healed.

Although I have chosen not to describe them in much detail here, other television programs and films have been produced that include noteworthy content on the subject of male rape. *Dress Gray*, a novel by Lucian K. Scott, was made into an NBC Movie of the Week starring Alec Baldwin and Hal Holbrook. First broadcast in 1986 and then again in 1988, the movie depicted the cover-up of a same-sex rape and murder at a fictional military academy. An excellent documentary simply titled *Male Rape* appeared on Irish television in 1995 and included six male rape survivors who speak about their experiences and how the rape has affected their lives. It has been rebroadcast several times since. In 1996 the investigative news show *60 Minutes* conducted a lengthy interview with the former president of Stop Prisoner Rape, Stephen Donaldson, shortly before his death from AIDS-related complications. That same year a British series about a female prison warden, *The Governor*, was axed by the Independent Television Commission over what it deemed to be excessively violent scenes, including a male prison rape. Also in 1996, the popular British series *Out of the Blue*, about a fictional South Yorkshire police squad, dedicated an episode to the investigation of a male rape.

As for other subject matter concerning male rape in major films, the 1970 version of *Fortune and Men's Eyes*, adapted from the stage play, has become somewhat of a prison movie classic. Rape behind bars is spotlighted as the ultimate expression of power between inmates in the isolated prison society. The prison rape scene in Todd Haynes's film *Poison*, inspired by the writings of Jean Genet, generated controversy when the American Family Association, a right-wing conservative group, denounced the film as pornographic. *Poison* received acclaim as the winner of the Grand Prize at the 1991 Sundance Film Festival. The American Family Association prompted Congress to scrutinize the National Endowment for the Arts (NEA) federal grant program. The NEA had awarded Haynes $25,000 for postproduction of the film.

The late 1960s ushered in two major movies with male rape content, including *Come Back to the Five and Dime Jimmie Dean, Jimmie Dean*, in which Cher plays a transsexual who describes how her male rape experience prompted her sex change operation. The 1969 movie *Midnight Cowboy* includes a scene in which the main character, a male prostitute, is raped by an acquaintance, although the scene is somewhat vague because the rape is implied rather than graphically shown. And in 1992, the movie *American Me* was released, about a Hispanic-American family involved with organized crime in East Los Angeles. The movie includes several graphic male rape scenes. One takes place in a prison setting and the others occur as part of the violent struggles the crime organization uses to maintain power.

The powerful depiction of male on male rape in popular media has only recently begun to change for the better. Examining the spectacle of male rape as it has evolved since the 1960s, more positive images are emerging in which fewer stereotypes appear, more practical information is offered through documentaries and dramas, and the topic is treated with the greater sensitivity and respect that it deserves. Some amount of insensitivity and under-representation of male rape in media will undoubtedly continue, but the charted progress of the last few decades is promising as an indicator of society's increasing willingness to recognize and confront sexual violence.

DARREN'S ABDUCTION

T he following account is the result of an interview
I conducted with a male rape survivor, whom I'll name Darren, in
early 1996. Darren is an upper-class, single, white man in his
mid-30s who lives in a large midwestern city. I first encountered
Darren anonymously on the Internet. He agreed to telephone me
long distance at a predetermined time to be tape-recorded as he
discussed his rape. I was struck by the details of his rape experience, both surprised by the tortuous events and impressed that he
actually survived. After transcribing the interview, I decided to
delete my questions from the text with his permission. What
remains here are only his words, which form the story of his
abduction and sexual assault by two strangers:

> It happened last fall in October of 1995. It was on a weeknight,
> about 8:30. I had been at the gym working out and I was walking
> out to my car. My car was pretty far away, at the other end of the
> parking lot. As I was almost to my car, I saw a van driving around

very slowly. I didn't think anything about it. I walked to my car and opened my trunk. I was putting my gym bag in my trunk, but I still had the trunk open when the van pulled up beside me. There were two guys in the van. One of them got out of the passenger's side and he started asking me for directions to a place. I started trying to tell him where it was and then he said, "Would you show us on the map?" I said, "yeah." It had seemed OK right then, it was just all happening really fast. At that point, he got out of the front of the van and opened the door to the back of the van as if he was going to get the map. He stepped up into the van for a second. When he turned around, he had a pistol in his hand. I was 2 feet away. He pointed it at me and said, "This is a robbery. You're not going to be hurt. You just need to do exactly what we say. We just want your money." He told me to take my gym bag and close the trunk. He told me to step in the van. He shut the door and was in the back of the van with me. They told me to lay down on my stomach. They pulled my hands behind my back and handcuffed me. One guy climbed up front and drove while the other guy stayed with me in the back of the van. The guy in the back with me said, "You thought this was a robbery, but we don't want your money at all. You're the kind of guy we've been looking for." Then he kept talking to the driver as if I wasn't there, saying things like, "We've really got a good specimen here. Look at this ass." I was wearing gym shorts and he kept telling the driver how good I looked in them. He started touching my butt and legs.

They drove for about 45 minutes, way out in the country to a house. They kept calling it the rape house, where they would kidnap guys and take them to rape them. It was definitely in the middle of nowhere. They told me multiple times that this is what they did, that they went to gym parking lots and looked for guys to kidnap. They took me into the house. It didn't have much furniture. They took me down to the basement, and they had a platform in the center of the room. They made me stand up on it, my hands still cuffed behind me. They walked around and looked at me and told me they were going to uncuff my hands. By this point they both had guns, and one of the guys uncuffed my hands. They told me to pull off my gym shorts and I did. They made me pull my T-shirt back behind my neck. All I had on was gym shoes, socks, and a jock strap. They made me get into different poses and positions for them for a long time. They held the guns on me the whole time. I was really scared because I was afraid the guns might even go off accidentally. I kept thinking I didn't know what they were going to do to me, that they might cut me up or mutilate me. They were touching themselves with one hand, masturbating while they were watching me.

Then they told me it was time for dance training. They turned on the stereo and said they had picked out a special song for me to dance to. It was a Village People song. They told me to put my hands up in the air and pump my butt. They told me to rehearse this dance over and over until I got it right. They told me I wasn't dancing right and that I would have to be punished for it. They kept rewinding the same song. They kept telling me they were going to train me to dance perfectly to that song while they held guns on me. They told me what a jock I was, that I must not have anything better to do with my life than live at the gym. One of the guys went to get a tape measure to measure my body and said he was going to prove what an asshole I was. They seemed to have a lot of anger directed toward guys who go to gyms. That was a big focus.

They told me to take my T-shirt off, that they were going to punish me for not dancing right. They put handcuffs on me and made me go outside. They told me they were going to punish me with a switch. They took me out to the edge of the yard where there were bushes and made me pick out branches. They took the branches and made sure they were good ones. One or two of the ones I picked out weren't any good, so I had to pick out new ones. We went back down to the basement and they made me get back on this platform, on my hands and knees, my hands still handcuffed in front of me. They used the switches on my butt and my thighs. While that was happening one of the guys stood in front of me, made me open my mouth, and he put his gun in my mouth. He held it in my mouth while the other guy was using the switch on my butt. He told me if I moved he was going to shoot me.

They started talking about how they wanted me to service their dicks with my mouth, but they couldn't have me do that because I'd probably bite them and that pissed them off. They said they really wanted me to do that but they couldn't trust me. By this point, I wasn't really terrified, but I was just miserable and tired of the whole thing, just thinking I wouldn't ever get out of there, just trying to get through it.

One of the guys started talking about how he was going to fuck my butt. They put me over a wooden sawhorse and made me lie across it. They pulled my jockstrap off and then tied my hands and legs to it so I was over it. Then they both took turns raping me. That went on for a long, long time, an hour and a half or so. They were constantly talking about me, sometimes to me, but more about me—the same things—like how much I deserved this because obviously I didn't have time to do anything but go to the gym anyway, this is what I got for going to the gym so much—that I deserved to be punished like this, fucking me. They kept calling me an asshole and a jock and a specimen. They seemed angry when they were fucking me because they did it so hard, with so much force. Earlier when they were using the switch on me, it was like they were trying to get every piece of anger or rage they had out on me. The rest of the time they were more sarcastic or condescending, more trying to humiliate or degrade me than angry.

One of them said he wondered what it would be like to be in bed with me. They handcuffed my hands behind my back and made me go upstairs to a bedroom. I had to get in the bed and they each got in bed on each side of me. They started feeling my body up. One of them took his belt and used it on my butt and legs. They stopped whipping me with the belt and I was crying. One of them started sticking his fingers up my butt, then one of them started sticking his dick up in me again like they did downstairs. He kept telling me he had made the decision that he wasn't going to take me back, that I was just going to stay there forever, they were going to put in a gym and build my body up and keep me there, all these fantasies and stuff. He started making me lick him with my mouth—his armpits, his butt.

Then they made me go back downstairs and they pointed their pistols at me again and put the music back on and made me start dancing again. Then I had the recollection that outside it was looking like dawn. I was in the basement, but there were windows down there. It was my first recognition that it was morning, because I had no idea what time it was. Then they put me back over the sawhorse, and one of the guys used a wooden paddle on my butt, and he made me count out loud every time he hit me with it. That was real intense and really bad. Then one of them fucked me with his dick again. They never did ejaculate, not even at the end.

Then they made me get dressed, and I got in the van with my hands cuffed again. It was morning. They drove me, and the van stopped. They tied a piece of ripped cloth around my face as a blindfold. One guy opened the door on the side of the van. He took the handcuffs off and told me to step out. I stepped out, and then I was just waiting for something to happen. The van left. They didn't say bye or anything. I waited a second, reached up, and pulled off the blindfold. There was no van there. I didn't know for sure where I was. I was beside an industrial building in an alley. I walked to the street and down half a block, and then back to my car a block away.

I couldn't drive my car, because they had kept my gym bag. My car keys and wallet were in my gym bag. I couldn't figure out what to do because I didn't want to tell anyone that this had happened to me. I sat on the edge of my car trying to think what to do. I wound up getting in a taxi and taking it to the building where I live. I told the doorman at my building that my wallet had been stolen, and he knew me, so he paid for the taxi. The doorman let me in my apartment, and I told them I had been at the gym and my wallet and keys had been stolen.

That freaked me out because they had my keys and my address, so the building manager had the locks changed on my door. I called in sick to work. I didn't go to the hospital or anything. I thought about calling a rape crisis center later that day after my locks got changed, but I thought it would probably be oriented toward women. I remember thinking they would be flipped out that I was calling and they wouldn't know how to handle me. My thoughts were that it would mainly be women working there and that they would mainly have a mind-set that they wanted to help other women that had been raped and that they wouldn't be very open to helping me, that I would somehow shock them and they wouldn't be prepared.

I was kind of freaked out that I might have contracted HIV or something. I wound up going to the doctor about a month after that for an HIV test. It came back negative. I first went to a licensed social worker who was really awful. He didn't seem compassionate, was very uncomfortable with me telling him what had happened. So later I found this woman psychologist out of a magazine. I went to her a whole lot—two and three times a week. I didn't want to talk to anyone else about this, nobody. I would never tell my family about being raped, not in a million years. I might tell a partner though, if I became close enough to him.

The guys that did this told me that they did this all the time, taking guys from gym parking lots. They made it sound like a routine thing. I kept looking in newspapers to see something about this, but I never saw anything. But then I thought, maybe most guys are just like me and they're not going to call the police. I wasn't about to call the police for something like this. I couldn't imagine calling them, and I had no information at all. I didn't have a license plate. The guys who did this were in their 30s. One guy might have been in his 40s. They were pretty intelligent in the way that they talked. They could have professional jobs.

The only thing that's changed in my sex life since then is that I really haven't had sex, hardly any, since that happened. I used to have it more. I have had sex since then, but I'm just now getting back into it. I just lost interest in sex. Well, actually, it did something really weird to me. I developed this whole spiritual outlook *that I didn't really have before it happened. I lost interest in sex, and I started reading lots of spiritually oriented self-help books. I started feeling like I had a connection with something bigger, whereas before I felt like I was more materialistic. It changed me in that way. I realized this there's a whole big universe out there and this is not that big a deal, just one thing that happened to one person.*

I have not been able to find any literature on the rape of adult men. I've been to big bookstores like Barnes and Noble, and I've been to the library. I found plenty of stuff about men being assaulted, but it's all about when they were kids, nothing about adults anywhere. I don't remember ever seeing examples of adult male rape in the media either—only in like prison situations, and not in film, maybe only in news stories.

Darren's experience of that night is certainly disturbing and although a reading of his story might sound somewhat cold and matter of fact, Darren often described the incidents with a voice of pain, remorse, and, at times, outrage. A number of aspects about this assault are representative of the larger phenomenon of male rape in society. The two assailants' treatment of Darren as an object rather than a human being is clear and very common as an inherent element of power in sexual violence, conveyed through their actions and even their words, referring to him as their "specimen." Their attempt to exert absolute control over him is exemplified by the way they forced him to dance, the severe beating, and repeated anal penetration. The two men who assaulted Darren seemed to have an intense, simultaneous love/hatred of traditional masculinity. At times they told him the reason for the degradation and humiliation was his "jock" body, whereas at other times they revered his masculinity—measuring his muscles, forcing him to strip and sexually perform, and so on. This contradictory expression is analogous to the attitudes of many men who rape women. These men sexualize their violence, claiming to be "turned on" and "excited" by their female victims' bodies, while at the same time indicating their hatred of femininity by using misogynist epithets. It appears in Darren's case there was a kind of "double bind" that most women experience—they are expected to be "real women," but are then punished for their conformity to rigid gender roles.

Darren's process of recovery after the abduction and assault is not entirely unusual. He began to cope in the months after his rape by expanding his view of life and the world, realizing that although his rape was significantly devastating, it remained a minor event in the larger scheme of things. This perspective is common among many spiritual ideologies and is a recurrent theme in self-help approaches to healing. The essay by Christopher Smith in Chapter Ten echoes the role of spirituality in recovery, although from a standpoint of more organized religion.

Like many other survivors, Darren made repeated attempts to find written information and looked for media representations of adult male rape, but with little success. Darren's concerted effort to find materials in bookstores was met with a stifling silence. Many male survivors interpret this void as a message that men are not raped and, therefore, the topic is not deserving of attention. Even more specifically, it is important to note Darren's vigilant eye on the local newspaper as he scanned for mention of others who had been raped by the same two men. The assailants made sure that Darren knew they had abducted others like himself, and even referred to the isolated location as the "rape house" in which they regularly conducted such activity. He recalled stereotypical portrayals of male rape in prison news stories, but none in film and nothing that came close to resonating with his own experience. As discussed in the previous chapter, many survivors like David continue to face this invalidating lack of male rape imagery in the media. The insensitivity of the few appearances that male rape makes in popular culture can further complicate the recovery, as indicated by other survivors.

Darren's anxiety and well-reasoned concern about contracting HIV infection as a result of his rape is also fairly common among male survivors. The risk of HIV transmission, especially by means of anal penetration, brings an added dimension of fear and crisis to the rape aftermath faced by survivors. These issues are more fully explored in the next chapter on the intersection of rape and AIDS, which continues with a consideration of broader medical concerns associated with men raping men.

EIGHT

VIRILE MEETS VIRAL
The Intersection of HIV and Same-Sex Rape

housands of pages of research and writing have been published exploring the transmission of HIV between men through penis-to-mouth and penis-to-anus contact. The bulk of this material, with only a handful of notable exceptions, operates within a context of presumption that men's risk for infection with HIV entails physical contact and the exchange of semen and blood voluntarily, always with mutual consent of the involved participants. Strangely, the concept of the rape of men and its relevant significance to HIV infection has never been explored in any breadth or depth. This glaring void could be attributed to a cultural denial that men are sexually assaulted as adults, or perhaps AIDS has become so intertwined with male homosexuality that consensual sex is always presumed. Maybe AIDS prevention efforts have chosen to focus on consensual acts in behavioral change models in the spirit of public health's mission to empower individuals to make healthier choices. The preservation of private choice in the sexual domain has become a hotly contested issue in the field of public health and public policy. A culture of self-restraint has long been emphasized by public health measures seeking to negotiate the rights of the individual with the safety of the community at large, but issues of nonconsensual same-sex risk behaviors have remained largely overlooked as they pertain to HIV infection and AIDS.

The psychological, social, cultural, and medical implications of the relationship between HIV and rape are vast and varied. Relatively little research has been conducted in this area, especially in the case of same-sex rape. Prevention and risk-reduction efforts have tended to concentrate on voluntary behavior, attempting to identify the motivation behind a willingness between individuals to engage in behaviors that facilitate the transmission of HIV. Stepping away from the convention of consensual sexual activity as a venue for measuring the transmission of disease, this chapter represents an attempt to identify patterns and draw meaningful connections at the intersections of same-sex rape, sexual behavior, and HIV.

ASSESSMENT OF RISK

According to Dr. Jordan Glaser of the State University of New York Science Center's Infectious Diseases Division, an exact measurement of risk for HIV transmission via same-sex rape is presently not possible.[1] The virtually limitless variables that could hinder or enhance HIV infection during a rape make even a rough estimation incalculable. As for same-sex sexual assault, a number of specific factors could determine the possibility that a male rape survivor will become infected as a result of being sexually assaulted by another adult male. These factors include, first and foremost, whether or not the assailant is infected. In most cases, especially in the case of acquaintance rape, a rape survivor may not know his attacker's HIV status, and speculation of the potential risk resulting from the assault can lead the survivor to ask, "What are the chances that I have become infected?" Obviously, same-sex penetration does not, in and of itself, cause HIV infection. The virus must be transmitted from one human body to another. If a survivor equates rape with sex (as we are socialized to do), and more specifically, same-sex rape with homosexuality, then he may irrationally deduce that homosexuality is accompanied by AIDS. This chain of logic, that same-sex rape = homosexuality = AIDS, has been legitimized by an extensive history of treating AIDS as a gay disease in the United States, beginning in 1981 when the immune system disorder was originally named gay-related immune deficiency (GRID). Same-sex rape may, therefore, instill greater fears of HIV infection than opposite-sex rape based on homophobic socialization that all gay men have AIDS and that same-sex rape is a sexually motivated act only committed by gay men.

Assuming the attacker could be HIV-positive, an assessment of risk will include several considerations, keeping in mind that risk of infection can never be exactly quantified because of the virtually limitless number of cofactors and variable conditions surrounding exposure to HIV:

1. *Was the sexual assault oral, anal, or both?* Anal penetration may create more risk for transmission than oral penetration, especially if the tissue of the rectal lining becomes torn, creating entry points through which HIV can enter the bloodstream. Recent reviews of research conducted on oral sex between men indicate that unprotected penis-to-mouth penetration is not a predominant mode of HIV transmission.[2]

2. *Was the weapon used in the assault a finger, penis, or some other instrument?* If the weapon was a penis, the possibility of contact with blood or semen increases risk. The use of a condom, other barrier devices, or lubricants with antiviral agents such as nonoxynol-9 may reduce risk. Nonpenile weapons, such as a finger or dildo, may still carry some risk if the assailant's blood or semen is on the weapon.

3. *Did the rapist ejaculate?* Some studies suggest that in the

majority of male same-sex rapes, ejaculation does not usually occur. Again, the presence of semen, beyond pre-ejaculatory fluid, increases risk. Although low levels of HIV have been detected in preejaculatory fluid, the most danger occurs when the rapist's semen enters the victim's bloodstream via the mouth or anus.

4. *What was the severity of physical trauma?* The severity of physical trauma may create tears in the oral or anal cavity that will allow an attacker's blood or semen (and HIV) to enter the survivor's bloodstream. Other physical injuries such as scrapes or cuts may pose similar risks.

5. *How many assailants participated in the rape, and with what frequency did the assault(s) occur?* Men who have been raped are more likely than female rape survivors to have been attacked by multiple assailants.[3] Understandably, the greater the number of individuals' blood and semen one comes into contact with, the greater the risk of infection. Similarly, a greater number of exposures to HIV will yield a higher incidence of infection. Gang rapes are frequently more brutal and last for longer periods of time, resulting in more physical trauma that may provide increased opportunity for HIV to enter a man's body.

6. *What was the health status of the assailant?* An HIV-positive individual may also be more infectious at certain periods over time, related to the stage of progression along a spectrum of HIV disease, drug treatment therapy, and other factors. In addition to the amount of virus in the bloodstream, now scientifically measured as "viral load," some strains of HIV are more potently infectious than others, usually described in medical terms as virulence. Higher virulence increases risk of infection. The differing viral subtypes and concentration of the number of virus in blood and semen will determine the likelihood of infection to some degree. Herein lies the distinction between exposure and infection. Whereas exposure simply means contact with the virus, infection results from a sufficient quantity of virus needed to successfully invade the host.

7. *What was the health status of the survivor?* The health status of the survivor should be taken into account as well, especially the competence of the survivor's immune system, which may determine whether an exposure to HIV results in an actual infection. If the survivor was under the influence of alcohol or other drugs, a high degree of emotional stress, poor diet, lack of sleep, and other variables of impairment that compromise the human immune system, HIV has more of an opportunity to overcome bodily defenses.[4,5]

For some men who were unaware or unsure of their HIV status before being raped, the assault may provide a previously lacking motivation or insight for them to seek out antibody testing. Some survivors may wish to be tested immediately after their rape, if only to establish a "baseline" of their HIV serostatus before the assault. Determination of HIV transmission from the assault will usually entail waiting the necessary minimum 12-week "window period," allowing the immune system time to generate enough antibodies to HIV to be detected by the ELISA (enzyme-linked immunosorbent assay) and Western blot HIV antibody test. The two components of this test detect the presence of HIV antibodies (ELISA), followed by a more sensitive confirmatory test (Western blot) should the first test come back positive. Increasing availability of PCR (polymerase chain reaction) testing will significantly reduce this necessary waiting period, as PCR testing detects the presence of virus rather than antibodies. For some survivors, the knowledge of exactly how they became infected may be just as important as knowing if they are infected. Although sexual assault may motivate some men to find out their HIV status, other men may experience an increased reluctance to be tested when faced with the very real possibility of infection. This reluctance may be part of a larger denial that the rape has occurred, or perhaps part of a very valid right not to know his HIV status until such a time that he is psychologically able to deal with the results.

The possibility of HIV infection may require some male survivors to share their rape experience with their romantic or sexual partners so as to avoid possible infection of these significant others. For a couple who had previously practiced unprotected sex within their monogamous relationship, a sudden change to protected sex and condom use without a revelation of the rape may raise questions from the survivor's partner. The unknowing partner may suspect the survivor has been infidelic, or the reverse, that the survivor suspects his partner has been cheating on him and demanding safer sex as a result of this distrust. A sudden halt to all sexual activity or specific sexual acts is also common, as many male survivors experience sexual dysfunction after their assault. This too can be a source of frustration or suspicion within a previously normal relationship.

HIV-POSITIVE SURVIVORS

We should not assume that every male rape survivor was HIV negative before he was assaulted. For rape survivors who are HIV positive, the possibility of reinfection is an important concern. Reinfection with a different strain of HIV can accelerate the progression of HIV disease, posing a danger to those already infected. The effects of male rape on HIV-positive men can also be devastating in a myriad of other ways: psychological stress associated with rape trauma syndrome may severely cripple an HIV-positive survivor's immune system, reflecting the fact that emotional states can strengthen or weaken physical health and wellness. Some other physical symptoms that may occur as a result of rape trauma include loss of appetite, nausea, insomnia, muscle stiffness, stomachaches, and headaches.

A compromised immune system will also lead to slower rates of healing from any physical injuries incurred as a result of the assault, increasing the likelihood of infection or chronic injury. Sexually transmitted diseases other than HIV, such as hepatitis, syphilis, and herpes (to name a few), possibly acquired from the attacker, may do further damage to one's immune system. Economic costs associated with the effects of sexual violence—legal, therapeutic, medical, loss of employment and wages—can increase the financial burdens of some HIV-positive individuals who may already be struggling to afford adequate housing and quality health care.

Concerns surrounding the compromised confidentiality of one's HIV serostatus may prevent HIV-positive rape survivors from seeking the support, assistance, and treatment they need for optimal recovery. Documentation of HIV status in one's medical chart or legal report has the power to endanger health insurance coverage, employment, family relations, and more. For example, evidentiary blood drawn from the male survivor for forensic analysis may create an opportunity for the breach of one's serostatus confidentiality. The survivor should be informed and asked for consent if an HIV test will be performed on a forensic blood sample. The survivor should also be instructed as to how the resulting information will be shared or withheld from himself and others.

As with other violent crime experiences, an HIV-positive man's sexual assault experience may provoke heightened anxieties about connections between seropositivity, vulnerability, societal homophobia, and mortality. The compounding of life-threatening or traumatic events may present a kind of cumulative trauma, melding many of the losses associated with HIV infection (length of life, quality of life, social stigma) and the losses associated with being raped (loss of personal power, loss of sexual control). This "multiplicity of survivorhood," accompanied by homophobia, racism, classism, and other forms of oppression, increases the difficulties faced by men who, once again, seek to transcend victimhood by reshaping themselves into yet another kind of survivor. The social construction of a male rape "victim" also carries the implicit duality of guilt and innocence so common with other conceptualizations of victimhood. We have recently witnessed the emergence of "innocent" victims of AIDS—hemophiliacs, AIDS infants, and blood product recipients—all in contrast to the socially deviant "guilty" victims of AIDS—homosexuals, bisexuals, injection drug users, and prostitutes.

Many social movements utilize survivorhood as a politicized identity and vehicle for mobilization. A comparative analysis of these survivor movements might reveal opportunities for coalition-building and greater understanding between human rights activists. This could foster collaboration, for example, between "people living with AIDS" and "rape survivors." Several parallels of "secondary victimization" can be noted between the support people of rape survivors and those of AIDS survivors. A comparison between texts such as *If She is Raped* and *When Someone You Know Has AIDS* reveals remarkable similarities in both style and content. With regard to people living with AIDS and rape survivors, no one deserves to be infected or assaulted. Just as the ACT-UP slogan reads, "All people with AIDS are innocent," no man wants or asks to be raped. As stated earlier, if rape is fundamentally defined as a lack of consent, then consideration of a man wanting or asking for rape is paradoxical.

HIV AND THE HOMOSEXUAL PANIC DEFENSE

In the case of recently popularized "homosexual panic" defenses in courtrooms across the nation, HIV and same-sex rape have been spotlighted as key areas of contention. The "homosexual panic defense" is a tactic employed in legal cases to justify violence against gay men, usually in situations where the assailant claims his attack was in response to the sexual advances of another man. One particular case study exemplifies how homophobia and AIDS-related fears are used as justifications to bolster a legal defense against charges of antigay violence. A judge presiding over a 1995 murder trial in Laurel, Mississippi, allowed the introduction of two slain gay men's HIV serostatus (acquired from the autopsy) as evidence in a court of law. The decision to allow the admission of this information was mired in community conflicts of homophobia, racism, and sexual violence.

In February 1995, a 17-year-old black male had been charged in the murder of two white gay men. The prosecution claimed the youth had murdered the two men in the midst of robbing them. The defense for the youth claimed the murder of the two gay men was an act of self-defense against attempted rape. The defendant justified the killing as a measure of self-defense within the context of his fear the two men might be infected with HIV. The specter of the predatory male homosexual, coupled with a sense of panic regarding potential HIV infection, provided a backdrop of persuasive argumentation. Judge Billy Landrum allowed the introduction of the two gay men's HIV status as evidence into court as a result of this defense strategy. In allowing the "AIDS panic" defense of the defendant, Landrum stated he believed the jury was "entitled to know the whole facts in the case."[6] His decision immediately attracted national media attention. Locally, white gay activists denounced the trial as homophobic, citing the court's equation of homosexuality and HIV infection, accompanied by a violation of privacy in both regards. African-American activists claimed the trial, and the white gay community, were fraught with racism to the point of resembling a modern-day lynching of the black youth for the murder of two white men in self-defense.

Catherine Hanssens, director of the AIDS Project at Lambda Legal Defense and Education Fund in New York, quickly condemned Judge Landrum's ruling in a statement to the Associated Press:

> We're aware of no case before this where a judge has actually said the HIV status of a victim is in any way related to someone's violent criminal behavior. In a climate where there has been a horrifying level of violence against people who are gay or lesbian or people who have HIV, this is pretty sad news.[7]

Widney Brown, program attorney with the New York City Gay and Lesbian Anti-Violence Project, expressed similar concerns: "Basically he has declared open season on people with HIV and other disabilities that are stigmatized. We think it's an appalling decision."[8]

Judge Landrum had initially sealed the coroner's report including the HIV antibody test results of the two slain men. Later, however, he allowed the defense lawyer to reveal to jurors that one victim had tested HIV negative, the other HIV positive. In doing so, Landrum allowed the slain victims to be blamed for the crime, implicitly conveying that, first, unfounded fear of HIV is a reasonable defense for murder, and second, suspicion that a gay man is HIV infected (simply because he is gay) is also, in and of itself, a reasonable speculation. The youth was eventually convicted of murdering the two men and sentenced to two life sentences in prison. Black and gay communities were pitted against one another while a dangerous legal decision marked a growing precedent of impingement on the rights and privacy of individuals with HIV. The trial evoked the popular stereotype of the homosexual predator, this time infected with HIV, prone to both violence and contagion.

Strangely, an almost parallel case occurred that very same year in Noblesville, Indiana. An African-American teenager was found guilty of voluntary manslaughter of an older white gay man. The race and sexual orientation of both men figured prominently in the trial and surrounding media coverage. According to the youth, he acted in self-defense because the gay acquaintance had made unwanted sexual advances. The defense attorney for the youth introduced the notion that homosexuality was strongly associated with AIDS, therefore, "Not just [the gay man] could have died, but [the youth] could have died from the gunshot or AIDS. Will you let [the gay man's] lifestyle kill [the youth]?"[9] Unlike the case in Mississippi, however, autopsy results of HIV testing performed on the corpse were not introduced as evidence, despite the defense attorney's use of the homosexual panic defense.

BLAME THE RAPE VICTIM AND SAFER SEX CAMPAIGNS

If a man has been raped by another man without the use of a condom, how will the rape survivor feel when, during a safer sex workshop or HIV test counseling, he is told he has been "irresponsible," "unconscientious," or "risk-taking" for not using condoms during previous penis-to-anus bodily contact? Sensitivity toward rape survivors in populations targeted for HIV education is sorely lacking, perhaps related in part to the tradition of public health attempts at encouraging communities to voluntarily change the behaviors that they can themselves control. The following excerpts from safer sex literature are illustrative of language that could be interpreted by rape survivors as blame-the-victim sentiments:

> *You can control whether or not you become infected with HIV—from the Illinois Public Health Department's 1992 brochure AIDS: See the Light*

> *The #1 rule is: Never let someone else's cum or blood get inside your body (and never let your cum or blood get inside someone else's body).—from Gay Men's Health Crisis 1991 pamphlet, Safer Sex Guidelines for Gay Men*

> *You have choices to make about whether, when, and how to be sexually active.—from Columbus, Ohio Health Department's 1995 brochure, Positively Sexual: Living with HIV*

> *Alcohol and drugs can cause you to make bad decisions—from Impact AIDS, San Francisco's 1988 brochure, Safer Sex For Gay and Bisexual Men: Man to Man*

The implicit message is one of choice and responsibility, but could be interpreted by many rape survivors as "It's your fault that he forced you to have sex," "You are irresponsible," or "You have made bad decisions and unhealthy choices." AIDS educators and HIV test counselors must become better equipped to tailor presentations and discussions with the assumption that rape survivors are a sizable percentage of their every audience. Rape crisis intervention skills and referrals should also be on hand, as frank and open discussions of sexual behavior may trigger a rape survivor to come forward about his experience for the first time, seeking support from an identified "expert" working in the field of sexual health.

I have served as an HIV test counselor at the Ohio State University's Student Health Services clinic intermittently since 1993, providing both pre- and posttest counseling for students who wanted to know their HIV antibody status. As an anonymous testing site, we were given standardized "risk history" forms by the Ohio Department of Health. These written questionnaires, to be completed by the patient, were designed to assess an individual's history of experiences that might have placed him or her at risk for infection. All of the questions relating to sexual behavior, however, were phrased in language that suggested conscious choice and consensual activity. After several months our AIDS Education and Outreach Program rewrote the form using more inclusive language and included a question about sexual assault. The number of positive responses to the sexual assault questionnaire item was surprisingly high, and we soon realized not only that rape was a high-risk experience that motivated men and women to seek HIV antibody testing, but also that we had engaged in blame-the-victim counseling with a significant percentage of our past patients.

Because we had never specifically asked patients to identify their unsafe sexual experiences as consensual or nonconsensual, we had undoubtedly been advising an invisible population of rape survivors to make "smarter" and more "responsible" choices. The underlying message in this language conveyed that patients were responsible for their rape as well as their consequential risk of infection. Similarly, if a heterosexual male rape survivor indicated he was penetrated by another man without a condom, the test counselor may inappropriately take this as an indication the survivor is gay and launch into a discussion of safer sex between men. This action redefines rape as sex while inappropriately challenging the survivor's sexual orientation. Few HIV test counselors receive sexual violence sensitivity training, and when rape-related content is included in test counseling training, the topic of same-sex rape is generally absent. This results in part from the lack of national standards in training HIV test counselors.

Before becoming a test counselor in 1994, I attended a 4-day training provided by the Ohio Department of Health, conducted by a man who billed himself as an HIV education consultant. Several times throughout the training, participants in the training class were instructed to comfort our anxious or emotionally distressed patients through a variety of forms of physical touch— from reaching out to hold their hands, laying a hand on their shoulder, or even wrapping our arms around them in a tight embrace if they began to weep. Uncomfortable with this advisement, I raised the issue of gaining consent before physical touch and reminded my classmates that patients with a history of sexual abuse may be harmed rather than helped by this attempt to comfort and console. I personalized my comment by adding that I was uncomfortable with anyone touching my body without prior permission. My suggestion was dismissed by the trainer. Less than 2 hours after I had stressed the importance of negotiated consent before physical touch between individuals, the trainer moved about the room while talking. Standing behind me, he placed his hands on my shoulders as he emphasized a particular piece of information. I was outraged that he had completely disregarded my earlier point, and amazed by the extent to which he took such a liberty with my body. The importance of connotations and meanings associated with physical contact between professionals and the clients they serve cannot be underscored enough, especially in a setting where sexual health is of primary relevance in the provision of quality care.

With the large numbers of men (and a percentage of them being male rape survivors) seeking HIV testing, a great deal of misplaced blame and insensitivity has become institutionalized as common practice. Greater collaboration between rape and AIDS prevention movements might foster the mutual understanding necessary to chip away at these damaging, albeit well-intentioned, protocols. A more interdisciplinary approach to sexual health, including sexual violence, is desperately needed to provide quality, integrated education, prevention, and treatment to survivors and non-survivors, HIV positive and HIV negative.

These connections across disciplinary and professional boundaries can conserve resources and create innovative approaches that simultaneously promote the negotiation of safer sex with the negotiation of consent. The negotiation of safer sex is, in part, the negotiation of sexual consent. After all, if a sexual activity is not consensual, one should consider defining the activity as rape. Consensual sex is not, however, synonymous with safer sex. Two individuals may very well consent to have unprotected sex. If HIV prevention and antirape movements could identify and agree on these conceptual relationships, perhaps health educators and risk-reduction workers could create more effective opportunities for motivating behavior change on a larger scale of health promotion.

I do not wish to depict AIDS and rape organizations as simply unfamiliar and in need of being introduced to one another. It has been my professional experience that many anti-rape organizations and service providers have been, for the most part, willing to address issues of HIV infection. The same cannot be said, however, for the reverse. Many AIDS groups still refuse to take any stance on the issue of mandatory testing for sex offenders, continue to discuss behaviors in ways that deny the possibility of sexual violence, and fail to understand the connections between rape, oppression, and HIV as a pandemic of society's undesirables—even when this negligence is brought to their attention. The mainstreaming of AIDS service organizations since the mid-1980s has been accompanied by establishing a distance from feminist and other anti-oppression movements in efforts to gain legitimacy in the eyes of private and governmental funders.

After coordinating a campus AIDS education program for 2 years, I was hired as the coordinator of Ohio State University's Rape Education and Prevention Program. Although I remained in the field of sexual health education and risk-reduction work, I soon realized my theoretical approaches and public speaking were self-contradictory. The problem resided in notions of the constituent elements of consent, and how consent is negotiated in situations of both safer sex and potential rape. As a rape educator, I have defined behaviors such as coercion and manipulation to be rape behaviors, that is, if someone employs coercive tactics to persuade his unwilling sexual partner to submit or relent, this constitutes rape behavior. As an AIDS educator, I conduct workshops to teach sexual communication skills to college students. Part of this skill-building includes the ability to convince one's partner to wear a condom, despite his reluctance to do so. Through role-plays and examples, participants are trained to become skillful in the art of coercion.

I have only recently begun to examine this contradiction in method and philosophy. How, as a rape educator, can I denounce coercion as a form of sexual assault while, as an AIDS educator, promote coercion in the interest of HIV prevention? The answer lies in a mentality of paternalism. I presume to know what is best for the population I educate, and through inscribing their values within a culture of self-restraint, I seek to protect them from themselves. Through this logic, I state that coercing an unwilling partner to engage in sexual activity is unethical, but coercing a partner unwilling to engage in safer sex is responsible and healthy. Populations that receive rape prevention and safer sex promotion messages may become understandably confused, for the two approaches can appear to be in direct contradiction to one another. By this rationale, rape and sex are once again conflated while glaring exceptions continue to deviate from basic standards of public health.

Along this intersection of sexual violence and fear of infection, two notorious court cases have attracted national attention in recent years. Although these cases involved the rape of women by men, they nonetheless demonstrate the ways in which communication surrounding safer sex and consensual sex becomes blurred. A man in Austin, Texas, successfully avoided one grand jury indictment on rape charges because his alleged victim asked him to use a condom. The female survivor told police the man, Joel Valdez, broke into her apartment and that she asked him to wear a condom when he expressed his intent to rape her at knifepoint. Valdez later constructed a defense by arguing that her request demonstrated consent to have sex with him. The decision sparked several courthouse protests. Following the public outcry, the county district attorney submitted the case to a second grand jury who returned an indictment against the man. He was later convicted of aggravated sexual assault and sentenced to 40 years in prison.[10] A similar argument was also attempted in 1993 when a defense lawyer suggested that a Washington, D.C., woman had consented to sex by asking a man to wear a condom. Jurors later dismissed this as an expression of consent, especially with the victim testifying her alleged assailant had a gun. The jury was divided on whether she gave consent in other ways, however, and the judge eventually declared a mistrial.[11]

Other public recognitions of condom use in sexual assaults have spawned legislation and research. In 1994, California Governor Pete Wilson signed into law a bill stating that any request made before a rape that the attacker wear a condom cannot be considered consent. That same year, Dr. Jav Kovar of Hermann Hospital's emergency room in Houston, Texas, reported that between 10 and 15% of rape victims receiving treatment reported that their attacker used a condom. Emergency room personnel speculated that the attacker may have worn a condom as protection from HIV and other STDs, and to leave less forensic and genetic evidence behind for prosecutors. Marilyn Lewis, head of the San Francisco Rape Treatment Center, has reported that 15 to 20% of her agency's rape cases involve the use of condoms. It remains to be seen if these cases involving the rape of women will eventually become trends among male rape survivors as well. One of the male survivors I interviewed told me that HIV infection was a major concern for him after he was raped and that "if I am ever in that situation again, I would ask that person raping me to use a condom."

A person's request for his would-be attacker to wear a condom does not constitute a desire to be violated. In analyzing the above two examples in which women asked their attackers to wear condoms, we should characterize the acts as "safer rape" rather than "safer sex." Asking or persuading one's rapist to wear a condom is a strategy of self-defense, not seduction. This is a thinly veiled, recycled attempt to depict women as "wanting it." Similarly, if a rape victim acquiesces or becomes compliant during the assault, often as a strategy for reducing physical pain or brutality, he or she is not responsible for the victimization. Simply put, cooperation does not equal consent.

Negotiations of sexual consent and negotiations of safer sex often overlap, creating tenuous areas between the dichotomy of rape and sex. The negotiation of sexual consent can be incredibly complex—much more than a simple, verbal yes or no, especially when safer sex is involved. Agreements based on when and how certain acts will take place are often the most relevant in attempts to prevent the transmission of bodily fluids. The gray areas beyond a yes-or-no duality quickly become apparent. For example, if a man agrees to sexual activity with a condom, and his partner refuses to wear a condom but still penetrates him, has a rape occurred? I would argue that yes, consent includes more than whether a specific act is mutually agreed on, but also the physical and social context within which the act takes place.

In an interview I conducted with a gay man who was raped by an acquaintance, a disagreement about safer sex marked the pivotal moment that a consensual act became distinctly violent. The survivor, Jonathan, clearly connected a disagreement over condom use as the turning point in a sexual encounter that quickly became an episode of brutal rape and physical abuse:

> He said he wanted to fuck me. I told him to put a condom on and he said that no, he didn't have to do that and that I would do what he said. He was bigger than me and he pinned me down, and so I had to let him do it. He didn't cum. After a while he stopped fucking me and started hitting on my face. And I tried to just resist it, thinking he would stop. Then he started hitting harder and harder and then started hitting me in the eyes.

Jonathan indicated that while he was being penetrated without a condom, his panic during the rape was exacerbated by his fear of becoming infected with HIV. This later motivated him to seek HIV testing from the local health department.

The recently updated sex manual, *The New Joy of Gay Sex*, suggests a more direct, cause–effect link between sexual assault and HIV. Scanning the contents of the book organized alphabetically like a sexual encyclopedia, I was surprised to find the term *rape* included in this volume. An excerpt of this entry reads:

> The increased frequency of date rape in recent years seems to be directly related to the fear many gays feel about contracting HIV Disease. Less willing to be sexually active, yet attracted to their partner, they appear indecisive; another may interpret the indecision as flirting. Should the misunderstanding continue, the partner may feel frustrated. If he has a violent streak in his personality, sexual assault may be the result.[12]

A relationship between the fear of HIV infection in gay male acquaintance rape should not be discounted, but attribution of one to the other is extremely reductive and fails to address a larger problem, namely, masculine violence and many men's lack of skills in communicating with each other to negotiate consent. This "fear of HIV = sexual assault" model remedicalizes and pathologizes the rape of gay men and rape by gay men once again in its attempt to draw strong causative links between illness, violence, and sexuality—the intersection of virile and viral.

This contextualization of male rape within the ongoing AIDS pandemic marks a dramatic shift in contrast to the first edition of *The Joy of Gay Sex*, coauthored by Dr. Charles Silverstein and Edmund White, and published in pre-AIDS 1977. A portion of the entry on rape from the original volume reads:

> *An experienced man, for instance, may pick up someone who is just coming out and fail to respect his limits. Overcome by lust, the experienced man may fuck his partner by force, without lubrication and without the partner's consent. Sex of this sort can produce psychological and physical damage.*[13]

The above statement is somewhat contradictory in a number of respects. Male rape is attributed more to "lust," and is more synonymous to "fuck"ing and "sex" than violence. The hypothetical example Silverstein and White conjure up does, however, point to the overpowerment that is fundamental to the act of rape—such as an inequity in social power (i.e., "experienced" versus "just coming out") and a failure to respect the limits of another (i.e., "without the partner's consent"). Although the psychological and physical dynamics of violation are clear, the definition is couched in sexual language, blurring the elusive boundary marking where sex ends and rape begins.

Most notable in this entry is the suggestion that a man who suspects he is about to be raped should prominently announce a fabricated sexually transmitted disease. The following self-defense strategy is offered to the potential gay male victim of rape: "If you find yourself in this situation, head off your adversary by saying, 'I'd love to get fucked by you. Unfortunately I have clap in the ass. How long does it take to get rid of the disease?'"[15] Interestingly, the 1977 *Joy of Gay Sex* guide offers the threat of a sexually transmitted disease (gonorrhea) as a protective measure against rape. In the later edition of this same book, the fear of a sexually transmitted disease (HIV) is identified as a directly causal element in same-sex male rape. This dramatic shift points to the social and cultural differences between HIV and other sexually transmitted diseases. HIV is bestowed with the ability to set into motion complex chain reactions of social behavior with inevitably disastrous results. Like HIV, other sexually transmitted diseases in the 1990s have also acquired a different ability to instill dread and fear within the age of AIDS.

INTENTIONAL INFECTIONS

When rape is used as an exercise of control within same-sex relationships, the power play of sexual violence takes on additional significance if the partner committing the rape knows he is HIV positive. "Like women, gay men are also victims of rape and sexual assault—violence that makes them prone to HIV infection. At its extreme, domestic violence takes the form of deliberately infecting a partner."[15] Patrick Letellier, a counselor at the Family Project in San Francisco and the coauthor of *Men Who Beat the Men Who Love Them* (a book on domestic violence in gay male relationships), offers an explanation for this rape behavior as a vehicle for infection: "I have talked to men who were infected by their partner and believed they were infected deliberately. It's the mentality of 'If I can't have you, no one can.' "[16] Frequently, men who rape know the stigma of sexual victimization they impose will brand the survivor as "damaged goods," making him less desirable in the eyes of others. Similarly, a positive HIV serostatus within gay male culture may also transform one into a social pariah. The combination of infection by means of rape causes a duality of harm in this way, increasing the rapist's likelihood of maintaining control and ownership of the survivor. In cases of both rape and HIV infection, survivors often report feeling dirty or unclean, guilty from their past experiences, and socially and sexually undesirable in the eyes of others.

Aside from acquaintance rape in gay male relationships, the threat of HIV infection from a stranger may produce other sorts of concerns. In one survey of 28 male rape survivors, 12 spontaneously reported that their attackers had used threats of HIV infection such as "You'll get AIDS now."[17] Clearly, the more distant the relationship between the attacker and survivor, the less knowledge the survivor will have in surmising his attacker's HIV serostatus. This lack of knowledge might escalate the survivor's anxieties by preventing him from being able to assess his own risk of infection.

The window period from time of infection until the survivor generates enough HIV antibodies to be detected with standard antibody testing can last several months. The anxiety of waiting through this window period is often increased by repeated testing. An HIV-antibody test procedure can produce a great deal of understandable tension and stress. To help alleviate this aspect of the clinical experience, practically all HIV testing includes some amount of pre- and posttest counseling. Sensibly, these discussions include a "history-taking" of an individual's personal experiences that might have put him or her at risk for infection. Each time a rape survivor is HIV-tested, he or she will be forced to relive the rape experience, recounting and explaining exactly how he or she came to be at risk. If HIV test counselors are not sensitive to issues of sexual assault, they risk instilling guilt or blame on the survivor without drawing any distinctions between high-risk acts that were chosen and high-risk experiences that were not willingly engaged in.

The ability to terrorize another person with a long-term threat of HIV and AIDS may represent a new and emerging form of continued power and domination wielded during and after sexual assault. A man who rapes another man and conveys the possibility of HIV transmission gains power and control over his victim not only from the immediacy of the physical violence, but also from the assurance and confidence that such a threat will provide ongoing fear, dread, and uncertainty. Knowledge of basic HIV transmission issues can be a double-edged sword in this regard. Marcus, a bisexual male rape survivor I interviewed, discussed

how his increasing level of HIV-related knowledge magnified his
fear of infection resulting from the rape:

> *Considering the way it happened, that fact that he went down on*
> *me, I didn't think of it as a particular risk. Even when I went in for*
> *my first two HIV tests, I didn't think of it that way, as a risk. As I*
> *learned more and more about HIV and transmission, sort of gradu-*
> *ally over the years, it began to worry me a lot more. Every time I go*
> *in to get tested it becomes more and more traumatic.*

Unlike Marcus's case, the "ignorance is bliss" principle might
apply to some survivors who lack an understanding of the prevalence and possibility of HIV infection. HIV education directed at
these individuals could be a catalyst for their self-perception of
vulnerability for infection. Those survivors who possess a higher
level of HIV-related knowledge may be acutely aware of their risk
to a psychologically disabling degree.

The specter of the gay male "AIDS avenger" has also been
popularized, in which gay men seek to intentionally infect others
via rape out of a twisted vengeance for their own HIV diagnosis.
This urban mythology has created a new form of homophobic
paranoia that angry gay men who are HIV positive might forcibly
transmit the virus to "innocent" heterosexual men as a form
of social revenge or anarchy. Many same-sex rape myths are
grounded in this irrational belief that gay men, given the chance,
will prey on unsuspecting heterosexuals and "spread" AIDS
among the "general" population. Similar to the expressions of
hatred that have been directed toward gay men who have donated
blood and presumably contaminated the national blood supply,
the fear that gay men will rape without regard for the biologically
hazardous consequences justifies some individuals' unconditional
homophobia. Numerous examples of such homophobic fears of
rape and AIDS have appeared in mass media, with probably the
most powerful and blatant being radio personality Howard
Stern's angry statement directed toward Larry Wert, general manager of the radio station WLUP. Wert allegedly had canceled
Stern's show and refused to pay the money owed to Stern from a
contractual agreement. Stern's broadcast message to Wert was,
"Larry, I hope you get AIDS and cancer. I hope a homosexual, a

deranged homosexual, rapes you in the buttocks and he has the deadly AIDS virus and you contract it after one sexual encounter . . . and then I hope you spread AIDS to your whole family."[18] Lesbigay Radio Chicago hosts Alan Amberg and Trish Koch responded promptly with a statement that "[Stern's] attacks are obviously intended to incite anger. We have a hard time accepting his use of violent gay stereotypes and hysterical information about AIDS."[19] Although Stern's comments may not have been motivated directly by homophobia, clearly he was conscious of the impact of such a statement in the midst of popular fears and stereotypes surrounding homosexuality and HIV infection.

HATE CRIMES AND HIV-BIASED RAPE

In the research article, "Gay Men as Victims of Nonconsensual Sex," which appeared in the *Archives of Sexual Behavior* in 1994, Ford Hickson (a professor of sociology at the University of Essex, United Kingdom) and his colleagues discussed the rape of gay men by heterosexual men as part of a hate crime, suggesting the specter of HIV infection acts as a deterrent against sexual assault during gay bashings: "The emergence of HIV, and its associations with gay men, may have made that group 'off limits' as potential targets for [sexual] attack."[20] In the preceding statement, Hickson made several assumptions in his consideration of the threat of HIV as a demotivational factor, first being that the heterosexual rapist is always seronegative, and therefore runs the risk of seroconversion should he rape a gay man. In addition, the gay man in such a scenario is either assumed to be infected, or necessarily perceived through a lens of homophobia to be HIV positive purely on the basis of his sexual identity.

At least one example that defies Hickson's theory can be found in a 1987 United Press International article refuting the rationale that a fear of HIV protects gay men from sexual assault. Gregory Herek, an assistant professor of psychology at the City University of New York Graduate Center, reported that "the spread of the deadly disease [HIV] may be inciting people who are already prejudiced against homosexuals to rape, kill and beat the people they dislike or fear."[21] After interviewing dozens of individuals who had physically attacked gay men, Herek concluded that AIDS has given homophobic people an excuse for violent acts, and that often the attacks were very sexual in nature, including castration, genital mutilation, and male rape. Interestingly, this article was authored by a UPI "Science Writer" and titled "Science Today: Violence Against Gays Linked to AIDS." Once again, the connections between HIV, gay men, and male rape are presented in a medical and scientific context. A more thorough analysis of male rape and medical science is discussed in the chapter on medical sensitivity.

Strangely, the rape of an HIV-positive person as an expression of power and hatred puts the HIV-negative rapist at risk for becoming that which is the object of his domination. In some cases of this form of sexual violence, a rapist may use other weapons besides his penis to forcibly penetrate his victim, creating a form of "safer rape" (in contrast to consensual "safer sex") where he is able to violate an HIV-positive person without putting himself at risk. There are several documented cases of women claiming (both truthfully and untruthfully) to be HIV positive in the face of an attempted sexual assault in an effort to deter her would-be rapist. Whether this will become a self-defense strategy to be commonly employed by men remains to be seen.

The disproportionate number of socially marginalized people infected with HIV in the United States has fashioned AIDS into a convenient tool for the blame of all social problems. AIDS has augmented and intensified the scapegoating of African Americans, Hispanics, men who have sex with men, and injection drug users, among others, holding them responsible for everything from an overburdened health care system to HIV-tainting of a blood supply that endangers "innocent" citizens. The New York City Gay and Lesbian Anti-Violence Project has documented numerous sexual assaults and other acts of physical violence against women, people of color, injection drug users, and gay men that were "HIV-biased," meaning the attacker chooses his victim based on perceived or known HIV-positive antibody status.[22] The identification of this trend further refutes the theory that fear of HIV acts as a safety mechanism, at least for gay men. As a population living in the midst of the ongoing epidemic, we sometimes search for a silver lining of AIDS, grasping for any beneficial by-products that bolster the slightest optimism. Although the equation of gay = AIDS may have afforded gay men and men perceived to be gay a degree of physical protection against bashings in some cases, in other instances it has clearly provoked and substantiated acts of violence.

In addition to the anxieties and fears surrounding HIV and AIDS, manifestations of hatred in the forms of misogyny (the hatred of women and femininity), and racism compound the motivation behind these attacks. The New York City Gay and Lesbian Anti-Violence Project, for example, has documented the verbal epithets used in conjunction with bashings. They reveal the frequent "double bias" in the mind of the attacker who uses such phrases as "AIDS faggot," "infected junkie," or "HIV bitch."[23] A 1991 study conducted by the National Gay and Lesbian Task Force Policy Institute found 12% of the antigay and antilesbian hate crimes reported nationwide were HIV or AIDS related.[24]

RAPE AS A RISK FACTOR FOR HIV INFECTION AND OTHER HEALTH PROBLEMS

We must also consider the possibility that rape and sexual assault may psychologically predispose men to HIV infection. The emotional consequences of being raped may put a survivor at risk for later HIV infection from other partners. Common post-rape conditions such as rape trauma syndrome, including posttraumatic stress disorder, low self-esteem, and increased alcohol and other drug use, can all be factors that increase an individual's risk for HIV infection. The effects of rape in lowering self-esteem and inciting depression are well documented, both of which may be risk factors for subsequent substance abuse, eating disorders, and unsafe sexual practices. One study conducted by researchers at the George Warren Brown School of Social Work of Washington

University in St. Louis found that a history of sexual abuse is strongly associated with HIV risk behaviors, and that sexual abuse is also related to a continuation or increase in those behaviors throughout adolescence and young adulthood.[25] If the rape of adult males is largely neglected and ignored by social and psychological research, a huge area is left unmapped that could expand our understandings of men's risk for HIV infection. The better our understanding of such risk, the more sophisticated and effective our risk-reduction strategies can become across time.

I do not wish to suggest, however, that rape is always a directly causative agent in increasing the likelihood a man will seroconvert as a result of voluntary engagement in unsafe sexual behavior after his assault. A number of social and cultural factors will help to shape the ways in which each survivor reacts and makes sense of his victimization. One interview I conducted with a gay male rape survivor exemplifies the individuality of reactions to rape. Steven, a 37-year-old gay white male living in the Midwest, identified a direct link between his rape experience at age 18 and his later survival amid the ongoing epidemic. Steven attributed his life and continued HIV-negative serostatus to being anally raped before 1980, the age of "pre-AIDS." Ever since the assault in his late teens, Steven has been psychologically unable to bear the act of anal penetration as a consensual sexual behavior with other men:

> I think if that [the rape] hadn't happened to me I'd be dead by now. Most all of my friends from that time who had the same kind of sex I did have gotten sick and passed away. It just so happens that the result of my attack left me unable to put myself at risk, which is partly a blessing and partly a nightmare. It's not the way I wanted to survive, but here I am.

Steven's psychological inability to physically be in the receptive role spared him from what he believes would have been a late 1970s and early 1980s participation in unprotected sex with the friends and lovers he has since watched die of AIDS-related complications. This is not to say that Steven's rape was necessarily a blessing. Ideally, men should feel free to choose from a full range of human sexual expression, unhampered by past trauma and

violent episodes. This particular instance yielded a lifesaving outcome, but at what cost in the limitation of the survivor's sexual
freedom and mental health? Such a limitation is a form of secondary sexual violence, for the "sexual" control in Steven's experience
extended beyond his rape, culminating in 20 years of restricted
behavior.

Another survivor I interviewed, T. J., also told me how his
rape experience changed his safer sex behavior. He said that he
sought out HIV testing:

> *because he didn't use a condom, and I had had unsafe sex in India. I*
> *was immediately afraid of being infected after I was raped. That was*
> *the first thing that went through my mind after my mind started*
> *working again. I thought, "This is something I need to be concerned*
> *about." That was good for me, to think in those terms because I*
> *didn't want to think that sex was over for me. Getting tested was the*
> *first thing I wanted to do, but then I found out I had to wait 3 to 6*
> *months. That was the first time I had ever got tested. That changed*
> *my sexual practices. Safe sex became a must for me after the rape.*
> *Everything opened up for me after that. I thought, "Damn, I need to*
> *survive this. I need to do everything in my power to try to get*
> *through this." So I went to get tested and that really helped. When I*
> *found out I was negative that really gave me a fresh look on things,*
> *like I had a second chance.*

HIV INFECTION AND PRISON RAPE

In addition to these male rapes that occur in noninstitutional
settings, prison rape can be difficult to manage as it relates to HIV
and AIDS. In most prisons, condoms are considered "contraband"
material; their possession and use are prohibited. With the
alarmingly high numbers of prison inmates being raped by inmates and correctional officers, often repeatedly by multiple attackers within a closed environment, HIV infection behind prison
walls has steadily risen in recent years. Prison officials have been
reluctant to distribute condoms for two reasons: They frequently
deny that rape happens at all in their institutions, and they fear
that condom distribution will be perceived by the public as con-
doning consensual homosexuality in prison. Even if condoms

were regularly distributed, male rapists may not use them, but any attempt should be made to ensure the safety and health of these men while they serve out their prison sentences. The brochure "AIDS Advice for the Prison Rape Survivor" published by the organization Stop Prisoner Rape even recommends making homemade condoms using rubber gloves or cellophane paper with rubber bands. The organization clearly states that, given the incredibly high prevalence of rape in prisons, they consider "a government ban on condoms in confinement to be a form of government-sponsored murder." As of 1996, only six prison institutions in the United States make condoms available to prisoners.

Stephen Donaldson, the former president of Stop Prisoner Rape, wrote in a 1995 *USA Today* editorial about how the fear of HIV infection has even changed how rapists select their victims behind bars:

> The widespread popular association of AIDS with homosexuals has put a greater premium on heterosexual anal virgins as preferred sex objects for horny convicts, and these can only be obtained through rape. More and more of those infected with HIV in this way will get sick with AIDS and add to the public expense as well as the private burden; once released, they will also spread the virus still further.[26]

Donaldson himself was raped countless times while incarcerated and eventually died in 1996 of AIDS-related complications. He believed he had been infected as a result of prison rape.

Stop Prisoner Rape publishes guidelines for prisoners to reduce their risk of HIV infection by making difficult choices under harsh circumstances. One of the recommendations is that prisoners who are "punks," and likely to be repeatedly raped during their stay behind bars, should pair off with one rapist (a "jocker") so as to limit the number of different sexual contacts. The punk/jocker relationship is typically respected in prison culture, and once other inmates are aware that a punk is the property of a particular jocker, they will consider him off-limits as a target for rape. The organization also suggests that victims should attempt to persuade a would-be rapist to accept oral sex in place of anal penetration, as this will reduce the risk of HIV transmission. In addition, prisoners who are raped should try to ensure that lubricant is used in an effort to limit rectal bleeding, which can be an opportunity for HIV to enter the bloodstream. Although these strategies may seem outlandish, they are a cruel necessity in environments where rape is the norm.

The very first documented case with medical evidence of a prison rape victim becoming infected with HIV while incarcerated came relatively late given the early 1980s beginning of the epidemic. While incarcerated at Illinois's Menard Correctional Center, Michael Blucker was gang-raped within days of his arrival at the institution. He had been sentenced to 10 years for burglary and auto theft. In June 1993, 6 months after he was imprisoned, Blucker was tested for HIV after he informed a nurse he had been raped. The results of the test came back negative. The gang raping of Blucker continued and in March 1994 he was tested for HIV again. This time he was informed he had tested HIV positive. Armed with documentation that proved he was infected during his prison stay, Blucker filed a lawsuit in federal court against the Illinois Department of Corrections to seek restitution for personal damages and reform in prison policy related to rape prevention. That lawsuit is still pending at the time of this writing. The prevalence of rape in correctional institutions makes forthcoming cases of this type a practical inevitability. Having examined the interrelationship between HIV and male rape, the next chapter expands this inquiry by considering how male rape is treated and viewed within the field of medicine.

MEDICAL SENSITIVITY

*I*n 1995 the American Medical Association released the report *Strategies for the Treatment and Prevention of Sexual Assault*, which included a section on rape of males under the heading "special populations." The document stated, in accordance with numerous other studies and professional opinions, that male rape survivors frequently do not seek medical attention after they are assaulted. Those who seek treatment often do so out of necessity, usually presenting at hospital emergency rooms with physical injuries. Few men seem to want medical care from a family practitioner or community clinic, and the prevalence of emergency room visitation serves somewhat as a barometer of reluctance to report male rape. The intense stigma of same-sex rape is enough to prevent most male survivors from obtaining the services they need unless physical injuries severely compromise the survivor's life or ability to hide the assault from others. Andrew, a survivor I interviewed, recounted the events immediately after his rape:

I knew I was hurt. The pain was pretty bad. I remember when I sat down in the car and locked the door, I felt the sensation in my pants of how wet I was. I remember thinking it was semen coming out. When I sat down I felt like I had to go to the bathroom, that I could not hold it. My pants weren't all the way up. I put my hand back there and when I pulled my hand back there was blood all over my hand. I knew I was hurt, that I had to do something. I started driving. I had no idea where I was, where I was going. I just drove. I really didn't know what to do. I was hurting and I remember thinking I've either got to kill myself or I've got to go to the emergency room. I didn't want to live through that. I didn't want to have to go to the hospital and know that they would have to look and they would know what happened to me. At that point I think I would have rather died. At that point I think I really wish they would have just killed me.

For Andrew, the decision to reveal his rape, even for emergency medical treatment, was perhaps worse than suicide. The role of such incredible shame cannot be underscored enough because some survivors may choose death over the pain and humiliation of stigma. However, timely medical care for male rape survivors can be crucial for a number of reasons, ranging from the prevention of sexually transmitted diseases to the forensic collection of physical evidence that could later be used for criminal investigation and prosecution.

Aside from the shame associated with revealing sexual victimization to strangers, male rape survivors may not consider medical help either because of a state of shock or because they may not immediately discern the potential benefits from such assistance. Only two of the survivors I interviewed sought medical attention. Jonathan, who did not, had a brief interaction with the police. (This account is detailed in Chapter Eleven.) After the police officers dismissed his report of rape, Jonathan felt so invalidated that he did not want to open himself up to anyone else in a way that would make him vulnerable to more of the same cruelty. He also did not, at the time, consider the necessity of a physical examination:

I think if they had told me why it would have been important to do it [go to the hospital], I would have. If they had said, "This may have been more serious than you think. We should go and make sure that you don't have any concussion or retinal damage or something," then I would have gone.

Sadly, some male rape survivors are either passively or actively discouraged from getting medical treatment during their first few interactions with people after the rape. If they are told the rape was "no big deal" or that they "must have really wanted it," they will not view their bodies as being in need of emergency care. Men, especially, are expected to endure physical pain and not rely on others. This masculine ideal feeds a form of conscious self-neglect.

MEDICAL TREATMENT

In 1996 I became a patient advocate with the Ohio State University Hospitals' Domestic Violence and Sexual Assault Advocacy Program, working primarily with adult male rape survivors in the hospital emergency department. As an advocate, my job is to represent the interests of the survivor and assist with the continuity of care throughout the treatment and collection of evidence, which can be an extremely difficult and emotionally trying process. Andrew described his hospital visit in detail, relating how the experience was at times cold and impersonal:

I got to the hospital. I went in. By the time I got out of the car I got my pants up. Other than being somewhat dirty, outwardly I didn't look like anything was too wrong. I walked in and saw the lady at the desk. I just lost it and started crying again. She said, "Are you okay?" I said no. She went and got a doctor. The doctor got me in a wheelchair and took me back to a room. He asked me what had happened. I told him very briefly, and he left the room. Some time later a nurse came in and made small talk, didn't say a whole lot. She asked me to take my clothes off, that the doctor needed to examine me. He came back in and did. He said there was quite a bit of tearing but that he didn't feel there needed to be stitches. It was mostly internal I guess. He said it would heal in time. He cleaned me up to some extent and put some antibiotic cream on me. He gave me several shots for different STDs. He talked to me a little bit about HIV and said that I should get tested before much longer and again

> *in 6 months. After I got dressed again, he gave me some instructions*
> *on eating soft foods. He gave me medication to take, some stool*
> *softeners. Then I went to talk with a social worker—a young man.*
> *He seemed supportive, but didn't know what to say.*

Rape advocacy programs can help to humanize the hospital environment, easing the trauma of medical procedures and providing support that may otherwise be unavailable in a typically understaffed and time-strapped emergency department.

The following outline of this treatment and evidence collection in a hospital setting is both idealized and abbreviated, a summary of events and procedures that are common in emergency room rape examinations. In many respects, this treatment is formulaic, following a commonsense flowchart of observation and action. Occasionally male rape survivors will arrive in emergency rooms presenting with nongenital, physical injuries and, because of shame and embarrassment, do not mention they have been sexually assaulted. It may not be until the medical examination has begun that the patient indicates he has been raped or that medical personnel suspect the patient has been sexually assaulted. Therefore, treatment for rape and collection of evidence could conceivably begin at any point during the hospital visit, not just at the time of arrival.

Consent

First and foremost, consent must be obtained from the rape survivor before the course of treatment begins. This is the standard procedure for any patient arriving at an emergency room, but can be especially empowering to a rape survivor who feels as if he has lost all power and control over his life. Being presented with basic options and the opportunity to make decisions will be the beginning of the transition from victim status to survivorhood. Some rape survivors may decline all or certain parts of medical examination and treatment. Despite what others may feel is best or most appropriate, these decisions should be respected if they are made within a context of informed choice. At times a rape survivor may be so deeply entrenched in crisis, ranging from hysterical to nonresponsive, that he may be psychologically unable to understand his options, let alone make decisions about his treatment.

Treatment of Acute Physical Injuries

Depending on the severity of physical trauma inflicted on the rape survivor, attention to immediately pressing physical injuries may take precedence. Conditions such as heavy bleeding (internally or externally), bone fractures, or concussions will receive priority. Once the patient is stabilized, further information will be gathered and less emergent treatment will resume. At some point the physician may also use a device called a proctoscope, which is inserted into the anus to examine the rectum for internal trauma.

Medical History

A physician and nurse will take a complete medical history from the survivor, including any current medications, allergies, disabilities, or recent illness. Medical staff should also ask the survivor if he has a past history of sexual abuse or domestic violence. Sexual history is of key importance, especially in determining the risk of sexually transmitted disease as well as creating a context for evidence collection. Any samples or materials collected during the examination could be from either the assailant or a recent consensual experience. Unless explained, asking questions such as the most recent sexual experience may confuse the survivor or create the impression he somehow is to blame for the rape. Questions regarding sexual orientation may also be a sensitive issue here. Heterosexual men who are questioned about their sexual orientation may feel as if their sexuality or manhood has been compromised or that medical staff are implying he has become gay as a result of same-sex rape. Gay male survivors may be reluctant to "come out" to medical staff, fearing homophobic treatment or the documentation of their sexual orientation in medical records.

Assault Statement

Details of the assault will be crucial in determining the administration of targeted treatment. For instance, knowledge of the exact kind of sexual contact will inform the determination of risk for possible sexually transmitted diseases. The detection of puncture wounds such as bite marks or knife stabbings might require a tetanus shot. The events leading up to, during, and after the assault are usually recorded in the patient's medical chart, including a characterization of the survivor's emotional state. Careful notation of these details can be crucial if the medical chart is subpoenaed by a court of law. Questions that begin with "why," "where," "what," and "how" can come across to the survivor as judgmental, such as asking, "What were you doing in his apartment?" or "Why didn't you struggle?" Careful wording and explanations to the survivor as to why these questions are important can help to alleviate a sense of blame.

Testing

Blood samples will be drawn from the rape survivor, to identify the patient's blood type and test for the bacterium that causes syphilis. Cultures are also commonly taken from three areas of the body: the throat, rectum, and urethra of the penis. Swabs for this purpose are inserted into each area, gently sweeping the mucous membrane, then preserved for later testing of possible gonorrhea, chlamydia, or other bacteria. This part of the examination may be especially traumatic for the survivor, a kind of secondary rape. Just as he has recently been violated by someone in a way that has stripped him of personal power, he is again faced by someone in a position of greater power and authority (this time medical), who will poke, prod, and penetrate his body in ways that are highly personal.

Antibiotic Prophylaxis

A high dosage of antibiotics, either oral or via injection, is usually administered to the survivor. In the event that his perpetrator was infected with a sexually transmitted disease, the prophylaxis will help to ensure that the exposure to disease does not result in infection. In addition to the immediate dose given in the emergency department, survivors may be prescribed more medication for further short-term treatment. Untreated sexually transmitted diseases can eventually cause permanent bodily damage such as sterility or neurological complications.

Discharge Instructions

The whirlwind experience of treatment, evidence collection, police questioning, instructions for home care, and social work referrals during a time of mental crisis will undoubtedly be more than any survivor could fully comprehend and commit to memory. Written instructions that include pertinent names, telephone numbers, medication instructions, and referrals are essential.

Payment and Billing Issues

Some states have allotted crime victim compensation funds available to reimburse victims of violent crime for medical and mental health expenses incurred as a result of their assault. Sometimes these funds are only accessible if an official report is made to the police within a designated time after the crime has occurred, usually 72 hours. Some states may only pay for the cost of the rape kit and evidence collection.

Many survivors, especially men, will want control over who they do and do not share their assault experience with among their family, friends, and colleagues. The billing of medical services through the mail or by provision of information to insurance companies might be a challenge for medical organizations attempting to ensure the utmost confidentiality for the survivors they have treated. Because of the intense shame associated with male rape, many men do not inform their spouses, parents, or employers. The reception of an emergency room bill in the mail at one's home or office address may instigate difficult questions posed by others.

FORENSIC COLLECTION OF EVIDENCE

The collection of evidence for possible later use in investigation and prosecution of the rape might not seem to be of much importance soon after a rape has occurred, but should still be completed. Some states have adopted protocols for the minimum standards of rape evidence collection, usually developed in conjunction with prosecutors, forensic scientists and crime labs, police departments, and emergency medicine specialists. Standardized "rape kits" are also available, complete with evidence bags, instructions for collection, and so forth. The survivor always has the right to refuse any or all of the rape evidence collection procedures.

Swabbings will likely be taken from the penis, urethra, mouth, anus, and other areas where a fluid or dried fluid may be found. Sometimes an ultraviolet light, called a Wood's lamp, will be used to detect the presence of any semen on the skin. These fluids may later be useful for DNA analysis to link the suspect to the crime. Defecation, urination, showering, and brushing teeth may all be natural responses for a victim after an assault, but this will likely destroy evidence that has remained with his body.

Hair combings from both the head and pubic area are taken in case there are any fibers or other materials that may be important for the investigation. In addition, pubic and head hairs will also be plucked from the survivor to serve as "standards." These standards can be used to distinguish between the hairs of the attacker and the survivor, or they may link the survivor to the scene of the rape (or sometimes the suspect if he has been apprehended and has the survivors' hair on his body). Saliva and blood are collected from the survivor for similar purposes. Fingernails are often clipped and scraped to obtain substances, such as the attacker's skin or blood, that may have been deposited there during a struggle.

One of the most important pieces of evidence can be the clothing the survivor was wearing at the time he was assaulted. There may be stains, fibers, soil, hair, or other elements on the clothing that could later prove to be very valuable. Even a tear in the clothing can represent evidence of resistance or struggle in cases where the attacker claims the experience was consensual. Many rape survivors will want to immediately change clothes after the rape, laundering them or throwing them away to dispose of the memories they may trigger. If possible, they should be saved in a paper bag.

If there are any physical markings on the survivor's body, the physician or nurse will want to take photographs of those injuries. These marks could be bite marks, bruises, lacerations, swelling, or any other visible abnormality from the assault. Typically, two photographs are taken of each area of the body. One set of these photographs is given to the survivor, and the other set is filed in the patient's confidential medical chart. If subpoenaed into a court of law, the photographs will be useful evidence. Written documentation of bodily markings should accompany the photographs in the patient's chart. Photography of the body may be a very humiliating experience for some survivors, especially those who are concerned their rape will become public knowledge.

The physician's responsibility in the process of evidence collection is threefold: to determine and document if penetration of the mouth or anus occurred, document signs of trauma, and maintain a chain of evidence. The physician's duty is not to determine if a criminal act has occurred or if a specific act was consensual, for this is considered to be the responsibility and domain of the court.

Some physicians may be reluctant to work with male rape survivors because of the possibility they could be subpoenaed to testify in court should investigation of the rape lead to an attempted prosecution. Careful documentation of observations in the patient's chart may later avert the need for the physician to be subpoenaed for testimony.

One of the final steps in the collection of evidence will be a police report. In the United States, if a person is treated for rape in an emergency room, the police are automatically called. The survivor, of course, can refuse to speak to the police, but the officers will still attempt to make a formal report and investigate the crime that has occurred. In most states, medical personnel are required to notify the police who have jurisdiction in the location where the rape occurred. Police do not have access to the survivor's medical chart without his consent or any other information that is bound by laws of confidentiality. The documentation may later be subpoenaed by a court of law, however. An interview with a police officer may put additional emotional strain on the survivor. He will be forced to recount the rape yet another time for another person, and may feel as if the questions being asked are couched in an attitude of blame or disbelief. They very well may be if the police officer is insensitive or ill-informed. Even the classic criminology handbook, *Practical Aspects of Rape Investigation*, includes no pertinent information that applies specifically to male rape survivors. The index includes only one page of material that mentions male survivors, and the book's preface ends with a special "Editorial Note" that makes brief mention of this omission by stating:

> While it is recognized that males are also victims of rape, the gender descriptor "she" is primarily used in this text. The male pronouns are also used at times when the female gender would be equally applicable [presumably in the context of referring to the perpetrator]. This is done in the interest of sentence structure and readability.[1]

Strangely, this manual was coedited by Ann Wolbert Burgess, the same professor of psychiatric mental health nursing who coauthored several research articles on adult male rape in which she calls for greater sensitivity and increased services for male survivors. Just as the "generic he" is inappropriate for referring to hypothetical individuals whose gender could be male or female, the "generic she" can be equally damaging in its erasure and invalidation of male rape survivors.

PRISON RAPE SURVIVORS

Sadly, the majority of rapes committed in prison are not reported or documented, and most men who are raped behind bars receive no medical attention even if they request it. Depending on the medical facilities available at a prison and the extent of physical injury, male survivors may be treated "in-house," or transported to a nearby community hospital emergency room. Usually these hospitals have standing contractual agreements with the prison institutions they serve in the event of necessary emergency room visits. Prisoner rape survivors are usually not provided with the same quality of care as nonincarcerated survivors for purposes of security and protecting the safety of medical personnel. Volunteers such as rape advocates are typically not provided to prison survivors because of the chance the prisoner may become violent. Greater care is used with the handling of necessary medical instruments such as syringes or glass while other items (such as inkpens or name badges) remain outside the examination room altogether as they could be used by the prisoner to inflict harm on himself or others. Sometimes a prison survivor's hands and feet are shackled, contributing to the survivor's sense of powerlessness and inability to make choices about what is happening to his body.

Social work assistance may also be of little help, as most prisoners are unable to access the majority of outside community resources, including counseling. Even if the local rape crisis hotline serves male survivors, many social workers will not offer this telephone number to prisoners because of a high rate of abuse. Sometimes prisoners will make harassing calls to the hotline prompted by the appeal of a largely female staff and 24-hour availability. Other prisoners may abuse the line with repeated calls, developing an emotional dependence on the hotline staffers beyond basic crisis intervention counseling. Although prisoners' needs may be legitimate, most crisis lines are neither prepared nor suitable for calls from incarcerated survivors.

MEDICAL LITERATURE: A CASE STUDY

Apart from the actual practice of medicine as treatment of patients, the area of medical research and publication is of great importance in its dissemination of information to the health professions. In 1979, the first article specifically devoted to the topic of male rape in a major medical journal appeared, titled "The Male Rape Victim: Evaluation and Treatment" in the *Journal of American College Emergency Physicians*. Authored by Dr. Josephson, a physician at the Memorial Hospital in Worcester, Massachusetts, the three-page article briefly discussed the sexual assault of both boys and men, particularly the lack of available information:

> The medical literature offers little guidance in the evaluation of male victims of sexual assault. The statutes are a confusing patchwork of conflicting and sexually biased laws. . . . The evaluation and treatment of the sexually abused male is similar to his female counterpart. Physicians and emergency department staff must be knowledgeable regarding their responsibilities to these patients and concerned with the medical, legal, and psychological ramifications of sexual assault.[2]

He presented the case study of a 27-year-old man who was raped in prison and concluded with a call for physicians' sensitivity to these patients.

The second major medical article dedicated to adult male rape survivors was published in 1980 in the *Southern Medical Journal*. "Examination and Treatment of the Male Rape Victim" was written by Dr. Arthur Schiff, a physician at Mercy Hospital in Miami, Florida, who had previously worked at the Dade County Rape Treatment Center. In his explanation for writing a "how-to" article on examination and treatment of adult male survivors of sexual violence, Dr. Schiff wrote, "Gynecologists and others who staff rape treatment centers . . . have been reluctant to examine and treat male victims, believing their duties to be limited to women. Consequently, many rape treatment center workers not only resisted the notion of examining men, but were not qualified for the task."[3] Dr. Schiff continued by posing a question that still has not been resolved in the medical treatment of male survivors: "Who, then, is most qualified to examine and treat the male victim: the urologist, the generalist, or the proctologist?"[4] The lack of a logical referral for male rape survivors requiring medical attention, in contrast to female survivors' standard direction to gynecologists, is indicative of the status of health care systems in most Western nations. For the most part, only women are viewed as possessing gender-specific health care needs, and a comparable men's health movement remains sorely lacking. Male survivors often fall through the cracks of health care delivery as an anomaly in this respect when rape is medically viewed as solely an issue of female biology.

Although Dr. Schiff's opening statements in this early text are progressively informative, the article is not devoid of insensitivity and harsh moralism. Before outlining techniques for treatment, Schiff encourages the examining physician to maintain a high level of suspicion toward the male survivor, noting that in many cases the "victim" is not really a victim at all, but an individual with ulterior motives who has fabricated his assault in a bid for attention. Schiff claims that if no anal or rectal injuries are seen in the male rape survivor on examination:

> the anus probably has not been penetrated unless the victim is a passive homosexual. To determine this issue, one may use several different techniques. In some instances, the very manner in which the victim positions himself for examination without being told is referential.[5]

This statement carries several alarming presumptions: that "passive homosexuals" are either unrapeable or do not sustain rectal trauma because of their sexual history, that a lack of evidence of physical trauma implies the act was consensual, and that a physician may be able to surmise the patient's sexual orientation by observing the comfort level or familiarity with which the patient positions himself for a rectal examination.

Dr. Schiff suggests the victim's sexual identity and sexual history hold legal relevance and therefore the examining physician's testimony must be prepared to account for documentation of consensual homosexual activity.

> *Although much of the forgoing may appear superfluous, in the rare instance that the case may go to trial, an attorney is sure to ask, "Now Doctor, can you state in all medical probability whether the victim is homosexual?" Even if the judge, on the objection of the opposing attorney, strikes the question from the testimony, the jury will have heard it.*[6]

Such a rationale presumes that doctors possess the uncanny ability to read bodies in such a way that they can determine an individual's sexual identity, regardless of that patient's own statement or declaration. The article has an overall condescending tone toward gay men and a blame-the-victim approach to working with male rape survivors.

Examples such as this serve as a reminder for the reasons that some cultural populations continue to harbor a distrust of traditional medicine. Much of this is grounded in a history of medical science used as a tool for social control of the marginalized and oppressed. Gay men and men of color, therefore, may be less willing than other men to seek medical assistance if they suspect the "treatment" they receive will do them more harm than good. At least until the 1970s, medical scientists attempted to "cure" gay men and transform them into heterosexuals with shock therapy, psychiatric drugs, surgical procedures, and more. AIDS has also cast light on homophobia in the medical community as gay men have been forced into close, prolonged contact with health professionals. Similarly, African-American men have been the object of unethical experimentation and medical neglect throughout history. The most well-known instance of this was the Tuskegee study, in which African-American men were cruelly denied treatment for syphilis and studied until they died of this curable disease. This experiment continued into the 1970s. Although the field of medicine has predominantly been used as a tool for healing, it has also unfortunately been wielded as an instrument to justify and enact homophobia, racism, and sexism.

MEDICAL PROGRESS

Fortunately, the above case study of Dr. Schiff's work does not exemplify a majority opinion on male rape within the scientific literature and medical practice. A great deal of progress has been made since the publication of that article in 1980, such as the work of the late Deryck Calderwood, former director of New York University's Human Sexuality Program. Dr. Calderwood made connections between unresolved psychological trauma and the manifestation of physiological health problems such as chronic and degenerative respiratory, cardiovascular, and gastrointestinal diseases. His conclusion emphasized the physician's role in the survivor's overall recovery and quality of life:

> *Physicians play an important role in the recognition and manage-ment of male rape. Their awareness that sexual victimization may be a basic or contributing cause of sexual dysfunction and other seemingly unrelated physical conditions allows prompt interven-tion and treatment. With such help more raped men will be able to cope effectively with devastating postrape trauma, and therefore regain physical and mental health, instead of having to live with unresolved problems for the rest of their lives.*[7]

In 1995 the American Medical Association released the report *Strategies for the Treatment and Prevention of Sexual Assault*, which included a section on rape of males under the heading of special populations, stating:

> *Sexual assault against homosexual males and men in prison popu-lations may be significantly underestimated and under-reported. In the gay male community, the stigma of reporting and legitimate concerns about discriminatory treatment may contribute to under-reporting. . . . Male victims frequently do not seek treatment or report the assault for fear of being labeled homosexual erroneously.*[8]

Only recently has the medical community begun to recognize male rape and direct serious attention to the treatment it deserves. As the stigma and shame surrounding male rape continues to slowly decrease, male rape survivors will presumably seek more and more medical treatment. Hopefully they will receive care from individuals with prior experience and knowledge in this area.

QUALITY AND SENSITIVITY

The assurance of quality and sensitive medical attention can be accomplished relatively easily, with only minor adjustments to existing sexual assault response protocols. One of these changes is the option for a male survivor to choose a male or female service provider. When female sexual assault survivors seek medical or any other form of care, they are usually paired with a female provider. Most women who have been raped do not wish to be dependent or in a position of lesser power with someone like the person who just violated them. Although this may be the commonsense norm with women, male rape survivors cannot be treated in a parallel manner. That is to say, some male survivors may prefer female providers and others may very much want a male provider.

A male rape survivor might feel shamed in the presence of a woman just after his rape, as if his masculinity has become suspect and embarrassing. He could also feel the need to remain stoic and unemotional for this same reason, not wanting to appear weak or vulnerable to the psychological or physical pain he may be experiencing at the time. Some male patients, not just rape survivors, simply prefer male doctors, especially for a physical examination that requires undressing or a proctological examination. Conversely, a man may feel similar to a female survivor in that he may not want a male health professional to be in a position of power and control over his body. Ideally, the survivor would be presented with a choice of providers. This not only helps to assure a high degree of comfort, but also allows the survivor to begin to make his own decisions about the course of his healing and survival, which is the first step toward putting the pieces of one's life back together. In addition to this choice, medical practitioners should be well trained in issues of sexual health, sexual assault, and domestic violence. Taking a thorough sexual history of all patients during routine and emergency examinations is of great importance, as this may reveal a recent sexual assault or provide a structured opportunity for the patient to raise any concerns or questions he might have about his or his partner's sexual well-being.

As another gendered concern for male survivors who visit an emergency department, some or all of the survivor's clothing may be kept by the emergency room as possible evidence of the assault. Many emergency rooms provide rape survivors with packages that include soap for showering, a toothbrush and toothpaste, and sweatsuits to wear home in the event that a friend or family member does not arrive with a change of clothing. Unfortunately, however, these sweatsuits are often available only in smaller women's sizes, or are clearly feminine in design (e.g., pastels, floral prints). This clothing is often donated by local businesses or purchased by community groups for this purpose. These organizations may not recognize the need for clothing to be made available to men as well, and the emergency department may not have the resources to purchase these additional amenities. The necessity of wearing this feminine clothing home may further demoralize a male survivor who feels as if his masculinity has already been stripped from him during the rape. It also invalidates the survivor, making him feel as if he is the only man to undergo such victimization.

RAPE IN MEDICAL SETTINGS

Although it is rare, the medical setting is sometimes the site in which a rape is committed rather than treated. As an act of power and control, health care professionals are in contact with individuals who are weak, unable to defend themselves, and vulnerable to sexual violence. From home health care to a family practice office to a surgical recovery room, rape can and does occur in these environments. These accounts regularly appear in the media, such as a situation in 1992 when a 34-year-old man was arrested for raping an elderly cancer patient. A spokesperson for the Suffolk County police told *Newsday*, "A 65-year-old man who was recovering from surgery in the hospital . . . was awakened by a man who said that he would pray for him. The man then sodomized the victim. He was arrested as he was attempting to leave."[9] A health care worker at the hospital said there was less security throughout the building as a result of a recently adopted "open house policy" during visiting hours. The policy eliminated the need for visitor passes in an effort to create a more welcoming and less institutional environment.

Most clinics and hospitals have faced complaints from male patients who claim their physicians have inappropriately touched, fondled, molested, or raped them. To avoid any misunderstandings about examinations and other medical procedures, all physicians should carefully inform their patients what they are about to do, why they are doing it, and what the patient can expect to feel, all before the act occurs. In addition, many physicians prefer to have a nurse or other witness who is of the same sex as the patient in the room during any procedure that involves genital contact or rectal penetration. Some institutions have implemented policies that demand the presence of this third party or make it an option available to all patients. Although this has become standard practice for many male gynecologists seeking to avoid malpractice and criminal law suits, it should also be considered for same-sex examinations.

THE HEALING PROCESS

A rape survivor's first few days and first few personal interactions after the assault will set the stage for the course of his recovery. His ability to heal, both physically and emotionally, can be severely enabled or impeded depending on others' level of sensitivity and the availability of vital resources. Male rape is frequently not reported to police, and medical professionals may very well be the first to come into contact with survivors who need treatment and cannot hide the physical, bodily evidence of their rape. Sensitivity and access to quality medical care after a sexual assault remain a crucial concern for all survivors of sexual violence.

TEN

SURVIVAL

by Christopher B. Smith

The following account, written by Christopher Smith, details a story of survival in spite of the intense stigma imposed by a society that fails to recognize and understand the rape of men. His experiences, sadly, are only unusual in that he has overcome the shame that suffocates most male rape survivors. His ability to speak openly about what has happened to him is both brave and extraordinary.

It was October 27, 1994. I was 24 years old and madly in love with the woman of my dreams, my wife Susie. Being highly ambitious people, Susie and I were known for having big dreams. Susie was busy working on her degree in nursing, while I was working as an engineer and going to school part time for an MBA. We dreamed of what our life would be like and had put into motion the necessary plans to make those dreams our reality. We looked forward with joyful anticipation to our children, our careers, and our home. Basically, we looked forward to life. Life was not always perfect, but when is it ever?

I was raised in a small town, so I was sheltered from many things as a child. I had always been a little frightened of new and unfamiliar things. Even though it wasn't natural to me at first, I had managed to become an outgoing person. Susie brought that out in me. She taught me to enjoy life more fully. I discovered that I liked to be involved in new activities and with new people. I enjoyed learning about their hopes and dreams, about where they were going, where they had been, and what made them tick. It was all very fascinating to me. Slowly, I overcame my shyness and now I feel comfortable approaching almost anyone and engaging them in conversation. It is that same friendliness, openness, and innocence that begins my story.

I will never forget how beautiful a day it was. It was more than beautiful, it was ideal. The perfect autumn day. Bright sunshine filled the sky, yet a gentle breeze kept the air warm and comfortable. I had worked all day, dying to be outside to enjoy the sunshine and colors of autumn. After I left work, I changed into my favorite pair of shorts and headed off to a local forest preserve to do some studying and enjoy the sights of the world around me before I went to school that night.

Once I reached the forest preserve, I drove around looking for a spot away from any other groups of people who were there. Although I like to be around people, I still prefer solitude when studying outdoors, so I wanted to avoid all potential distractions. I noticed a small circular drive off the main road. There was a shelter, a wide open field, and numerous picnic tables spread over the area. Best of all, there wasn't a car or person in sight. I had found my spot. I parked and made my way to a nearby table and began to read.

After some time had passed, I noticed a man walking in my direction from the parking area. When I looked up, I noticed that a truck had been parked next to my car. I assumed that he had just pulled up. Nothing unusual stood out about this man. He looked like any other person who may have driven his truck to the forest preserve to enjoy the nice day. As he approached, I smiled and said hello. He returned the greeting and paused by the table. He was dressed casually, wearing a light brown jacket. He wore glasses and had well-groomed shoulder-length hair. Although I didn't talk to him very long, he seemed to be friendly. He was the type of person I would expect to meet either at work or in one of my business classes. There was absolutely nothing about his appearance or demeanor to suggest any other conclusion. He was just like me.

After a while, something didn't seem quite right. I can't really explain it except to say that I was slightly uncomfortable. Something in his appearance had caught my eye. Then, just as suddenly as I had become uncomfortable, I became horrified. I saw what was troubling me. This ordinary man standing before me had a gun handle sticking out of the side of his jeans! I tried to hide my reaction, because the thought of being this close to a stranger with a gun truly terrified me. I felt an overwhelming urge to leave.

The man's demeanor swiftly changed and I believe he knew that I had seen his gun. Suddenly, he wasn't so easygoing, he was very orderly and matter of fact. He asked me to walk over to his truck and in my nightmarish trance, I obeyed. Millions of thoughts raced through my head. I quickly began to inventory the contents of my wallet and my pockets, convinced that I was being robbed. How inconvenient! I knew that if I just did what he wanted, my life would not be in any danger.

We reached the back corner of his truck. I looked at the truck itself and noticed that a cab attachment had been placed over the bed of the truck. He motioned me toward the rear of the vehicle and suggested that I get inside. My mind raced even more furiously. I reasoned that he apparently was going to drive me around for a while, rob me, and then just push me out of his truck somewhere along the road. But I knew that if I did just what he wanted, my life would not be in danger.

He opened the window to the back of the truck and I began to climb in. As I climbed in, the true motive of his plan began to unfold before my eyes. Straight ahead of me was a mattress. It had been turned sideways so that it would fit inside the truck bed. There was a pillow lying to the side on the mattress. In the back corner of the truck bed was a blue duffel bag. The sight of these objects had just begun to register in my brain when I felt his hands on my back push me into the truck. Before I could support myself on my knees, he placed his left arm firmly on my back. His right arm reached around my waist and began to mess with the button on my shorts and then began to work the shorts down to my knees. Reality slowly overcame the shock and I realized what was about to happen to me.

During those next minutes, my thoughts were scattered and often blurred. I remember his comments about me and how I looked to him. He told me over and over how much he was going to enjoy me. I would try to move, yet he would only allow me to roll, always pushing down on me. I know that at some point during this time, he had managed to remove all of my clothes and pull my shirt over my head. He had also managed to get his jeans down to his knees. He rolled me over onto my back, pinned my shoulders down with his knees, grabbed my head by the ears and forced me to participate in oral sex. All the while he commented on how good it was. Each word made me more and more sick. I wanted to puke all over him. How dare he say those things to me! My mind was so flooded with fear, I didn't know what to do.

After a while he informed me that he was going to make me feel really good. He rolled me back over onto my knees and pushed my face down into the mattress. The pit in my stomach grew as I realized what he was about to do, but I couldn't really believe that it was going to happen. What made me feel even worse was that as much as I did not want him to perform this evil act, there was absolutely nothing I could do to prevent it. I couldn't move from him in any direction. I was completely disoriented. Everything around me seemed to be moving in super slow motion. I felt like I was watching some horrible movie about my life and not really experiencing any of this terror. I then did the only thing that I had the power to do—I prayed. I prayed that if this was going to happen, then, please God, do not let me be hurt and do not let me catch any type of disease from this man.

As I completed my prayer, I felt the cold, wet lubricant being applied. I tried again to move, but it was impossible. The screams and tears were building up inside of me. The instant I was able to collect my thoughts, I felt him force himself inside my body. The physical pain combined with complete humiliation was over-whelming. It is an experience that defies description. I have never wanted to scream so badly in all of my life. But my screams were choked by fear and the disgust I felt each time I heard him emit his words and sounds of pleasure. I managed to pull a few words together: "Please stop. That hurts." This seemed to excite him further. This disgusting excuse for a human being had the nerve to enjoy himself while he tortured me! I tried to pray some more to escape from what was happening but my thoughts were continu-ally interrupted by pain and disgust. I remember biting down into the mattress to stifle any sound that I may make. I didn't want him to have the joy of knowing how much I was hurting.

There were other horrible things that took place in the back of the truck that day, but I still cannot bring myself to write them down. Finally, after what seemed like hours, the sounds, the words, and the pain all ended. I couldn't move my body, so I turned my head to see what he was doing. He had moved back to the corner of the truck. He was removing the condom he had just used. For a very brief moment, I felt a sense of relief. He then looked at me with a bizarre smile on his face. He didn't say anything, but he looked as if I should be clutching his heels and thanking him for this huge favor he had just done for me. I didn't say a word to him. I wanted only to leave and bury my shame. I put on my clothes, crawled out of the truck, jumped into my car, and drove away.

Humiliation doesn't even begin to describe how I felt. Neither does cheap, degraded, used, abused, or violated. Although all of those words are pieces to the overall puzzle, no word or set of words could ever capture the emotional state that I was in. I was surrounded by the enemy, being bombarded from all sides. There did not seem to exist a place where I was safe. My soul was engulfed with turmoil and pain.

After I left the forest preserve that day, there was no thought more paramount in my mind than to get as far away as possible. I drove around in my car, not really knowing where to go or what to do. I remember stopping at a traffic light and catching a glimpse of my face in the rear view mirror and noticing that I looked ragged.

My eyes were red, puffy, and sore and I realized that I must have been crying quite hard.

The scene unfolded over and over again. It was like watching some bizarre movie of my life, but it only contained back-to-back footage of this event. The tears were now rolling down my cheeks and filling my eyes so that I could barely see the road signs and traffic around me. I could not even begin to comprehend what hideous events had just taken place. I was in complete shock that I could allow something like this to happen to me. To me, of all people.

I stopped at another traffic light and tried to look at myself in the mirror again, but I looked away. I was too ashamed to even face myself. After all, I was now a miserable rotten person because this had happened. As I looked out of my window and onto the field next to the road, my thoughts turned toward Susie. I was worried how this might hurt her if she knew, then realizing that I would need to somehow tell her. But, if I could just get home and be with her, I would be safe again.

Somehow, I managed to make it home. I do not even remember what route I took to get there. Obviously hours had passed, because the sun had almost set when I pulled into the driveway. I remember noticing how dark and empty the house seemed from the outside. I walked in and made my way upstairs to the bathroom. Once again, I caught a glimpse of myself in the mirror and I took the first long look at myself since everything had happened. The reality of the attack was setting in. It was no longer a dream or a vision. It was no longer something that I couldn't believe had happened. It was all too real. All of the anguish and shame was taking hold.

Suddenly, I was overcome with energy. I had to remove this black mark from my memory. I took off the clothes that I had been wearing and threw them into the wash. I then proceeded to get in the shower and scrub myself harder than I ever had before. With each stroke, the scalding hot water washed another layer of filth and disgust that covered me down the drain. Soon it would all be gone.

Susie had been out picking her mother up at the airport. They arrived home later that evening. I did not want her mother to have any idea what had just gone on. But, despite my best efforts to keep everything inside, Susie knew something was wrong. She took me aside and was able to get me to tell her what happened. She wanted me to be comfortable, so she called two very close friends of ours and asked them to come to the house. It took them a while to do so, but between the three of them, I was convinced to go to the hospital.

Once at the hospital, I was whisked away to an examining room, while Susie was forced to stay behind and deal with the paperwork and the hospital red tape. I am still amazed at how Susie was able to keep things together enough to rationally deal with the whole situation. I was a complete mess, but Susie, even though I know she was dying inside as well, was able to be in control when she needed to be. I don't know if I could ever thank her enough for all she did that night. Without Susie, I don't think that I could have survived even this part of the ordeal. I am so thankful to God and so fortunate that she is in my life and that she loves me the way she does.

Once inside the room, I was asked to remove all of my clothes and await the arrival of the nurse. I sat there, naked , on top of a cold examining table, frightened and all alone. I felt even worse and more humiliated than before. With all of this time on my hands, my mind took me back to the forest preserve. I relived every action and word. It was like I was still there. He told me how good I looked and how much he was going to enjoy me. I could still feel his arm on my back, holding me down so hard that at times I couldn't breathe. I was very disturbed by the notion that he may have thought that I wanted this to happen.

Finally, the nurse entered the examining room once again. This time she had a box tucked underneath her left arm. She informed me that I was going to be required to go through a rape kit. She explained that the rape kit was used to collect evidence and that this evidence would be stored until such time that it is needed for a trial. The more she explained, the more jumbled and garbled her words sounded to me. Everything was still in some bizarre haze. I tried as hard as I could to focus and pay attention so that I would understand everything that was about to happen to me. But I couldn't, I just wanted to go home.

The nurse began to methodically go through the steps in the kit. She took my arm and explained that she needed to take a blood sample. My mind instantly shifted to the possibility of AIDS or other sexually transmitted diseases. I remembered that he had used a condom and, therefore, the risks were reduced, but there was still cause for concern.

Next, hair samples needed to be taken. For this, I could have no assistance. The nurse handed me a small black comb. It reminded me of a comb that I used to carry in the pocket of my jeans in grade school. Following her directions, I combed through my hair at various points around my head. I collected and plucked approximately 50 hairs from all over the top of my head and placed them on a small square paper that was folded and placed in an envelope along with the comb. The nurse returned with a second square and comb and instructed me to similarly supply the same quantity of hairs from my pubic region. The hairs were again placed into an envelope and into the kit.

Finally the doctor returned for the swabbing. The doctor was required to swab every, and I do mean every, opening in my body with these really long versions of Q-tips. The swabs were basically a long, very thin wire with a cotton tip. The nurse stood by as the doctor collected three swabs per area. All there was to do was close my eyes and pray that this would be the end. The swabs were packaged, identified, and returned to the kit. The kit was then sealed.

As the nurse and doctor left, I was given a gown to put on. I put on the gown and walked over to the restroom area. I stared at myself for the longest time in the mirror over the sink. As I looked, I began to piece together and understand what all had just happened to me. I had just sat naked on a table in front of two complete strangers, having every hole in my body invaded by long wires with Q-tip ends that emerged covered with my own blood, after combing and plucking out my own pubic hairs one by one, after being left alone in a cold examining room, after wandering aimlessly for hours, after having been raped and emotionally traumatized earlier that afternoon. I was scared, embarrassed, and feeling all alone in the world. But it wasn't over yet.

In walked two of the forest preserve district's finest who were responding to the hospital's call. The officers seemed the exact opposite of each other. One was older, gentle, and kind, and the other was younger and gruff. They had arrived to take my statement.

It all seemed routine. It was a lot like what I had seen happen in the movies and television. First, they asked for personal information—my name, address, occupation, and so on. Then they took my statement of what had happened. I reconstructed the story the best that I could under the circumstances.

Then I told the story again. Then again. They asked questions. They interrupted. They told the story back to me, but changed things. They inserted information that I did not provide. Questions sprayed at me from every direction like bullets from a machine gun. Everything became so cloudy and confused.

"Was his jacket red or brown?"

"Did he gesture with his left hand or right?"

"How's your marriage?"

"Did he show you the gun?"

"Was he wearing tennis shoes?"

"Do you have any friends who are gay?"

I looked for Susie, but she was gone. I was trapped in the examining room with people who didn't understand, who didn't care. I wanted only to go home. I wanted to go to sleep and wake up so that it would all be over. To leave these horrible officers and be with someone who understood, someone who cared.

Then more questions. More changes. I wanted to scream at them. I needed to make them realize they were torturing me. They were questioning my every move, my every word. The more they spoke, the more I believed that I was responsible for what happened. That I deserved it. That I wanted it.

Then they asked the question. The question that I will remember to my dying day. The question that still raises nothing but complete rage in my soul.

"Why didn't you just run? He wouldn't have shot at you, it's too hard to hit a moving target. I would have just started running. Why didn't you run?"

If only I had my wits about me at this point.

"Why don't you hand me your gun, start running down the hall, and you tell me if I hit you."

Maybe I could have done something differently. But, then maybe I would be dead. I believe with all my heart that I did everything that I could within my power not to have any harm come to me and stay alive. I did not ask for this man to enter my life. I did not ask him to threaten me, to humiliate me, or to use me as an object to satisfy his sick desires. I have just one question for these officers and for anyone else who might question me in any way. Why would I go through the extreme humiliation and pain that I went through, not to mention the anguish that would follow, if there was anything else in the world that I could have possibly done? Couldn't these detectives see that? If this man had mugged me instead of raping me, the police probably would have spent their time convincing me that I had done the right thing to save my life. But, because it was rape, suddenly everything I did was questioned.

After being degraded and humiliated in so many different ways, I had reached the lowest point ever. I was convinced that I was a terrible person. I didn't even feel recognized as a human being. No one in their right mind would treat a human being this way. I was also convinced that I should have been able to avoid the whole attack in the first place. I have heard of people fighting their attackers and being able to escape harm. I was not good enough to do that either. I had been treated as a worthless animal and didn't view myself as being much better. Not to mention that I felt stripped of every ounce of masculinity that I once possessed. After all, the majority of the world just might believe that a "real man" would not allow this to happen to him.

What would everyone think of me when they heard what had happened?

Within 24 hours of the event, Susie and I were sitting on the couch across from a Christian therapist who we had been referred to by our church. I remember experiencing many different emotions that day. I was completely devastated by what had happened. I was uneasy telling anyone else about it. I was comforted that Susie was there right by my side. I was anxious at the thought of being "in therapy." The discussions were very general and concerned why we were there. We talked awhile about how we wanted to handle the news with other people and about ourselves. I mostly remember leaving his office still in a daze from the emotional storm that had just hit me.

The first several months of life following were very erratic. I can cite several instances where life as I knew it was on the verge of blowing up in my face. There were so many times that I just wanted out. Seeing my loved ones hurting so much because of me broke my heart over and over and only intensified the emotion of wanting out. I must admit that suicide, although a fleeting thought, did cross my mind. Because I was working and going to school, I had a hard time scheduling therapy appointments and keeping them. Many times I was out of town and could not make it back in time, needing to cancel at the last minute. I was not dealing well at all.

I continually frustrated myself by trying to act the way I thought I should, by responding to my therapist's questions the way I thought I should. I wanted to be strong. I wanted to be an example. But, no matter how functional I appeared to others, I was dying inside. My mood was changing what seemed like every couple of hours. Therefore, I was a royal pain in the butt to all of the people who mattered in my life—my friends, my family, and many times my own wife. My marriage suffered. My relationships suffered. My spiritual well-being suffered. My work suffered. I sank to depths lower than I ever thought possible.

I looked for other outlets to network with other men in my situation. I found a blockade down every path. Many of the rape crisis lines that I called were rude or did not know how to handle me. Those that were helpful had information that was so out of date that despite their best efforts, they were of little help. I searched for books or articles to read. The reality is that there are more outlets for criminals than victims. Furthermore, the help for victims of sexual crime is mostly for those who have experienced childhood trauma. The handful of groups for rape victims are totally dedicated to female survivors. Although all of these things are good, the lack of understanding or even concern for my predicament is still a source of frustration.

After months and months of frustrating work, things slowly began to fall into place. And then, it hit me suddenly like a bolt of lightning and it all became crystal clear. I was too preoccupied with other concerns. I was too busy trying to act strong, yet not acknowledging my weaknesses. I was covering up my true emotions with nice words and thoughts. I was not acknowledging my feelings. I was so determined to not let this event define me. I did not want to be known as "the guy who let another guy rape him." So, I tried very hard to cover it up. To try to make it all go away. I would be known for accomplishments at work or in school or through my church.

What I needed to realize was that as much as I hate what happened, as much as I want to erase it from memory, as much as I want to dream that it never occurred, the truth is that it happened. It happened and it has made me into the person I am today. I cannot go back and change the past, so why should I try to hide it and hope that it goes away? The reality is that this is my life. That is a fact. But, I must not forget that I have the power to control how it is defined in my life. Do I let it consume me or drown my enthusiasm? Do I fight to make things better for others? Do I fight to educate an uneducated society? Do I fight to right all of the wrongs that exist? Do I run and hide?

It had been almost 2 years since everything began for me. I have gone through many emotions and many changes. In some ways, I am a much different person than before and I am pleased with some of those changes. I have learned to express my emotions better and not keep them to myself. I think that I am able to stand up for myself more effectively. I have a renewed passion and strength.

I would be lying if I said that I am no longer affected. I accept that this is always going to be in my life. There are times when my heart feels as if it were going to break. Sometimes I am still filled with an unbearable sadness in my soul. Sometimes I dream about it all over again. But, I do not mourn over these facts. I have decided to live in spite of them. After all, it is my life, not some criminal's.

My focus now is to work to fix some of the problems our system has. Susie and I have pursued communications with the hospital and the police about how our situation was handled. I am continuing to look for organizations and outlets that are dedicated to the issue of male sexual assault. I want to do whatever I can to help them. I am continuing the work with my therapist and have found my own personal modes of expression to deal with all of the emotions surrounding this event.

The saddest reality is that the victimization that occurs as a result of a crime such as rape does not end at the completion of the crime. It continues. It follows the victim home. It dwells in the examining rooms of hospitals. It thrives in courtrooms and police districts. It lingers in the lives of victims everywhere and shapes their lives. Hopefully, someday I can contribute to ending some of the senseless procedures that further traumatized me and others in my situation. Hopefully, I will continue to realize my own power in becoming victorious. In spite of everything that has happened, Susie and I continue to dream about our future and look forward to sharing our lives together. I am not sure that there will ever be an end to pain and suffering in this world. But it would be wonderful to see that day arrive in my lifetime. Until that day comes, however, I pray that all of us who struggle can remain focused on the beauty that is life and the great power that dwells within us. Together, we cannot be defeated. We are survivors.

Christopher's experiences with the hospital medical examination reinforce the points made in the previous chapter about the importance of quality and sensitive treatment. Perhaps the most distressing part of his post-rape interactions with professionals is the antagonism he faced from the police officers who questioned him. Essentially, the officers treated Christopher as though he were the suspect, and in many ways he was. His masculinity, heterosexuality, and honesty all became suspicious in the context of stereotypical beliefs that men are not raped, and if they are, they must have somehow wanted or deserved it. The next chapter turns to a critical inquiry of exactly how legal statutes and law enforcement both define and interpret the act of men raping men.

ELEVEN

POLICING THE LAW

*T*he legal issues surrounding male rape are complex and often contradictory. As Chris Smith detailed in the previous chapter, police officers who work with male rape survivors can sometimes be insensitive and perhaps administer more harm than good. In addition to contact with law enforcement individuals, the very wording and philosophy of legal codes vary greatly when addressing sexual violence. In his article, "Dancing With the Patriarchy: The Politics of Sexual Abuse," Atlanta therapist Jim Struve wrote of the connections between present-day rape and the historical underpinnings of law related to sexual violence. The concept of "chattel property" has traditionally been the basis for positioning women as the property of their husbands. This serves to define a husband's rape of his wife to be a legal impossibility, and the rape of another man's wife as a kind of property damage:

> *The norm of chattel property is based on the concept that men have ownership of their wives and parents have ownership of their children. . . . Within our culture, the concept of chattel property is most readily embodied as male privilege. Members of society are conditioned to believe that men, by birth, have the privilege to control. This is especially prevalent—and dangerous—in the commonly held belief among men that they are guaranteed the right of sex upon demand. Male privilege . . . creates the framework for a pervasive rape mentality.[1]*

Feminist legal reform over the past several decades has sought, in part, to revamp these archaic laws that only protected women from rape in the interest of preserving the property of men. Instead, many laws have been redefined to make rape a crime of personal devastation and an atrocity more damaging than other forms of physical assault and battery. At times this reform has involved the gender-neutralization of legal language that has customarily defined the rapist to be male and the victim to be female, or restrictively defined the act of rape as the forcible penetration of the vagina by the penis.

U.S. RAPE LAWS

In the United States, rape is legally defined on a state-by-state level, and the statutes differ widely in terminology and applicability. Many states, for example, no longer employ the term *rape* at all, but have instead adopted language such as *sexual battery*, *unlawful sexual intercourse*, and *criminal sexual conduct*. Some states' primary rape statutes are either gender specific in naming the sex of the offender and victim or define rape to be vaginal penetration without consent. Anal rape is often classified under a different crime, such as "deviate sexual intercourse" (in Alabama, Missouri, New York, and Oregon) or "forcible sodomy" (in Utah and

Virginia). In some states, anal rape and vaginal rape are considered to be crimes of equal severity (i.e., Class A felony), and in a few states (such as New York) anal rape is considered to be a less severe crime than vaginal rape.

Apart from this classification of severity, legal terminology that separates anal and vaginal rape may appear, on the surface, to be simply a matter of superficial language that bears little consequence in rape survivors' lives. For men who have been raped, however, these distinctions can hold great symbolic meaning in terms of validation and the ways in which they make sense of their victimization. Imagine, for example, how a male rape survivor might feel if he reports to the police, "I've just been raped," and the police respond by saying, "No, you weren't really 'raped,' you were forced to engage in 'criminal deviate conduct.'" This distinction of anal rape as some form of "crime against nature" (as it is defined in Idaho) reinforces the idea that male rape is more of a sexual perversion than a form of violence.

In 1985, legal scholars Ronald Berger, Patricia Searles, and W. Lawrence Neuman examined the rape and sexual assault laws of the 50 states and District of Columbia. They found that of the 51, 13 were restricted to male offender and female victim, 1 was restricted to male offender and male or female victim, and the remaining 37 used gender-neutral terminology for both offender and victim. As of 1995, the primary sexual assault crime statutes were restricted to male offender and female victim in 13 states, and the remaining 38 use gender-neutral language. It is apparent that even in the last 10 years, few advances have been made toward our country's legal recognition of male rape.

Below I have selected six states that represent the range of ways that rape is legally defined and dealt with, so as to provide examples of the practical implications of these definitions. A complete state-by-state listing of primary sex crimes in the 50 states and District of Columbia is given in Appendix 3 of this book. These statutes are discussed as they existed in 1995. Continuous rape reform may have already changed some of these definitions.

Georgia

Georgia defines rape as "carnal knowledge of a female forcibly and against her will. Carnal knowledge occurs when there is any penetration of the female sex organ by the male sex organ." If a man is found guilty of raping another man in Georgia, he would be charged with the dual offense of "sodomy/aggravated sodomy." Sodomy is defined as submission to any sexual act involving the sex organs of one person and the mouth or anus of another person. Male rape would be classified as aggravated sodomy, which is defined as sodomy enacted with force and against the will of the other person.

Idaho

Rape in Idaho is defined as forced vaginal intercourse. Penetration of the anus or mouth is considered to be a "crime against nature." A consensual sodomy conviction in Idaho carries a minimum 5-year sentence, but male rape carries only a 1-year minimum sentence. The maximum sentence for both crimes is life in prison. It is interesting to note that consensual anal intercourse is deemed to be more criminal, carrying a heavier sentence than nonconsensual anal penetration.

Maine

In Maine, rape has traditionally been defined as sexual intercourse without consent, where sexual intercourse is "penetration of the female sex organ by the male sex organ." Anal rape in Maine is classified as a "sexual offense." Both are considered to be Class A crimes. A court-appointed commission conducted a 1996 study of gender bias in Maine's legal system. The study found that women are less likely to receive the legal assistance they need, but the panel also reported that in some cases men were more underserved than women, citing the example of male rape survivors.

Michigan

Michigan's sexual assault statute, now called "criminal sexual conduct," was revised in April 1975 to include same-sex rape and also gender-neutralized the definition of the perpetrator (i.e., it became legally possible for women to rape men). Michigan was one of the first states to adopt gender-neutral language in the United States. Some time later, in 1983, Michigan State University officials became puzzled when, in less than 1 year, four men reported having been raped by other men. Local law enforcement and university administrators remained unsure if the dramatic increase in male rape was an increase in actual incidence or simply higher reporting of the crime. The coordinator of the Michigan State University sexual assault and safety education program suggested the recent modification that gender-neutralized the state of Michigan's rape law may have created a climate in which men felt more comfortable in reporting the attacks.

Ohio

Although Ohio's definition of rape is progressive in that it is gender neutral, the state still carries the crime of "importuning" under its array of sex crimes. The code states, "No person shall solicit a person of the same sex to engage in sexual activity with the offender, when the offender knows such solicitation is offensive to the other person, or is reckless in that regard." This section of the code applies only to adults who are members of the same sex, and same-sex propositions are defined, in and of themselves, to be offensive. In effect, the importuning statute criminalizes same-sex negotiation of consent. It is not illegal to have sex with someone of the same sex, but it is illegal to ask that person to have sex; this precludes the possibility of establishing verbal, mutual agreements about sexual interaction. As this law predominantly applies and is enforced with same-sex encounters, a number of vital concerns become apparent. For example, importuning discourages not only the negotiation of consensual sex, but also the negotiation of safer sex. Sexual assault is more likely to occur if one is unable to explicitly ask permission for physical touch or to express boundaries and limits.

New York

In New York, the crime of rape involves sexual intercourse without consent, but sexual intercourse is defined as the penetration of the vagina by the penis. Under the statute of sexual misconduct, anal rape is classified as "deviate sexual intercourse" which is defined as sexual conduct between unmarried persons that involves contact between the penis and anus, mouth and penis, or mouth and vulva. Rape in the first degree is a Class B felony, whereas sexual misconduct is only a Class A misdemeanor. Clearly, the rape of a man is considered to be less severe and damaging than the rape of a woman.

This distinction between rape and sexual misconduct has had a number of serious implications, including what kinds of evidence can be used in the event the case goes to trial. In 1996 a Manhattan State Supreme Court judge ruled that men who are victims of sexual assault can introduce evidence of rape trauma syndrome to justify why they did not immediately report the attack to police or other authorities. Lawyers in the case had argued that a male rape survivor could not introduce evidence of the syndrome because in the state of New York, rape is defined as an act of violence that occurs between members of the opposite sex. Justice Felice K. Shea later decided that individuals may suffer from rape trauma syndrome as a result of different kinds of sexual assault, not just rape, and that scientific literature supports a general acceptance that men as well as women can suffer from the syndrome.

INTERNATIONAL RAPE LAWS

Outside of the United States, adult male rape is legally recognized and unrecognized in a variety of ways. As discussed earlier in the chapter on male rape and sexual identity, most Asian countries restrict their definition of rape to male penetration of the vagina. Below are some other international examples of male rape statutes.

England

Created in 1976, the Sexual Offenses Act in Great Britain defined rape specifically as the nonconsensual penetration of a vagina by a penis. In February 1993 the British government rejected a bill that would have reformed the existing rape law to include both marital rape and male rape. The government justified the defeat of the bill by stating the reform was unnecessary as marital rape and male rape were already covered under other existing criminal offenses. Male rape was defined as "buggery," carrying a lesser penalty than that of rape. In the previous year, 1992, there were 320 male rapes reported to British authorities. On July 11, 1994, the United Kingdom House of Lords finally decided to extend the definition of rape to include the act of men raping men based on evidence of the severe impact rape has on male victims. The change in the legal definition of rape was decided without a vote, and the offense of male rape was recognized for the first time in English legal history.

Romania

In 1994 the *San Francisco Chronicle* reported that:

> In a small Romanian city, a gay man was raped by two other men in February 1993. When he reported the crime, prosecutors told him that, being gay, he must have wanted it. The victim was tried under Romania's law against consensual homosexual acts and sentenced to a year and a half in prison.[2]

Although Romania may legally recognize the rape of men, the law affords no protection to survivors if they are not believed when they report their assault. Cases similar to this, in which male rape

survivors are punished rather than the offender, are discussed
later in this chapter.

Russia

Homosexuality was first criminalized in Russia during the
18th century under the rule of Peter the Great. Sodomy was eventually added to the legal codes of Soviet Russia in 1933 at the
height of Stalin's reign. Article 121.1, banning homosexuality, created an intensely homophobic environment for gay and lesbian
people in the former Soviet Union, justifying official persecution,
discrimination, and imprisonment. Pasha Masalasky, a gay activist in Moscow, served a 3-year prison sentence for consensual sex
with another man. He described how his sexual identity brought
harsh treatment in prison:

> In Russian prisons there is a very strong hierarchy which is adhered
> to by the prison officers as well as the other prisoners. . . . Homosex-
> uals are forced to do all the dirty work. . . . The officers use gay men
> for sexual gratification and no one tries to help them.[3]

Once again there is a contradiction in the imprisonment of a gay
man for consensual sex, and once in prison he is forced to engage
in the same physical act with those who supposedly enforce and
uphold these laws.

On April 29, 1993, President Boris Yeltsin signed the repeal of
Article 121.1, although the signing remained relatively unpubli-
cized for several weeks. Kevin Gardner, the American director of
the Moscow branch of the International Gay and Lesbian Human
Rights Commission, commented to the newspaper *Moscow News*
that implications for the repeal would range from definitions of
sexual violence to improved health care for gay men. He spoke of
the repeal as being:

> "a gigantic step forward for the gay community" but more had to be
> done. "People in the provinces still don't know about the repeal, we
> have to tell them. We have to make sure that the new penal codes do
> not consider homosexual rape any different than heterosexual
> rape."[4]

Gardner launched a campaign to publicize the repeal and ensure that gay and lesbian citizens were aware of their new rights, including a greater recognition of same-sex rape.

MALE RAPE AND SODOMY STATUTES: REPERCUSSIONS OF REFORM

In 1990, Missouri state representative Sheila Lumpe intro-duced a bill to reform sex crime statutes. The bill would have criminalized marital rape, made the rape law gender neutral, and raised the age of consent. The bill faced defeat amid controversial publicity in the *St. Louis Dispatch*. Republican conservatives and homophobic citizens claimed the wording of the bill would have legalized same-sex consensual activity. Lumpe reworded the bill so that it would not contradict or affect the state's law against sodomy. Nevertheless, the bill was eventually defeated. The ho-mophobia associated with the bill was cited as a factor in the defeat. An editorial by the *St. Louis Dispatch* commented:

> *Some legal eagles noted that the wording of Rep. Lumpe's bill, drawn from federal statutes, might have the consequence of legaliz-ing homosexual sex between consenting adults. Well, the state of Missouri isn't about to do anything that would drag its medieval sodomy law anywhere in the vicinity of the late twentieth century, so Rep. Lump agreed to revise the wording to prevent that inter-pretation. . . . However, this little brouhaha only goes to underscore how urgently an educational campaign on privacy rights is needed in this state.[5]*

A similar situation arose in February 1993 when Democratic Representative Jim Martin sponsored House Bill 666 to reform Georgia's rape laws. The bill, however, included a measure to eliminate the state's sodomy statute. Martin had previously made attempts to repeal Georgia's law that criminalized consensual sodomy. The Georgia Coalition to End Sexual Assault (GANESA), a coalition of rape crisis organizations across the state, had sought out Martin to sponsor the bill because they believed he would tackle the sodomy component as well. An article in the *Atlanta Journal and Constitution* explained:

> Mr. Martin and GANESA members acknowledge that the current rape law could be strengthened and expanded without bringing in the emotionally charged issue of sodomy—but they argue that the law prohibiting consensual sodomy is one of the "root problems" of the rape law now on the books. The "confusion between morality and criminal conduct" is part of the problem, Mr. Martin said. By bringing morality into the courtroom, as sodomy does, juries find it difficult to convict someone of sexual assault if the woman has done anything to make her vulnerable to assault, he said.[6]

Later that year in October, Martin continued to defend and explain the connection between sodomy and rape reform. Again, the *Atlanta Journal and Constitution* reported:

> The bill faced fierce opposition, however, from a conservative religious organization named Family Concerns because the bill would also repeal Georgia's law against consensual sodomy in an attempt to strengthen jurors' understandings of the value of sexual consent. . . . Representative Jim Martin, sponsor of the bill, explained, "It's more important than ever to do away with the sodomy laws because . . . some of society's moralistic attitudes about sex are responsible for our treatment of sex crime victims."[7]

Proponents of the bill criticized Family Concerns for confusing morality with criminality, and even the *Atlanta Journal and Constitution* took an editorial stance against Family Concerns, stating:

> How odd that a group [Family Concerns] claiming to be dedicated to protecting children now opposes efforts to get sexual predators off the streets. Have these conservatives gone soft on crime? Apparently, Family Concerns is not as interested in convicting criminals as in meddling in the private lives of consenting adults. . . . Unfortunately, Family Concerns doesn't want the law to apply only to people who force sex on others. It wants the state to criminalize private behavior that it doesn't like.[8]

Morality arguments are commonly used to blame women and men for their assault, citing provocative clothing, consumption of alcohol or other drugs, and more. Similarly, same-sex rape (aggravated sodomy) in Georgia has been difficult to distinguish from same-sex consensual sex (sodomy) since they were coupled as a dual statute. The majority of public discussion about the bill focused on the rape of women, however. Disagreement over the technical language in the bill and controversy over the repeal of Georgia's 160-year-old sodomy statute eventually caused defeat of the proposed legislation.

Most of the states that classify and name vaginal rape and anal rape differently use the term *sexual intercourse* for distinction between the two, with sexual intercourse meaning penis-to-vagina penetration. By default, anal intercourse becomes something other than significantly "sexual," as evidenced by some of the terms for anal rape that do not connote a sexual element, such as *criminal deviate conduct* in Indiana. A reluctance to define the anal rape of men as a "sex" crime may be related, in part, to societal homophobia. If one recognizes the forced penetration of a man's anus as sexual assault, one is also forced to consider its opposite, that is, anal rape is defined by a lack of consent and therefore distinguished from consensual anal sex. If anal rape is acknowledged, then the existence of consensual anal sex is implicated. In a society that attempts to erase or deny the possibility and practice of anal pleasure, the mentioning of anal rape may incite a taboo of perversity. A legitimization of the crime "anal rape" may therefore be perceived by some as a legitimization, or at least recognition, of anal sex. This may be especially true in states that do not define forced penetration of the anus as rape, and simultaneously do not recognize the existence of anal sex via the condemnation of it through punitive sodomy laws. If sodomy laws represent some form of recognition that anal sex occurs between individuals, therefore needing to be outlawed, states without these sodomy laws might fear a new recognition of anal sex through acknowledgment of anal rape.

Several legal cases in the last 30 years have attempted to manipulate sodomy and rape laws to actually benefit those who have committed crimes of sexual violence. I found more than 20 rape cases that had been appealed by the alleged rapist on the basis that the gender-specific language of a state's rape law made the charge of rape unconstitutional. This argument of gender bias stemmed from state statutes that made it a criminal offense for a male to sexually penetrate a female without her consent, but did not similarly protect males from nonconsensual intercourse or did not allow for the possibility of a female perpetrator. The constitutionality of these gender-specific rape statutes was upheld in all but four of these cases. Only one of these involved male rape victims or female perpetrators—the rest were men who had raped women.

In the case of the *United States v. Brewer* in 1973, Paul Brewer, a convict in a federal penitentiary in Pennsylvania, was convicted of sodomy, but challenged the ruling on the basis that the state sodomy law was only enforced with prison inmates and not in the general population. Besides the fact that the act of sodomy Brewer committed was forced on another male inmate, his argument was also denied for the following reason:

> Pennsylvania sodomy statute, while perhaps constitutionally suspect as to consensual sodomy between adults in general population, is constitutional as applied to consenting adults in prison in Pennsylvania, in view of the fact that inmates are in need of protection from sexual and other assaults encountered in prison.[9]

In essence, the court ruled that even consensual same-sex acts behind bars were forbidden in an effort to discourage all sexual conduct, including rape, and that this was in the best interest of the prisoner. This case is interesting because it reveals the court's constant contradictions as to what exactly defines "consent" and "nonconsensual sodomy." At one point in the court's response, it is explained that "prison rapes are a serious problem. . . . Perhaps forward-looking legislative and administrative reforms with respect to conjugal visits will alleviate the problem of prison rape."[10] Although it seems the court fancies itself as progressive, it believes rape to be a sexually motivated act that other sexual outlets such as conjugal visits would alleviate. Two other reasons the court gave for refusing to distinguish between consensual sodomy as legal and nonconsensual sodomy as illegal are:

> (1) the threats of violence which may cause a victim to "consent" to sodomy, and as a corollary, the difficult in proof, and (2) the very tense and potentially dangerous situation existing within the prison confines as opposed to society at large. These additional

factors convince the court that "consensual" sodomy between prison inmates may be validly prohibited.[11]

The court states its recognition of prison rape to be a serious problem, but rather than addressing the problem infringes on the rights of the victim. The criminalization of both consensual and nonconsensual sodomy without regard to consent is, most of all, a convenience to the court. If consent is a nonissue, the court does not have to spend any time determining if force was involved. Instead, all parties can be charged equally, even at the risk of punishing the male victim of rape.

In the 1980 case of the *People v. Coulter* in Michigan, a rather creative argument of gender bias was used. Convicted of committing sodomy in Marquette Prison, John Coulter and Ruben LaVictor appealed on the basis that the sodomy statute was gender-biased as it treated male same-sex penetration much more harshly than if it had occurred between two women. Their appeal was denied because woman-to-woman penetration did not fall under the Michigan sodomy statute. The sodomy charge was upheld and the court adopted the holding in *United States v. Brewer* that any violation of prisoners' privacy is for their own good in the deterrence of prison rape.

In the 1974 case of *Washington v. State of Florida*, the defendant appealed a sodomy conviction after he had raped a male inmate in Seminole County Jail in Washington. He appealed on the basis that sodomy requires one to "carnally know" another. The defense claimed:

> rape can only apply to the rape of one sex by another, wherein a pregnancy might occur, and that it does not apply to unnatural sex in a homosexual relationship. As authority for this proposition, Appellants cite an Alabama case in which carnal knowledge was defined as being "sexual intercourse, that is the actual penetration of the male sexual organ into the sexual organ of the female."[12]

The court denied the appeal on the grounds that carnal knowledge includes more than just sexual intercourse and that under constitutional law men and women should receive equal protection from sexual assault.

In the 1973 case of *Brinson and Wilson v. State of Florida*, defendants Brinson and Wilson had been convicted in a Circuit Court of the crime of sodomy for raping a man in Raiford prison. Legal reform had determined that sodomy was no longer punishable as a felony under the sodomy statute, however. The court struggled with finding a way to impose felonious penalties for the crime of sexual violence even though same-sex rape was not covered under the criminal definition of rape. The only alternative seemed to be charging them with a misdemeanor of assault and battery. They explained this alternative as unjust, for the punishment did not fit the crime:

> it is sure to come as a monumental surprise to the victim of Brin-
> son and Wilson . . . that they who perpetrated such a base and
> degrading sexual assault of forcible oral or anal sodomy upon them
> are to be punished no more for their transgressions than one con-
> victed of spitting on the sidewalk.[13]

Eventually the court reversed the sodomy conviction and instead convicted the men of forcible carnal knowledge. Even though carnal knowledge was defined as involving a female victim, the court substantiated the conviction on grounds of gender equality and constitutionality:

> In our view, the body and mind of a victim of a forcible sexual
> assault is no less outraged because the penetration by the assailant
> occurred in the anal orifice . . . rather than in the vaginal orifice. In
> either case, it is a gross invasion of the privacy of one's body which
> cannot be tolerated by a civilized society. . . . Moreover, we hold that
> males are entitled to the same protection from degrading ravish-
> ment and sexual assaults, regardless of the orifice involved, as are
> females.[14]

This case, although it took place in the 1970s, is a prime example of how the lessening or repeal of sodomy laws can have a negative impact on a male rape survivor's recourse against his attacker. Had the court not forced a reinterpretation of the forcible carnal knowledge statute, the two rapists would only have been charged with a misdemeanor carrying a maximum sentence of 60 days in the county jail.

If we work to repeal sodomy laws in states that have gender-specific rape laws, we may be stripping some male rape survivors of their only suitable legal protection. Gay political movements seem to have failed to consider this by-product of demanding the repeal of sodomy laws in the United States and other countries. They may win the right to participate in oral and anal sex legally, but do so at the expense of many gay (and other) men who have been raped or need legal protection from same-sex rape. On the other hand, if we allow sodomy laws to remain in their current form, male rape survivors are silenced and stigmatized in the fear that they have participated in a criminal act under the most literal interpretation, which sometimes does not distinguish between forcible and consensual penetration. This results in the legal system actively participating in "blame the rape victim" to the degree of actual punitive measures.

In these states where consensual same-sex sodomy and same-sex rape are conflated, the rape survivor is faced with a complexity of additional threats. If a man reports being raped to authorities, and they disbelieve him (which frequently happens in instances of male on male rape, as in the case of Andrew described later in this chapter), the authorities may determine that the physical encounter did take place, but was consensual. If this occurs in a state with a sodomy law, the male rape survivor is faced with a dilemma that is threefold: (1) He loses the ability to pursue legal recourse against the rapist, (2) he may face false reporting charges for supposedly fabricating a crime that did not occur, and (3) he may be faced with sodomy charges himself if investigators determine he participated in the act consensually.

Such was the case in a 1991 situation at Barnard College in New York. On November 22 of that year, a 19-year-old gay male visitor at Barnard College reported to local police that he had been raped at knifepoint in the basement of a campus dormitory by a male stranger. The police, however, decided a rape had not occurred and subsequently investigated the incident as sodomy, which is illegal in the state of New York. The severity of this charge in New York can range anywhere from a misdemeanor to a felony, depending on whether force was used and what kind of force. The *New York Times* reported that the survivor "said that police had not taken his complaint seriously and were treating him differently because they believed he was gay."[15] A similar situation occurred in Romania, as mentioned earlier in this chapter, when a man reported having been raped and was charged with sodomy by authorities. These sex crimes that do not take into account the element of consent are particularly dangerous for male rape survivors. Sodomy laws lose their proscriptive power against the act of rape in our society, outlawing the consensual physical act between two people in addition to, or rather than, the sexual violation of one person by another.

THE HOMOSEXUAL PANIC DEFENSE

Other violent crimes are sometimes committed that are not acts of sexual violence, but are purported to be self-defense responses to attempted same-sex rape. Numerous legal cases of assaults and murders have surfaced in recent years in which a man has beat or killed another man, claiming he did so in response to an unwanted sexual advance. In trials of these cases, the defendant often invokes the "homosexual panic defense," stating he was so panicked by a homosexual advance that, fearing he would be raped, he lashed out in violent rage as a form of self-defense. In a 1993 case in Durham, North Carolina, Brian Elgin Laws allegedly murdered a man named Earl Wayne Handsome. Laws himself confessed. Handsome was stabbed 18 times and beaten with a ceramic vase. The defense lawyer for Laws contended that he acted in self-defense to repel a "homosexual attack." Defense lawyer Eric Michaux argued to the jurors that "nothing can be more devastating to a 19-year-old kid" than a homosexual attack.[16] The focus of the trial quickly shifted from a discussion of self-defense to a normalization of physically violent homophobia.

A similar defense was used in 1989 by Donald Taylor, a man in Grafton, West Virginia, who stabbed Malcolm Davies 34 times after waking up one night to find Davies raping him. Taylor said he had been drinking, passed out on Davies's couch, and woke up in Davies's bedroom. In his testimony, Taylor admitted the excessive stabbings but claimed the action was in self-defense. The United Press International newswire reported:

> A clinical psychologist who examined Taylor said he went into a "homosexual panic" when he stabbed Davies. Prosecuting attorney Susan Tucker told the jury in closing arguments that a blood trail showed Davies went from the bedroom to the front door in an attempt to escape, but hesitated at the door. She said Taylor then stabbed Davies 15 times in the back and then repeatedly stabbed him after he was lying on the floor.[17]

In this case the violence was in response to an alleged rape, not just a sexual proposition. The jury sentenced Taylor to life in prison with a recommended mercy that he be eligible for parole after 10 years.

Perhaps the most notorious case of alleged homosexual panic occurred in Michigan in 1995. Scott Amedure had appeared on the television talk show *Jenny Jones* in an episode dedicated to secret admirers. The objects of the admirers' affection appeared on the show, not knowing exactly who their secret admirers were. Amedure revealed his crush on Jonathan Schmitz, who later claimed not to have known his admirer would be a man. Three days after the taping of the show, Schmitz killed Amedure with a shotgun and told police he had done so out of his anger for being humiliated on national television. When the case went to trial, Jeff Montgomery of the Detroit gay and lesbian civil rights organization called Triangle Foundation said, "We know from our work that in almost any case in which there is a gay murder victim, there is a tendency to try and blame the victim for his or her own demise. There have been people who have said Scott is to blame for going on that television show."[18] Schmitz was eventually found guilty of the crime.

Gary David Comstock, a professor of ethics at Wesleyan University, has demonstrated that the concept of "homosexual panic" is antiquated and invalid as it is currently being used in legal defense strategies. Although homosexual panic was included as a condition in the 1952 *Diagnostic and Statistical Manual* of the American Psychiatric Association, it is no longer held to be an officially recognized disorder. It was first defined "as a psychological disorder in which neither sexual advance to the patient nor violent attack by the patient of another person are causal or symptomatic."[19] Comstock suggests that defense attorneys regularly attempt to use homosexual panic as a defense because "juries are more likely to sympathize with a defendant who claims to have killed because of confusion and rage experienced during a same-gender attack than with one who claims to have difficulty controlling his violent behavior generally."[20] In essence, defense lawyers attempt to pander to the jury's homophobia by portraying gay men as sexual predators. Heterosexual men's homicidal response is then constructed to be an involuntary defense mechanism that, although perhaps unhealthy, is to be expected in many ways. This puts the victim on trial and shifts blame and suspicion away from the perpetrator.

MILITARY LAW

Earlier in this book I described male rape in military environments, focusing on the dynamics of single-sex institutions as they influence sexually violent behavior. U.S. military organizations operate under a federal legal code rather than follow the individual laws of states and countries in which military bases are located. Parts of this code render sodomy illegal and also prohibit men and women from serving as openly gay or lesbian individuals. President Clinton's approved "Don't ask, don't tell" policy stated that gay and lesbian people may serve in the military as long as they remain celibate and do not reveal their sexual identity. Like some state statutes, the policy and law that bind branches of the military are often more harsh in their punishment of consensual same-sex sexual behavior than some forms of sexual violence. For example, on August 19, 1994, the ACLU Foundation of Southern California charged that the Navy penalizes homosexual activity by officers and sailors more harshly than it punishes service members found to be engaging in child molestation, rape, or incest. The *Los Angeles Times* reported that Jon Davidson, senior staff counsel for the ACLU Foundation,

> made public a memo written by Navy Capt. Fred R. Becker Jr., legal
> counsel to the Bureau of Naval Personnel, which concedes that a
> Navy dentist who pleaded guilty to committing sodomy on his 16-
> year-old son last year is being kept on duty under a rehabilitation
> program. By contrast, he said, there currently are more than half a
> dozen cases pending of homosexual officers and enlisted men who
> have been ordered discharged from the Navy simply for declaring
> that they are gay—without even having been charged with actual
> homosexual activity.[21]

What seems to be a double standard is in fact a rank ordering of criminal behavior, communicating that sexual activity between consenting adults of the same sex is more reprehensible than sexual violence committed by a man perceived to be heterosexual.

In June 1993, Petty Officer Albert Ruggiero was sentenced to 7 years in prison after being convicted of two counts of "homosexual rape." The Associated Press article covering the sentencing added: "The attacks have intensified debates about President Clinton's plan to end the ban on gays openly serving in the military."[22] Retired Admiral John Dalrymple, executive director of the Navy League, seized the opportunity to equate homosexuality with same-sex rape in a distortion for discriminatory purposes: "What this shows is that homosexuals cannot be expected to remain celibate while on active duty in the military."[23] He added that allowing gays to serve only would make the "situation" (i.e., sexual violence) worse. None of the media coverage surrounding the assaults actually stated whether Ruggiero self-identified as gay or straight, but the implication is clear: He committed homosexual rape, therefore he is a homosexual.

These presumptuous statements made in 1993 by military leaders look rather unfounded and reactionary in retrospect, taking into account the Tailhook sexual harassment scandal and the scores of Army women who stepped forward in late 1996 and early 1997 to report they had been sexually assaulted by their male superiors. The latter situations occurred frequently in training situations where male officers had an inordinate amount of power over female recruits. Using Admiral Dalrymple's logic, one could easily conclude that heterosexuality is not compatible with military service and that no amount of discipline or training can possible reign in the unbridled sexual predation of heterosexual men. Interestingly, national military organizations have been unwilling to consider that perhaps it is the culture of the military, not its individual members and their personal backgrounds, that fosters a rape-prone mentality.

POLICE INSENSITIVITY

As with the field of medicine, male survivors' interactions with police officers can either be a great deal of help or an experience that leaves them more damaged than before they sought assistance from others. Of those survivors I interviewed who reported their rape to authorities, all but one had an intensely negative experience. The one survivor who was the exception had only a neutral interaction—neither helpful nor overtly detrimental. The most common complaints I have heard from male survivors who I interviewed and have worked with professionally have been disbelief, mockery, homophobia, or a combination of all three from police officers. I do not believe that the majority of police officers intend to be malicious or insensitive, but rather lack the necessary training and experience in working with adult male survivors of sexual violence. The shock and surprise that many officers display when confronted with a male rape report quickly transform into reactions grounded in the many stereotypes about same-sex rape. In these cases, the survivor is not only denied the benefit of a proper investigation, but risks internalizing such insensitivity to the degree that he may actually begin to believe that the experience was not rape, that he must have wanted or deserved it, or that such a crime is no worse than any other physical, nonsexual assault.

Law enforcement officials can, on occasion, be a survivor's first point of contact after the rape, sometimes even before medical attention, a call to a rape crisis hotline, or assistance from loved ones. The first revelation of victimization to another person can establish a psychological precedent for the survivor, indicating how he can expect others to react to him. When I interviewed

Jonathan, he described in great detail how he had been beaten and raped by an acquaintance in a hotel and was walking home when he was able to flag down a police cruiser. Jonathan thought he had made his way to safety at that point, but he was mistaken:

> *I was all bruised and my face was black and blue. I had vomited all over myself. I lived all the way on the other side of downtown, so I started walking home. I saw a police car coming down the street so I stopped him. I told him that I was just raped. I was wearing a leather armband on my right arm, and I was wearing a T-shirt and jeans and boots. It was clear that I was gay to anybody who knew anything. So I stopped him and told him that I wanted to get home. And he said, "Do you want to press charges?" and I said "I don't know" and he said, "Well, we're not your taxi service" and drove away.*

The callous attitude of viewing rape solely within the context of filing paperwork or pressing criminal charges can communicate to the survivor that he does not deserve assistance unless he is willing to risk the possibility of further humiliation. Jonathan was acutely aware that the officer had identified him as a gay man, especially because the incident occurred during the weekend of the city's annual gay and lesbian pride celebration. Even for male rape survivors who are not gay, the perception that rape equals homosexuality can motivate police to denigrate any survivor, regardless of his sexual identity. Andrew told me that after he had been gang-raped and treated at a local hospital, he was further debased by those he thought would aid him:

> *When I was with the social worker, he encouraged me to call to the police and report what had happened. I thought, I don't want this to happen to anyone else. I called the Denver police that night at the hospital. I called and was connected with a detective. I told him where I was and I told him what had happened. He said, "Well, probably, you really wanted this to happen. You wanted to have sex with a man, then you got scared. And now you want to say it was something else." I just hung up.*

Rather than seriously consider the possibility that men can and do rape other men in our communities, some people prefer to rationalize their disbelief of male rape by formulating a more plausible tale of regretted sex. This line of questioning and analysis is similar to the classic interrogation of female rape victims that suggests she is to blame for her assault. Just as she might be asked, "What were you wearing that night?" or "Why did you go back to his apartment?," male survivors are posed with similar questions. In the previous chapter, Christopher Smith remembers an officer asking him, "Do you have any gay friends?" and questioning why he didn't just run from his attacker because, even though the attacker had a gun, "it's hard to shoot a moving target." In an article published in *On the Issues* magazine, rape survivor Fred Pelka recalled police asking him why his hair was so long and if he did drugs.

Richie McMullen of the London-based male rape organization Survivors speculates that police mistreatment of male survivors is tied to a culture of masculinity within law enforcement professions:

> *Perhaps . . . most police officers are themselves males who value masculine activity, therefore themselves and their institutions, very highly. Police work, like prison work, involves the officer in having power and increased status over other members of the community. . . . The actual and feared stance the police take when an offence is reported explains, in part, why others refuse to report such a serious crime. Indeed, many male victims report that the treatment they receive by the police and in the courts is worse than the offence itself.[24]*

Until law enforcement officials are able to more fully support male survivors and recognize the crime of same-sex rape, we are not likely to see an improvement in the reporting of male rapes that typically remain hidden. In addition, if male rape is not punished or publicly seen to be a devastating act of criminal violence, there will be no deterrence of men who participate in same-sex rape behavior. This extends beyond the realm of state and local statutes to encompass federal law, such as Title VII, which bans sexual harassment in workplace environments.

MALE RAPE AND THE WORKPLACE

In October 1991, Joseph Oncale was working on an offshore oil rig, one of a seven-man crew. Oncale reported that he received repeated rape threats from his co-workers. One day while Oncale was showering, a man allegedly entered the stall and pinned him to a wall while another man attempted to shove a bar of soap into his rectum. Oncale said he complained twice to his company's top official on the oil rig but received no results. Two weeks later he quit his job and filed a sexual harassment lawsuit against the company. The case was thrown out by a federal trial judge who ruled that same-sex sexual harassment is not covered under Title VII. Part of the Civil Rights Act of 1964, Title VII prohibits workplace harassment of a sexual nature against employees of the opposite sex. Oncale appealed the ruling and the case has reached the Supreme Court. At the time of this writing, the Court has not yet decided if it will hear the case.

Similar cases of same-sex sexual harassment in the workplace have occurred elsewhere. Roger Fleenor, an employee of Hewitt Soap Company in Dayton, Ohio, claimed that he was sexually harassed and assaulted during a 2-week period in August 1992. One of Fleenor's co-workers allegedly exposed his genitals to Fleenor, threatened to force him to perform oral sex, and shoved a tape measure into his buttocks. Fleenor filed a sexual harassment lawsuit, which was dismissed on the grounds that Title VII does not cover same-sex sexual harassment. However, the Equal Employment Opportunity Commission, a federal government agency, has ruled that victims of sexual harassment and harassers can be of the same sex. Resolution of this discord between government organizations has not been reached, nor is it likely an agreement on the matter will be made anytime soon.

One rape survivor I interviewed named Paul told me that he had been raped in his workplace. The office was not simply the physical, coincidental site of the assault, and he described how the power relations within his company set the stage for the rape:

> In 1992 I was a manager for a large retail outlet in [a large north-eastern city]. My supervisor had offered me a promotion and lots of perks if I would agree to sex. It was couched in such a language that it was subtle. I told him that I was not interested, in so many choice words. As a result, the following Monday I was raked across the carpet and told that I would be fired for a serious violation of

company policy. This policy did not exist, but he made one up. After this meeting I returned to my office and after arriving I tried to pretend that nothing was wrong. A few moments later, this man arrived at my office. I felt very uncomfortable with him being there but I could say nothing. I already had enough on my mind. I was trying to figure out what to do to get out of this mess. Deep down I knew that I had done nothing wrong, but I felt powerless. As I got up to leave and go home, he cornered me and raped me. It has caused me and my family nothing but pain and grief. I am married with three children. I would not wish this on anyone. And no one knows what I am dealing with because none of my friends can empathize. I have not worked since 1992 and it is doubtful that I will ever work again. I have tried but I cannot get the fear out of me that it could happen somewhere else. I trust no one and if I feel closed in or threatened, I panic or respond violently.

Paul's workplace victimization indicates the magnitude of impact that male rape can have on a survivor's ability to economically support himself and his family. In addition, the psychological trauma of sexual violation in an environment that is meant to be professional and, at the very least, safe from interpersonal attacks severely exacerbates men's sense of vulnerability in the world.

Knowledge that this vulnerability is not policed, even in writing, is contradictory to the very principles of law as a protective force in our society. Law is not only used to enforce fairness and equality, but serves as a system of ethics that attempts to define an idealized political reality. The infusion of morality and religious belief into legal statutes has created rape laws that are sometimes harshly judgmental of female victims, deny the existence or severity of same-sex rape and sexual harassment, and confuse consensual sexual behavior with sexual violence. Although feminist-driven legal reform has succeeded in alleviating many of these problematic effects, some local and national legal codes must be improved if male rape is to be recognized and punished as a crime of personal devastation that damages the integrity of individuals and communities.

TWELVE

MEN WHO ARE RAPED: A PROFEMINIST PERSPECTIVE

by Rus Ervin Funk

I was gang-raped by three men who didn't like what I had to say. Perhaps they were threatened, maybe they were scared, or maybe they were just plain mean. Regardless of why or how, three white men jumped me after I presented a series of workshops and discussions on "Rape and Racism" in a small southern community.

It was April. A cool, quiet, and very clear evening. I walked back to where I was staying, feeling that high that you get after you have just nailed a presentation or did something really well— that you knew you did well. I was thinking about the presentation and the discussion—and was aware that I was walking in an area where, if I were a woman, I wouldn't be walking alone. However, I felt full of energy and it was a beautiful evening. As I neared the home I was staying in, a white pickup truck screeched to a halt next to me. One man jumped from the truck, hitting me with a pipe as he landed, breaking my collarbone (thankfully he missed my head). The others then joined him, beating me severely, and sexually assaulted me anally and orally.

During the attack, they made several references to the workshops and presentations I had offered in the community: "How can you talk about stopping rape when you can't even stop your own?" "Do the nigger boys you love so much give it to you this good?" "Does this feel good to you too?" "Is this rape, or maybe it's racism?" Although there was no evidence that they were at the presentation that particular evening, they obviously knew of me and of the work I was doing in their community. They knew what I was up to, and clearly didn't like it. The comments they made haunt me to this day whenever I speak out in public.

After the attack, they left me there. Thankfully another car passed not long after. The driver contacted the police and ambulance and I was taken to the hospital. I was in the hospital for 3 days and then released to go home and continue my recuperation (both physical and emotional). At the same time, the police were working to catch the guys.

I had become known in the town and the surrounding area for my work on the issues of ending men's violence and confronting racism. As is generally the case, when white men do what women or people of color do, men tend to get more recognition, applause, and support. My work included speaking, organizing, and training, in addition to working at a battered women's shelter/rape crisis center.

I was (and continue to be) a rebel-rouser against the social supports that allow and encourage men's violence against women, children, and other men. The men who raped me were hoping and acting to shut this rebel down. They acted in one of the more extreme measures to punish me for acting out of what John Stoltenberg[1] describes as the "myth of manhood," and to threaten me (and other men) to continue to behave in ways that keep the myth alive. By beating and raping me, not only did they hope to keep me "in line," but they also hoped to make an example out of me so that other men would know the danger of stepping out of our prescribed roles. Men's rape of women is a hateful act designed to reinforce male supremacy. So is men's rape of men.

You may ask how a white boy from a small town in Texas came to be invited to speak, train, and organize on issues like rape and racism. My university required that we volunteer at a local service agency during our first year. I chose to work at the local Women's Center—a joint battered women's shelter and rape crisis hotline. My experience there taught me more, and more deeply, than anything I could have possibly imagined. It also set me on my path toward becoming a revolutionary against the revolting notions of gender and gender roles, racism, and homophobia. Working at the Center (I ended up staying there for over 3 years) taught me what it means to be a responsible human being. It also taught me more about white and male privilege than I ever cared to know.

Not long after I began working at the Center, my supervisor, a Latina lesbian who wasn't too sure what to do with me, told me something that, at the time, I didn't understand, but has become one of the major principles in my life. She said, "you are clearly committed to ending child abuse and child suffering. But if you are serious, as opposed to just being committed, then you are also committed to ending war, street violence, battering, pornography, rape, racist violence, and all other forms of violence and abuse." With that, she left the room. At the time, I was 18 and really only wanted parents to stop hitting their kids.

I spent the next several years at the Center struggling with Delma's words. I also struggled with what it meant in the context of one of the lessons I was raised with: "if you're going to bother to believe in something, live it." I wasn't sure I knew how, or if I wanted to live the kind of life that demonstrated my as yet unclear belief in a nonviolent, nonabusive world. I didn't even know what one looked like. During most of my time at the Center, I didn't even know this is what I believed. I simply did what seemed to make the most sense. I didn't have any particular vision in mind, nor was I working toward any goal. However, as I continued to act, the lessons Delma offered became increasingly clear.

As I struggled with these lessons, I continued to work at the Center—going to the hospital at all hours with raped or battered women or children (I don't recall a man ever requesting services

for being victimized), accompanying those who had been victimized through the court system, meeting them in the middle of
the night after they had fled their violent husband or boyfriend
and taking them to the shelter, confronting (and being confronted
by) abusive men, and providing community education. I worked
at the Center at the same time I was living in an all-male dorm at a
medium-size university in southern Texas. It was through the
process of speaking out against men's violence against women
and children that I began (literally and figuratively) to find my
voice. It is here that I realized that I needed to be involved in
working to stop men's violence at the same time that I provided
support services to the women, children, and men who were being
victimized. I needed to raise the awareness of the issues of men's
violence, that there are things that each of us can do to stop it, and
if we all do what we can, we will end men's violence.

It was in this situation of my growing awareness of men's
violence against women, and growing understanding of the subtle
ways that men express men's oppression, that I, while living in the
men's dorm, first began to glimpse how men act so as to keep
other men acting like men. It would be a bit of an understatement
to say that the men in my dorm and the men in my life were not
supportive of my work at the Center or my growing awareness. At
best, they were tolerant. At worse, they were downright vicious.
One holiday season, my dorm exchanged "secret buddy" gifts. I
had been working at the Center for about 2 years at that time, and
had become quite outspoken in the dorm, on campus, and in the
community. My "secret buddy" offered me a beautifully wrapped
package of a doll baby covered in ketchup.

As personally painful as this gift was, there were several
messages that, although probably unintentional, were clear and
undeniable. This "gift" made a joke not only of me, but also of the
work I did, and the lives of the women and children who were lost
because of men who took this "joke" a little too far. It was certainly
a thinly veiled threat to me to quit questioning men's roles and
men's relationships with women. And it was a glaring statement
of the lack of concern most men have for the lives and pain of
women and children.

The ketchup obviously represented blood, but the doll baby continued to confuse me. Did it represent a child who had been beaten or a woman? After all, adult women were, and are, referred to as both "baby" and "doll." Or was it meant to represent me? Any way I took it, it was mean, it hurt, it scared me, and set me up to feel even more isolated than I had before receiving it. The options were increasingly clear: Either I stop speaking out for women's lives, and against men's violence, or risk losing my bond with my "brothers" in the dorm and in the community.

What I didn't realize immediately was that this kind of bonding is most dangerous—to women and children certainly, but also to men. It is this brotherhood, made by our connection with each other that is based solely on the fact that we have a penis, which we prove by putting into someone else (and not receiving), that leaves us as men more isolated and more vulnerable. We see men's vulnerabilities in the statistics of men in prison, men who are addicted, men who commit suicide, men and depression, and so on. All of these are attempts to either fill the emptiness most men complain of, or ease it—an emptiness based on a superficial bonding.

I didn't understand until several years later how this "gift" demonstrated how lightly men take men's violence when men are the targets. Men are expected to handle our pain "stoically" and alone. If men feel pain, we aren't supposed to acknowledge it, and certainly not ask for help, for this would reinforce the feeling of a "lack of masculinity"—a feeling based on the notion that "men" aren't supposed to be victims in the first place.

Not only do men not know how to ask for help, but they don't know how to respond when others ask for help. Men tend to want to "do it," "fix it," or otherwise "take care of" the problem, but rarely know how to support, acknowledge, or listen. As one man said to me in a workshop I offered recently on responding to people who had been raped, "you mean I'm supposed to just sit there and not do anything?!?" To him, as to most men, helping or supporting means going out and doing something—beating up the guy who did it, taking our friend to the hospital, calling the police . . . doing something. To sit and hold a friend, not make any decisions, and quietly remind a friend that the rape was not their fault, feel to many men like not doing anything.

The rape that I experienced as well as the gift that I received are but two examples of the extremes to which men will go to make sure that other men continue to act in ways that support male supremacy. Men have a fairly limited and limiting role by which to define manhood. In this image, men are supposed to maintain control—of ourselves and the events and people around us, particularly those who are seen as weaker or more vulnerable (such as "the weaker sex"). Men, according to this image, are supposed to act in ways to protect and honor women and children. It is an unspoken irony that men are supposed to protect women from the very men we are also supposed to be bonded with.

This "honor" is another form of domination. If men decide which women to put on a pedestal (generally white, heterosexual, and Christian women from an economically privileged background), men also decide when and why to knock women off the pedestal. Based on the best statistics available, it is just the men who are supposed to protect "our" women and children who are most likely to hurt, abuse, and kill them. More women are raped, abused, assaulted, burned, beaten, and killed by their male lovers than by all other categories of men combined. Together, men acting in these prescribed roles keep women and children vulnerable, and keep men from being fully human.

Through my work at the Center and my growing (albeit stuttering) awareness, I was challenging these roles. Not only was I questioning the ways that men acted in everyday life, and in particular in relations with each other and with women; but I was forcing the men in my life to do the same. I became increasingly uncomfortable about the ways that men related with women and the kinds of assumptions made. I wasn't sure of what role men should have in the lives of women, but I was beginning to believe that the role I had always believed to be true reinforced women's vulnerability. By definition, these roles set men up to be the violators of women—a role I didn't want for myself, and wasn't sure

I wanted for other men either. As my questioning and conviction increased, so did my acting and speaking out against these roles.

I became more active in organizing events around the community and on campus. I spoke more regularly, and at times almost nonstop. The campus I attended in 1987 still had sex-segregated dorms. The women's dorms were locked, "for their protection," at 10 P.M. on weeknights and 1 A.M. on weekends. It never made sense to me to lock women out (often, women weren't in the dorm at the time they were locked and were therefore forced to wait outside the locked doors until security would come by to let them in) to keep them safe. As I became more aware, active, and assertive, I initiated a proposal to lock the men's dorms. "Rather than locking women out to keep them safe, lock the men in." This project didn't win me a whole lot of fans with the men on campus.

As my awareness grew, the jokes that had always been so funny weren't so funny, the pornography I had always understood as being entertainment (sic) and my right (sic) became less enjoyable and less of a right. The ways men interacted with the women in our lives, which had always seemed so appropriate, weren't. This not only made me uncomfortable but it also made the men in my life uncomfortable. I was changing but I didn't know what I was changing into or what the ramifications would be. They didn't want to think about how they related with the women in their lives—they just wanted to relate in the time-honored way of southern college men. They didn't want to question their use of pornography, they just wanted to use it. They didn't want to hear about battered or raped women, they wanted to deny it. Just from my being and my process, they were forced to look at things they'd rather not, and this was a threat to their roles, their comfort, and for some of them, their access to victims.

Because I struggled and we were living in such close quarters, they struggled. Because I questioned out loud, they questioned. Like me, they didn't know where that questioning would lead or what would result from their questions. Unlike me, they didn't plan on asking these questions, and didn't really want to look at the answers. What they knew was that I made them question, and that made them uncomfortable. Being men, they responded like men do to being uncomfortable; they became controlling, abusive, and violent.

The men who raped me were acting in a more extreme way than the men who gave me the baby doll, but the motivation was the same: They were acting to protect their privilege and position. In the dorm, I was unknowingly and haphazardly threatening our position. By the time I was raped, I was consciously and deliberately threatening men's position—a position that needs to be questioned, threatened, and, frankly, eliminated.

But my being raped wasn't and isn't the end of the story.

I was raped after working at the Center for several years. I had become articulate, out loud, and proud in my self-definition as a profeminist who supported women and children when they weren't in the room. I hadn't realized that I had made it personal until I was lying in the hospital recovering. I seriously considered giving it up. I vividly remember lying in the hospital bed wondering what exactly I was doing. I never meant to be a martyr and still have no desire for that. I questioned why I was speaking out for women and children if speaking out meant I could be beaten so severely and raped by three thugs. To be hated, to be despised this desperately, was not part of my plan.

I realized that I didn't have to do this work. I could leave the feminist movement at any time. I didn't have to keep speaking out for women's lives, and for the rights of children. I didn't have to continue. I could have left the hospital and left the movement. As a man involved in the feminist struggle, I realized that I always have the opportunity to decide to stop speaking, acting, organizing, and writing. This is one of the expressions of privilege that men have who are involved in the movement. My involvement is a choice. With the opportunity to "abandon ship" comes an added obligation and an added vulnerability. If men are involved and supportive of feminism for women, then men have the obligation to make sure that what we do is respectful and accountable. We must ensure that what we do doesn't inadvertently cause more harm than good.

Almost as soon as I realized that I could stop, I also realized that if I left, I'd leave a part of my self as well. I had become personally involved. Somehow I had stopped working at the Center for the women and children, stopped speaking out for "them"; somehow (and to this day I couldn't tell you how this occurred) I began working for my own liberation and freedom. I couldn't articulate it then, but I realized at a very deep and personal level that my work for the rights of women and children to be free from the threats of men's violence meant that I was working to remove myself as a threat.[2] I came to understand that it is as liberating to live free from the threat of being a victimizer as it is to live free from the fear of being victimized.

But my story isn't over, for there were other men who also didn't want their privilege and position threatened or questioned, which my coming out as being sexually victimized threatened in yet a different way.

As I proceeded with the criminal prosecution, I was strongly encouraged to leave out the sexual assault part of the attack. The district attorney felt strongly that we could get a longer conviction if we ignored the rape, and proceeded with a prosecution of assault, assault and battery, assault with a deadly weapon, assault with intent to inflict grievous bodily harm, and others. Although it wasn't my decision whether or how to proceed with the prosecution, the district attorney listened to what I had to say. I seriously considered her recommendations, but realized after talking with feminist friends and allies that I couldn't ignore the rape. It was a part of the attack, and for me to ignore that part would be to deny the very issues I had so strongly advocated to bring out of the closet.

In retrospect, the district attorney was probably right. We probably could have gotten a longer conviction had I left the sexual aspects of the crime out of the charges. However, I am still convinced that I and my feminist friends and allies were right in speaking the truth, regardless of the outcome.

The defense attorneys went after the fact that I was a self-defined profeminist and that I had been working at a women's center for so long. They used my work as an advocate and educator against me by implying that as an expert I could have stopped the rape if I really wanted to. This analysis is fueled by two more assumptions of manhood: that men are the automatic experts of whatever it is that men speak about and that men can always successfully defend themselves if they really want to.

I realize as I look back at this experience that these men, and the men in the jury, and men in general, do not want to identify men as being victimized by sexual crimes because there is no way to see men as "victims" and still as men. This, of course, is a myth, but one that is held onto strongly by most men and many women. Men, so goes the myth, are supposed to handle our own problems. Whether it's asking a friend for help to carry a box, asking for directions, or acknowledging we've been raped and need some help, men don't. If men do, their masculinity is somehow jeopardized.

For men to recognize and acknowledge that men are raped, otherwise victimized, and sometimes need to ask for help means that men must acknowledge the degree to which we are vulnerable. There is no way in the current myths of manhood to acknowledge being vulnerable and still be a man.

The rape I went through was an extreme example, but extreme examples can often be used to underscore a common theme. The theme of the rape of men is that rape, regardless of the perceived gender of the victim, is a weapon of male supremacy. Most men say, "I'd rather die than be raped." Being raped, supposedly the most emasculating thing that can be done to a man, is one of the weapons that keeps men acting out and in the manhood myths. Men who are or are perceived to be effeminate, men of color, and men who act up and act out of the prescribed roles of male supremacy are at a greater risk of being raped, and the threat of rape is extremely effective in keeping men acting like men.

As a writer, therapist, and activist, I've come to realize how important language is in defining our understanding of the world and, often, in defining ourselves. Our language not only describes our view of reality, it also shapes our view of reality. I was raped, I was victimized (this wasn't the first nor would it prove to be the last time), but I was never a victim, and am not a survivor. Going through that experience does not define who I am or what my role(s) are in life. I am a person who happens to be male who was raped. I am also a person who happens to be "white,"[3] who has been pistol whipped, beaten, assaulted, arrested, and threatened. None of these experiences, not even the totality of these experiences, identify or define who I am. These were experiences, not roles, and not identities. I refuse to grant them that much power in my life.

Men who are raped are similar to women and children who are raped. They experience many of the same feelings and responses, and often feel less secure in asking for help from services or programs that are available, especially those that have been traditionally viewed as being for women. As when women are raped, it is a personal tragedy and a political crime. Rape is used by political beings for political purposes. To effectively work against rape, and support those who have been raped, we must confront the myths of manhood as we simultaneously support those who have been victimized, and hold accountable those who do the victimizing. It's a package deal. As I wrote in my book *Stopping Rape: A Challenge for Men*, I want a world without rape. This means a world where children, women, and men aren't raped; but it also means a world where men aren't raping. It's up to us.

THIRTEEN

GENDERED CONFLICT

*W*hile I was an undergraduate intern at Ohio State University's Rape Education and Prevention Program (REPP) in 1992, I worked with the woman who was coordinator at that time, Willa Young, to make services and programs more inclusive for male survivors. Our rape prevention program was part of a larger unit called Women Student Services. Similar to many other college campuses, our sexual violence prevention efforts were grounded in the equivalent of a university women's center. Together, Willa and I struggled with the mission of REPP and the implications for inclusion of male rape. We wondered, "If this is an act of violence perpetrated *by* men, *against* men, is it appropriate work for a women's organization to take on, especially given our limited resources that have been earmarked to benefit women?" At the same time, the mission of the program was to increase awareness and prevent sexual violence, which includes the rape of men as well as women. We eventually decided that as the overall mission of the organization was to challenge sexism on campus, the inclusion of male rape was germane to this end. Gradually the two of us began to redefine rape from being an act of violence committed solely against women to an act of misogynist violence, expressed as a hatred and devaluation of all things feminine, and saw male rape as very much bound up with the gendered oppression of women.

In the previous chapter, Rus Ervin Funk enumerated a number of these connections between sexism and the rape of men. His rape, in fact, was the direct result of his profeminist activism that challenged the norms of racism and sexism. As demonstrated by the men who assaulted him, rape is essentially a political weapon that is wielded by those who have more power over those who have less power. It should not surprise us that rape is also sometimes used against men who step out of line in the same way that it is used to keep women in subordination to men. A political understanding of sexual violence explains a number of these relationships by foregrounding the use of power before a simple focus on the biological bodies that are involved in the act.

The everyday struggle to incorporate and accommodate the needs of sexual assault survivors, however, draws us back to a tangible reality. In addition to theoretical understandings of male rape, difficult questions of leadership, safety, privilege, and the dedication of precious resources have arisen in antirape movements, sparking gendered conflict. Organizations have toiled over the consideration of allowing men into the safety of what have traditionally been women-only spaces. In most antirape activism, men are still classified as rapists or potential rapists and women are classified as victims or potential victims. And of course, these classifications are true, albeit limiting. We also know that men can be raped and women can be perpetrators of sexual violence, although to a much lesser extent. In a 1995 editorial piece published in *USA Today Magazine*, Stephen Donaldson (former president of Stop Prisoner Rape), scholar Cindy Struckman-Johnson, and several other antirape activists wrote:

> Traditional legal concepts of rape as gender-specific as well as now outdated concepts that rape is a "woman's issue" and men always the oppressive enemy, never the fellow victim—have obscured the

> reality that this crime of violence can be inflicted on men as well as
> women. Such views, now largely abandoned by rape counselors and
> clinicians, still influence the actions, and even more the rhetoric, of
> too many rape and victim activists, who in pamphlets, public
> statements, and articles still refer to victims only as women. This
> picture still dominates the mass media.[1]

The fact that men can generally be either rapists or survivors, and
that some individual men can be *both* rapists and survivors, creates a danger to the antirape movement, for the inclusion of male
survivors necessarily runs the risk of including perpetrators. Even
though many men do not directly engage in rape behavior, all men
benefit from the existence of rape in our society. Rape is one of the
chief vehicles of sexism, and all men receive some form of privilege from that sexism. Again, issues of trust are a major concern
when men enter leadership positions within the antirape movement and are expected to work, without reservation, to abolish
male privilege, including their own. Many men outside the rape
movement frequently invoke the subject of male rape as a way to
deny the existence of male privilege and to attack feminist ideology.

BACKLASH

Too often, male rape is brought up in discussions or cited as a
reason that feminism is oppressive or shortsighted. The growing
"men's rights" movement in the United States is grounded in a
philosophy that women have more power than men in most respects and that men are the true victims of gender inequality.
These men attempt to use examples of situations in which men
supposedly suffer more than women, and their claims include:
Only men are forced to register for selective military service, men
are expected to be the breadwinners in nuclear families, men are
frequently denied custody of their children after divorce, more
men die of prostate cancer than women of breast cancer, and so on.
A common case made in this rhetoric is that men who are raped do
not receive the treatment and services they deserve, and that
feminist rape crisis organizations not only turn male rape sur-

vivors away, but intentionally humiliate and degrade them in the process. Feminism becomes equated with man-hating, and the feminist goals of gender equality are translated into a power struggle of self-righteousness and finger-pointing.

A male survivor named Jim Senter wrote about the intersection of gender and rape in the profeminist magazine *Changing Men*:

> The statement, "Rape is a crime against women," tells me that I was imagining things. It tells me that a significant event in my life didn't happen. This denial of my experience, pain and blood angers me. The rage I feel in response to these statements is similar to the response women have when they are told by police, "You weren't raped. You really wanted this to happen."[2]

Although I agree that rape is a crime against women, I disagree with the statement that rape is *solely* a crime against women. There is a difference between gender-neutralizing rape for purposes of applicability and inclusivity (as with legal statutes, for example) and attempting to deny that gender is not related to rape in any way. This finer distinction needs to be made, lest we risk a knee-jerk removal of gender as an important element in sexual violence.

From my past work as an AIDS educator, I have witnessed a parallel predicament. In the early 1980s, AIDS was conceptualized and referred to as a gay disease. AIDS activists worked hard to broadcast the slogan that "AIDS is not a gay disease" in the hopes that everyone would recognize their own risk and take the necessary measures to protect themselves from infection. Eventually, however, a disproportionate majority of resources and targeted intervention became directed toward heterosexual populations, despite the fact that gay men continued to constitute the bulk of new infections. Gay men's insistence that "AIDS is not a gay disease" soon came back to haunt them, for it provided a homophobic justification to abandon the crisis of gay men dying from AIDS. This is an important lesson that can help to circumvent a similar situation as the recognition of male rape expands. The reductive rhetoric that "rape is not a crime against women" could potentially foster a neglect of the rape of women in both treatment and prevention as male rape attracts attention.

In a 1993 *On the Issues* magazine article, rape survivor Fred Pelka strongly criticized the attempts of the mythopoetic and men's rights movements to completely gender-neutralize the cause and effects of rape. He denounced the idea:

> that rape is a *"gender-neutral issue,"* and thus has nothing to do with sexism. What is ironic about all this is that what little ac-knowledgment there is of male victimization generally comes from the women's stop-rape movement. To the extent that male sur-vivors can tell their stories, it is because of the foundation laid by feminists. So this woman-bashing is as ungrateful as it is gratu-itous.[3]

Pelka continued by drawing attention to many men's lack of understanding between victimization and oppression, with the distinction between the two being "that while many women, and some men, are victimized by rape, all women are oppressed by it, and any victimization of women occurs in a context of oppression most men simply do not understand."[4]

As noted earlier in this book, one of Camille Paglia's favorite criticisms of feminist movements is their supposed inability or unwillingness to address the rape of men. Of course this is another of Paglia's broad-based generalizations, and as the following sec-tions demonstrate, feminist organizations have responded to male rape in a myriad of ways ranging from contempt to compassion. But overall, male rape has been addressed and acknowledged by feminist organizations and social movements more than any other entity.

A VALID CRITIQUE?

It remains unclear, however, exactly where a valid critique of antirape organizations and social movements ends and a backlash against feminism begins. Even in my research, I was sometimes confused by certain statements of what appeared, at least from a surface reading, to be insensitive. Take, for example, the following quote from the October 12, 1983, issue of the *Washington Post* in which writer Elisabeth Bumiller discussed Gloria Steinem's latest book, *Outrageous Acts and Everyday Rebellions*. In the article, Bumiller described Steinem's recognition that revolution takes time:

> *In the meantime, however, she contents herself with everyday rebellions. She won't get married, says she never wanted children, and has written that if men could menstruate "they would brag about how long and how much." She thinks that sons-in-law sleep their way to the top, says that someday she's going to yell, "Oh, you love it honey!" during a male rape scene in a movie theater, and doesn't go to parties because, "I would, in about 10 minutes, turn into this person who's saying this saucer goes with that cup."[5]*
> *[emphasis mine]*

In context, the above quote is 13 years old, and Steinem had used the turn-about method of gender role swapping as a tool for revealing the double standards applied to women. One can begin to see, however, how easily such statements could be misinterpreted as an intentional statement about male rape rather than a rhetorical device used to reveal gender-based inequities.

On an episode of the television talk show *Geraldo*, the former president of Stop Prisoner Rape, Stephen Donaldson, addressed some rape crisis centers' resistance to deal with male rape:

> *I'm very angry at . . . the hypocrisy of a lot of the women that are running their rape crisis centers. They think that rape has to be a woman's issue only and that men have no role. . . . And there's a lot of people who are giving lip service to male survivors, but are doing absolutely nothing about it. The same people will say, "Well, yes, we'll treat males." You look at their public statements, you look at their literature. All they talk about is female survivors, female victims. They're still giving the impression in their literature that there's no such thing as a male survivor, which is counteracting everything that they're saying.*

Andrew, one of the survivors I interviewed, told me how he had reached out to a rape crisis center in suicidal desperation, only to be met with hostility: After being gang-raped in a public park, Andrew had eventually returned home to contemplate his future, when:

> *Around 1:30 or 2, part of me wanted to die. There was part of me that still wanted to live, separate and apart from all this. I remember*

looking up in the phone book the rape crisis center. I thought, "I'll call and there will be someone I can talk to, someone who under-stands." I called, and the lady who answered, who was a volunteer, I told her that "I was sexually assaulted tonight and I just got back from the hospital and I'm having a pretty rough time." She asked what happened and I briefly told her. When I did she got real angry. She said basically that what I was telling her was a lie, that I was getting off on it, that I was probably sitting there masturbating while I was telling her this and that she wasn't going to let me do that. She hung up. I'm real angry still that she did that. In retro-spect, she's probably the reason that I'm still alive. I was so angry and so hurt at her response that I was determined to fight it, determined that the place that I should have been able to find help was not going to treat me that way. I was so angry. The fight was more important to me at that point than dying was, maybe because I knew where she was. Looking back I think, I couldn't fight the men who did this, but I could fight her, I could fight that organization and I wanted to fight back.

The next morning I called the rape crisis center. I was pretty angry, still hurting quite a bit although the doctor had given me some pills for pain. I asked to speak to the director of the center. . . . When the director got on the phone, I remember just screaming at her. I'm surprised she didn't hang up. There was so much emotion, I didn't know what to do with it. She didn't hang up, though. She stayed with me. After I calmed down she said, "Tell me what's going on." I told her what had happened. She was mortified. She was very apologetic. She said there had been some guys calling the rape crisis line and talking very graphically, sexually, and they were mastur-bating during the time they were doing that. She said it's no excuse for what she did, but she probably assumed it was another one of those calls. She asked what she could do to help, and I said, "Noth-ing, I don't want anything from you or your organization." She said there was a male who volunteered with the organization and that she would like me to talk with him. After she talked with me for a while I agreed to do so. We agreed that I would call back that evening and that she would have him available to talk to me. I did call back that evening. I talked to him for four to five hours that night. He is, bar none, one of the neatest men I've ever met in my life—very supportive, very encouraging, very understanding, pa-tient. He became my support in all that.

Most volunteers at rape crisis hotlines have historically been trained to be suspicious of male callers, especially given the prevalence of abuse from men who are not survivors but call hotlines to intimidate and access women for sexual gratification. The unfortunate side effect is that many hotline staffers have become so conditioned in their reaction to male callers that some survivors slip through the cracks and are further damaged by being mislabeled as perpetrators. In Andrew's case, however, the rape crisis center *was* prepared in some ways to meet the needs of men, for they had a male volunteer on their staff who was trained to work with male survivors and eventually did an excellent job. The *San Francisco Sentinel*, a gay and lesbian newsweekly, dedicated its September 22, 1993, cover story to male rape. Lucinda Ramberg, with the San Francisco Rape Treatment Center at San Francisco General Hospital, told the *Sentinel*:

> *Rape crisis and treatment centers were set up to address the needs of women and historically when men have called, they have been treated as the perpetrator because the counselor is completely unprepared to deal with men as rape victims, even in agencies where a female victim could get sensitive counseling.*[6]

The issues of receptivity and preparedness are key to the controversy of whether or not rape crisis organizations serve men. If rape crisis centers are not willing to meet the needs of male survivors, they should at least be able to direct them somewhere else. If a center has decided to address male rape, the willingness must be more than symbolic and they should be adequately prepared and trained to fulfill their adopted mission.

Men's work within these agencies has also been tenuous. The survivor I interviewed named Marcus had sought employment with a sexual assault service agency where he provided technological assistance. His first professional interaction with the agency generated a fairly immediate misunderstanding related to gender:

> *I remember in the interview, the executive director liked me a lot and she said, "It will be great to have somebody working here who doesn't have any of their own personal issues with sexual assault." She totally made that assumption. And I said at the time, "Well, actually, I do." Much later I talked to her about it and told her I had been assaulted and she was welcoming at that point. She had gotten to know me and actually really liked me.*

A number of men have been important for this particular agency, including a man who's been on the board since its foundation. However, a lot of people would call up, not clients, but activists and say, "There's a man answering the phone?" And that was quite disturbing for a number of people. It was not a crisis hotline, but a business line. Actually women who called up and were in crisis and had mistakenly called the office line responded uniformly very positively.

At many points there was discomfort with the fact that I was a man, mostly on the part of activists from other agencies. A man on the board told me that when he first started, the women from [another local rape organization] wouldn't talk to the board of directors of our rape crisis center as long as he was in the room because he was a man and that made it unsafe.

The decision of an antirape organization to address male rape usually raises a subsequent decision of how, and to what extent, men should be involved in the delivery of and advising about the provision of those services.

MEN IN THE MOVEMENT

At different sexual assault conferences across the country, I have attended numerous panels and workshops on the theme of "men's role in the antirape movement." Some of these workshops have been incredibly productive, with thought-provoking conversation that openly encouraged the exchange of ideas. Other workshops have been less productive, however. Perhaps the most surprising aspect of these has been that the question of, "Should men be a part of the antirape movement?" continues to be asked. For the most part, I find this question to be practically obsolete. Men are already a significant part of the movement, and they always will be. This is not to say that there should be no women-only space within the movement or that men must lead the movement, but if men are doing most of the raping and a significant number of men are raped, the problem of sexual violence in our society cannot be solved in a gender vacuum.

Marcus described his experience from a luncheon held at the National Coalition Against Sexual Assault's 1996 conference in

San Francisco, during which a keynote speaker responded to an audience member's question about male survivors:

> *The keynote speaker—it was very clear what her attitudes were about men. It was made explicit when someone asked her the question, "Given that men are the perpetrators of the vast majority of violence against women, how do you feel about men taking positions of power in the movement?" Her response was that men have a role in educating other men not to be violent and that men who are sexually assaulted have important stories to tell, but because they are not raised as women, they do not belong in this movement. She received a standing ovation for that comment which was rather disturbing to me. Everybody who was there at my agency, which was about ten people, looked at me and smiled at me encouragingly because they could see that was difficult for me. I had a very positive experience from my own co-workers. I have good relationships with them, but it was rather difficult to hear the keynote speaker basically telling me that I shouldn't be there.*

At that same conference, I left stacks of information about male rape on the public tables that all participants were free to use in sharing their materials. Three times in a 2-day period, every flier and brochure disappeared. Everyone else's materials remained, and it became clear that the information I left was not just wildly popular, but was being confiscated and discarded. As I made more frequent visits to the table, one stack of my materials disappeared within 20 minutes. Clearly the inclusion of information about same-sex rape and male survivors was incredibly threatening to someone at the conference.

These situations raise difficult issues that will not be resolved any time soon. The extent to which men become involved in antirape organizing, and in what capacity of leadership and power, are serious concerns because they will determine the success, vitality, and survival of efforts to end sexual violence. A partnership between men and women is necessary to do this work, but that partnership is only beginning to be delicately negotiated. Marcus felt invalidated and dismissed as a survivor and antirape activist, but still continues his quest to work against sexism and misogynist violence. In fact, soon after the conference he became the cochair of the National Coalition Against Sexual Assault's survivor caucus.

SUPPORT AND EMPATHY

Thwarting the claim that women in general and feminist women in particular are insensitive to male rape and cruel to male rape survivors is not a difficult task. Most of the male survivors I interviewed and have worked with professionally have had incredibly supportive women in their lives and positive (in addition to some negative) experiences with sexual assault service providers.

After Jimi Sweet had been raped at Cleveland State University in Ohio, he wrote about his experience in an opinion column for the campus newspaper. (Jimi's story is detailed in Chapter Two.) Unsure how the community would respond to his graphic description of what had happened, Jimi expressed surprise at the amount of positive reactions he received, and who those reactions came from:

> *I really wasn't looking for [support] from other people because I didn't think anyone else would understand. I dealt with it on my own. After the column was printed it generated tons of interest. I got a lot of cards from women, of all people, who were raped and sympathized with what happened.*

Among the pages of the infamous *Hite Report on Male Sexuality*, male rape survivors described how their rape experiences had changed the ways in which they viewed and related to women. One of the male interviewees stated, "I have never raped a woman. I doubt that I could. I learned firsthand how quickly men can turn an innocent situation into rape and how helpless a woman can be against strong men."[7] Another man said, "I have never raped a woman, though I have wanted to."[8] He continued by describing his brutal rape in a county jail:

> *What it did to my body was so very less important, torn flesh, bleeding and all, than what it did to my mind. That, in fact, is what men don't grasp about raped women who "haven't been hurt." . . . That costly understanding explains . . . why I have never raped a woman . . . and why I never will.[9]*

The survivor I interviewed named Jonathan discussed his revelation of rape to women who were close to him:

*I shared it with my supervisor and another employee. My coworker
was a woman who, as it turned out, the next week had been raped in
Jamaica. My supervisor later said, "Well, it [the coworker's rape]
was different because you brought yours on yourself." I guess she
said that because I chose to go home with him. I felt pretty bad, the
only thing was that my coworker was fair enough to say no, it
wasn't any different, that it was the same thing.*

When I asked him if he felt his supervisor's judgmentalism was
gay related, Jonathan responded by saying:

*No, I don't. She was a lesbian, by the way. Surely a little bit of it was
gay related, because it was disregarding what the gay culture is
about, disregarding that gay culture sometimes involves sex with
people who are virtual strangers. But you still don't expect them to
beat you up, you know?*

Another survivor, T. J., had this to say about his relationships with
women after he was raped:

*And then I met this woman, she was the head of the Association of
Women Students [AWS]. She was British, and she understood all of
my British sarcasm. We started talking to each other about what the
whole conception of rape was. That was the first time I made the
connection, "That was rape." At the time it was incredibly empowering. I really had no idea how to frame anything. This helped
incredibly. The more I was accepted by AWS, the more I became
profeminist, and the more I became conscious of what the power
dynamics of rape are. The more I became conscious, the more I
became active in profeminist issues.*

T. J. also said that "it has changed the way I have sex with
women—to the point where I am a pain to them, because I ask for
permission constantly. I want to make sure I don't want to put
them in the position that I was put in."

Although many women were immediately supportive of T. J.,
others were taken aback by the idea that men are raped. He said,
"When I talked about it with women antirape activists, I get the
same confused look as any person who is being exposed to rape
[of women] for the first time. It is something that is not talked
about, even in the rape literature." These are important dialogues
between men and women that must continue to our mutual benefit if antirape efforts are to ever build effective alliances in working

toward our shared goals. Indeed, these conversations are necessary because men have been, and will continue to be, part of the antirape movement. Some men speak out as survivors, some men challenge others on their rape behavior, and some hold leadership and professional positions. This is, for better or worse, the reality of today's world.

We must continue to engage in self-reflexive evaluation of antirape movements and organizations, always questioning if the criticisms related to male rape are valid or used as a convenient tool for backlash against feminism. Women and feminism are not to blame for the harsh insensitivity and stigma that male rape survivors continue to face. The true culprit is a patriarchal culture that perpetuates the hatred of all things feminine, enforces rigidly defined gender roles that place men in positions of power over women, and punishes nonconformity to these exploitive relationships. This is the essence of conceptualizing rape as an act of misogynist violence. Hopefully the dialogue between female and male survivors, and women and men in general, will increase and continue to strengthen our efforts to stop rape.

FOURTEEN

INITIATING CHANGE

Over the last 10 years, the services available to male rape survivors have increased dramatically. The sensitivity of those who provide these services has also risen, albeit incrementally. When taken in isolation, however, these are temporary and reactionary approaches to the problem of male on male rape. Treatment and services may address the aftermath, but do not confront the social forces that perpetuate and silence the rape of men. A more integrated set of initiatives is desperately needed if we are to successfully create social and cultural change on a larger scale. The following suggestions provide a tentative roadmap for implementing this work:

EDUCATION

One of the first steps in creating change must be comprehensive education. The lack of information and comparative wealth of misinformation on male rape is appalling. First, a general awareness that men can be raped, and are raped, is necessary. This awareness will also help to put a dent in many men's denial that they could never be sexually violated simply because they are male. This awareness must also be accompanied by public discourse, generating conversation and ideas related to the phenomenon of same-sex sexual violence. Although public discussions of anything related to sex or sexuality can be discouraged and are often controversial, we must take these risks to confront that which has remained unaddressed and neglected for far too long.

The opening of this conversation can have some immediate and drastic effects. For example, in a 1993 interview with *The New York Times*, male rape survivor Charles Meyer described how he had spoken publicly at Connecticut College about his sexual assault, and soon realized he was not the only man who had experienced rape. "All of a sudden, men started coming out of the woodwork to tell their stories."[1] One of the survivors I interviewed, Andrew, described the enormous validation provided by a book on sexual violence that he had read and the importance of knowing that anyone actually cared about the issue:

> Some time after the assault, my psychologist recommended Mike Lew's book Victims No Longer. I bought it. I started reading it, and I read the whole thing through. I didn't eat, I didn't do anything, I just read it all the way through. If you've read it, it's a fairly lengthy book. Some of the things he wrote in the book were things I was going through. I remember on the back cover is a picture of Mike. Whenever I felt like no one understood, whenever I felt very alone, I would open the book and look at his picture. And I would know there is someone out there who does understand.

In addition to a reduction in isolation and correction of misinformation, other educational endeavors will help to reduce the stigma and shame of male rape. Dispelling the myths associated with consensual homosexuality, for example, will lend considerable support to public understandings of rape as an act of violence, not to be equated with gay male sexual behavior.

PROVISION OF SERVICES

The provision of services to male rape survivors and their support people will continue to be crucial, and as male rape is discussed more frequently, more male rape survivors will feel comfortable in stepping forward to ask for the treatment they so desperately need. This may include anything from counseling to law enforcement, medical care, temporary housing, and a wide range of referrals. In addition to availability, these services should be of increased quality and more accessible to a range of survivors, including those of lower income. Presumably, more significant others of male survivors will also need counseling and support that is tailored to this form of violence.

A few simple, concrete measures related to male rape could be enacted almost immediately, if not for the conservative moralizing attached to them. The best example of this is the availability of condoms to prisoners. Currently considered contraband material in all but a handful of prisons, the honest admission that rape occurs with great prevalence behind bars necessitates protecting these prisoners from not only the sexual violence, but also HIV infection and other sexually transmitted diseases. Low in cost and logistically simple, condom distribution is seen by corrections officials as more of an endorsement of homosexuality behind bars than a protective measure that could and would save lives.

For male survivors to take advantage of services, organizations must make them available in ways that are as safe and confidential as possible. Numerous times while working at OSU's Rape Education and Prevention Program, male students have dropped by to visit me and ask for information about male rape "for a paper" they were writing. Some of these men would ask detailed questions; others would offer supposedly hypothetical scenarios for me to evaluate. Yet others would simply slip the written information I gave them into their backpacks and hurriedly leave. I call some of these men my "invisible clients," and although it pains me to see them struggling with the isolation of being a male rape survivor, I recognize their need to reach out for assistance in ways that entail little or no risk.

Even the most subtle of changes, such as altering the language of a general pamphlet on sexual violence to be gender inclusive, can have dramatic effects. Survivors who, in any way, perceive service providers to be open and willing to address male rape will often come forward for support. Most male rape survivors have preconceived notions that rape crisis centers, telephone hotlines, and hospital advocacy programs will only work with women who have been assaulted. Although sometimes this is true, the public visibility of the organization can support this image even when it is not the case. If all of the organization's resources (pamphlets, brochures, volunteers, support groups, workshops, and so on) are women specific, male survivors may not be able to envision themselves as recipients of that program's services.

RESEARCH AND WRITING

Whenever I have conducted sensitivity trainings or spoken publicly about male rape, one of the first questions I am asked is, "Exactly how much does this happen?" Sometimes people want national statistics, and at other times they are curious about the incidence and prevalence of male rape in their own local communities. Many police departments do not track or record the rape of males in the same way they do with females, and the lack of available information, especially quantitative information, is usually taken as a sign that no problem exists whatsoever. Prison rape is usually left out of both national and local statistics on sexual violence—more evidence of society's general conclusion that prisoners are less than human and somehow deserve whatever cruel abuse they receive behind bars.

As for writing on the topic of male rape, there continues to be a void in available materials in which male rape survivors speak aloud, telling their own stories in their own words. For the most part, men who have been raped have been studied and written "about," rather than speaking for themselves. This reinscribes male rape survivors as objects rather than subjects who are in control of their lives and experiences. Unfortunately, some male rape research has done more harm than good to male survivors because of misinterpretations and representations filtered through the homophobia and sexism of researchers presenting their findings. In addition, a great deal of male rape literature appears in scholarly journals, written in an academically discipline-bound language that is inaccessible to the average reader.

Even these scholarly investigations of same-sex sexual contact between men continue to be fraught with methodological and ideological problems that have not been resolved. The most notable example of this has been the construction of a gay history that includes the treatment of rape between men as homosexuality or consensual sexual behavior. Perhaps the most popular debate of this nature is the biblical parable of Sodom and Gomorrah, in which a male angel is sent to earth and is later raped by a man. Some claim that God's wrath, the destruction of the city, was evidence of a condemnation of homosexuality. Others claim the sin was not anal penetration between men, but inhospitable treatment of a visitor and sexual violence inflicted on another. Although this is an example of debate over the interpretation of religious scripture, it becomes clear that the implications for using a history of rape to inform and fortify contemporary gay identity and community are wide-reaching.

PREVENTION

Prevention can be broken down into several tiers: primary, secondary, and tertiary. Primary prevention would consist of precluding a situation in which a man would even be faced with the possibility of rape. This would entail drastic social and cultural changes that would prevent men, first and foremost, from ever attempting to engage in rape behavior. For this to occur, males would have to be socialized from a very early age not to objectify others, not to dominate and oppress, to be cooperative rather than competitive, and devalue physical aggression as a suitable method of venting anger or resolving conflict. Unfortunately, most cultures denounce males who do not embrace these values, using gay-baiting and other tactics to enforce compulsory, hegemonic masculinity.

Secondary prevention would include such tactics as assertiveness training or self-defense classes that prepare men to defend themselves in the event they experience an attempted rape. Men are usually assumed to possess some kind of innate ability of physical prowess that enables them to protect themselves from assault. Most men do not take assertiveness training or self-defense courses (apart from aggressive martial arts) for this reason, as if it is an admission of weakness and compromised masculinity. In addition, many men face other forms of vulnerability as they live in less than ideal situations of poverty, labor exploitation, abusive relationships, and more. Secondary prevention may not be a perfect solution, for there are few magic bullets that solve any problem, but these attempts can substantially reduce the risk of rape occurrence.

Tertiary prevention would limit the aftereffects of rape, such as medical attention to prevent sexually transmitted disease infection or counseling to lessen the degree of posttraumatic stress disorder. Another tertiary preventive technique could be a change in the rape survivor's life to lessen the chance that he will be raped again in the future, such as leaving an abusive partner or an inmate's isolation from violent prisoners. This category would hopefully involve action taken against the rapist, such as a harsher punitive action or better attempts to reform offenders' behavior. All of the above prevention strategies go hand in hand with some form of education as discussed earlier, but the difference between simple education and prevention is found in behavior change. For individual and collective behaviors to change, there must be cultural support for the desired alteration, peer influence that validates the behavior, internal motivation, adequate resources to make the variation possible, and a complex system of rewards and punishments that determine the outcome. The leap from knowledge to behavior change represents the most difficult passage to cross in our attempts to generate understandings of sexual violence that will create a lasting impact on everyday life.

LEGAL REFORM

Several changes in law and law enforcement are necessary before male rape can be adequately recognized and addressed. First, consensual sodomy must be decriminalized. As discussed in Chapter Eleven, male rape is often equated with consensual sexual behavior in legal statutes. This exacerbates the general cultural confusion between rape and sex. In addition, if a male rape survivor comes forward to report that he has been raped in a region where sodomy is a crime, he not only runs the risk of being disbelieved, but also could have sodomy charges pressed against him if for some reason authorities deem the act to be consensual.

Aside from sodomy laws, sexual assault statutes should be gender-neutralized or rewritten in such a way that the rape of men is a crime that is recognized and equal to that of the rape of women. The purpose of this reform is not to diminish violent crimes committed against women, but to acknowledge that men are also raped and deserve an avenue for justice and recourse against their attacker. Similarly, sexual harassment should be legally established as including same-sex sexual harassment, under both federal Title VII law of the Civil Rights Act as well as in workplace policies that condemn such behavior and ensure accountability.

Police officers must receive sensitivity training in regard to all forms of sexual violence, including male rape. In the early 1980s, a male rape sensitivity program was mandated for Seattle police officers in which they were led through a guided imagery exercise. The mental narrative asked officers to imagine they were being raped as a kind of role reversal to generate empathy and understanding. This exercise was later used as the basis for the 1985 made-for-television movie *The Rape of Richard Beck*. Although an admirable attempt, the training assumed that none of the audience members could have or had been raped, and that men cannot be sensitive and supportive without experiencing firsthand the exact same violation. Law enforcement officials should begin to incorporate same-sex sexual violence information into their training not only for reasons of sensitivity in working with survivors, but also to improve investigative techniques, ensure the proper collection and preservation of evidence from male bodies, and provide adequate service to gay and lesbian communities.

POPULAR CULTURE

Cultural change is absolutely critical if we are to expect any success with the above measures. No awareness campaign or public forum will yield progress if we fail to challenge mass media representations of male rape that are inaccurate, misleading, or judgmental. No amount of public education about male rape will be effective if, in our personal lives, we fail to challenge "don't drop the soap" jokes or support homophobia. Even our language must change as we work toward a use of terminology that accurately reflects the distinctions between the rape of women, men, or both in our communications about sexual violence. A more pervasive transformation of rape culture is necessary, and this can only be achieved through a multifaceted approach that demands collaboration and alliance across professional, disciplinary, gender, racial, class, sexual, and other traditional boundaries. Envisioning a culture that does not condone, support, justify, or excuse any form of rape behavior may be difficult, but can also be inspiring as we simultaneously look back at the rapid progress made by anti-rape movements and look forward to the future of eliminating the obstacles that impede further progress.

THE FUTURE

My own rape experience has radically shaped my life in many aspects, influencing my academic work, professional goals, personal relationships, and political ideology. Having lived many months in an oppressive environment and surrounded by men who hated me, I had adopted a victim mentality that, in some ways, became a self-fulfilling prophecy. The ability to resist personal and political violation came to me slowly over time and has been accompanied by a great deal of anger. Earlier in Chapter Two, I discussed anger as a negative by-product of surviving rape that can be potentially detrimental to a survivor's healing process. Certainly this may be true in many respects, but anger can also be the single most powerful tool that, when channeled and wielded properly, produces the motivation to speak and act with courage and conviction. In my professional work and interviews with male survivors, I saw that wonderful anger time and time again as these men broke their silences, all against the incredible odds of societal humiliation.

Despite our ongoing efforts, male survivors continue to slip through the cracks of the legal system, medical services, media attention, research endeavors, and the national antirape movement. These cracks contribute to male survivors' invisibility and perpetuate the intensity of stigma and shame associated with same-sex sexual violence, hampering recovery as well as preventive work. If it is true that the current societal treatment of male rape is comparable to that of the rape of women 20 years ago, we surely have our work cut out for us. Now is the time to organize and create change in these spaces that say male rape does not exist. In effect, the beginning of a new antirape movement is upon us. Perhaps together we can conquer the rape culture we live in before it conquers us.

ENDNOTES

CHAPTER 2

1. Susan Brownmiller, *Against Our Will: Men, Women, and Rape* (New York: Simon & Schuster, 1975), p. 258.
2. Nicholas Groth, *Men Who Rape* (New York: Plenum Press, 1979), pp. 118–141.
3. Arthur Kaufman *et al.*, "Male Rape Victims: Noninstitutionalized Assault," *American Journal of Psychiatry* 137.2 (1980), pp. 221–223.
4. Deryck Calderwood, "The Male Rape Victim," *Medical Aspects of Human Sexuality* (May 1987), pp. 53–55.
5. Bruce D. Forman, "Reported Male Rape," *Victimology: An International Journal* 7 (1984), pp. 235–236.
6. Susan Sorenson *et al.*, "The Prevalence of Adult Sexual Assault: The Los Angeles Epidemiologic Catchment Area Project," *American Journal of Epidemiology* 126.6 (1987), pp. 1154–1164.
7. Andi Rierdan, "How Shame and Fear Take a Toll on Men Who Are Raped," *New York Times* 4 July 1993, sec. 13CN, p. 1.

8. Jeffrey McMenemy and Susan Croili, "Man is Charged With Raping Woman; Victim Says Attack Occurred Near Daniel Boone Campground," *Chapel Hill Herald* 20 September 1994, p. 3.

9. Deborah Rozansky and Ohio Coalition on Sexual Assault, "Sexual Assault Needs Assessment for the State of Ohio," 1988.

10. Bureau of Justice Statistics' 1994 National Crime Victimization Survey, *Bureau of Justice Statistics Bulletin* April 1996.

11. Richard Geist, "Sexually Related Trauma," *Emergency Medicine Clinics of North America* 6.3 (1988), pp. 439–466.

12. Kaufman.

13. Ann Burgess and Larry Holmstrom, "Rape Trauma Syndrome," *American Journal of Psychiatry* 131 (1974), pp. 981–987.

14. Michael Myers, "Men Sexually Assaulted as Adults and Sexually Abused as Boys," *Archives of Sexual Behavior* 18.3 (1989), p. 209.

15. P. L. Huckle, "Male Rape Victims Referred to a Forensic Psychiatric Service," *Medicine, Science, and Law* 35.3 (1995), pp. 187–192.

16. Alfred W. Kaszniak *et al.*, "Amnesia as a Consequence of Male Rape: A Case Report," *Journal of Abnormal Psychology* 97.1 (1988), p. 101.

17. Patricia Frazier, "A Comparative Study of Male and Female Rape Victims Seen at a Hospital Based Rape Crisis Program," *Journal of Interpersonal Violence* 8.1 (1993), pp. 65–76.

18. Peter Goyer and Henry Eddleman, "Same-Sex Rape of Nonincarcerated Men," *American Journal of Psychiatry* 141.4 (1984), pp. 576–579.

19. E. Carmen, P. R. Ricker, and T. Mills, "Victims of Violence and Psychiatric Illness," *American Journal of Psychiatry* 141 (1984), pp. 378–383.

20. Kaufman.

21. Nicholas A. Groth and Ann Wolbert Burgess, "Male Rape: Offenders and Victims," *American Journal of Psychiatry* 137 (1980), p. 808.

22. Fred Krueger, "Violated," *Boston Magazine* May 1985, p. 140.

23. Jim Senter, "Male Rape: The Hidden Crime," *Changing Men* Spring/Summer 1988, p. 20.

24. Dusko Doder, "Male Sex Abuse Seen in Yugoslav War," *Boston Globe* 28 July 1993, sec. 4, p. 3.

25. Marty Baumann, "Toll From the Ethnic Unrest," *USA Today* 8 July 1993, sec. A, p. 8.

26. Jennifer Scott, "Rape Used as 'Ethnic Cleansing' Weapon in Bosnia," *Reuters Newswire* 2 July 1996.

27. Julian Borger, "Rearguard Action in Split," *The Guardian Foreign Page* 29 July 1996, p. 10.

28. Paul Hofheinz, "Soviet Union Heading for a Showdown," *Time* 6 August 1990, p. 36.

29. Michael Hedges and Peter F. Sisler, "Escapees Say Iraquis Kill Babies, Torture," *The Washington Times* 6 November 1990, p. A9.

30. "Alleged Rapist Abused Retarded Patients," United Press International 27 May 1986.
31. "Suit Claims AIDS Received From Sex Abuse," United Press International 22 May 1993.
32. Scott Sonner, "Male Rapes Motivated by Hatred," United Press International 22 August 1985.
33. "Male Rapes Cause Alarm in Utah," Associated Press 28 August 1993.
34. Dwight C. Daniels, "Two Men Arrested in Taunting, Beating of Gay in Hate Crime," *San Diego Union-Tribune* 17 May 1994, pp. 4–5.
35. Ginger Orr, "ATF Agents Blamed After Racist Fetes; Gatherings Draw Ire of Elected Officials," *Chicago Tribune* 22 July 1995, sec. News, p. 3.

CHAPTER 3

1. Stephen Donaldson, "The Rape Crisis Behind Bars," *The New York Times* 29 December 1993, p. A11.
2. Stephen Donaldson, "Sex Among American Male Prisoners and its Implications for Concepts of Sexual Orientation: A Million Jockers, Punks, and Queens," Lecture delivered at Columbia University on 4 February 1993.
3. Helen Eigenberg, "Male Rape: An Empirical Examination of Correctional Officer's Attitudes Toward Rape in Prison," *Dissertation Abstracts International* 50.11 (1990), p. 50.
4. Ibid, p. 51.
5. Curtis Krueger, "The Color of Red," *St. Petersburg Times* 15 December 1996, p. 1F.
6. David Hunter, "Sexual Abuse of Military Recruits Should Not Be Tolerated," *Knoxville News-Sentinel* 3 December 1996, p. A11.
7. Ibid.
8. *20/20* (ABC) 6 April 1995; quoted in Deborah Mendez, "Air Force Academy Alters Simulated Rape Training," *Austin-American Statesman* 8 April 1995, p. A4.
9. Jennifer Bloom, "Brockton Officials May Seek Charges in Hazing," *The Boston Globe* 6 April 1990, sec. Metro, p. 22.
10. William Plummer and Jerry Johnston, "Fit to Be Tied: The Hazing Humiliation of a High School Athlete Has a Utah Town in a Snit," *Time* 13 December 1993, p. 52.
11. Russell Blinch, "Canadian Hockey in Shock over Sexual Assaults by Coach," Reuters Newswire 6 January 1997.
12. Peggy Reeves Sanday, *Fraternity Gang Rape: Sex, Brotherhood, and Privilege on Campus* (New York: New York University Press, 1990), p. 171.

13. Rus Ervin Funk, *Stopping Rape: A Challenge for Men* (Philadelphia: New Society Publishers, 1994), p. 17.

CHAPTER 4

1. Paul Cameron, *The Gay 90's* (Franklin, TN: Adroit Press, 1991), p. 50.
2. Ibid., p. 51.
3. Groth, p. 124.
4. Groth, p. 124.
5. David F. Duncan, "Prevalence of Sexual Assault Victimization among Heterosexual and Gay/Lesbian University Students," *Psychological Reports* 66 (1990), p. 66.
6. Ford C. I. Hickson *et al.*, "Gay Men as Victims of Nonconsensual Sex," *Archives of Sexual Behavior* 23.3 (1994), pp. 281–294.
7. Caroline Waterman *et al.*, "Sexual Coercion in Gay Male Relationships: Predictors and Implications for Support Services," *Journal of Sex Research* 26.1 (1989), p. 118.
8. David Island and Patrick Letellier, *Men Who Beat the Men Who Love Them* (Binghamton, NY: Harrington Park Press, 1991).
9. Scott Powers, "Study Finds Gay Domestic Assault Common," *Columbus Dispatch* 24 October 1996, p. 5C.
10. Mike Royko, "500,000 Gay Men Don't Have to Take Abuse From Partner," *Chicago Tribune* 10 December 1996, p. 3.
11. Ibid.
12. *Charlie Rose*, WNET Educational Broadcasting Company, 30 January 1995.
13. Ibid.
14. Camille Paglia, *Vamps and Tramps: New Essays* (New York: Vintage Books, 1994), p. 33.
15. Ibid., p. 304.
16. William Gordon, "Male Rape: Tragedy, Fantasy, or Badge of Honor?" *Christopher Street* August 1992, p. 9.
17. Ibid.
18. Ibid.
19. Hickson, p. 284.
20. Gail Diane Cox, "A 'Good Soldier' Stands Accused of Assault," *National Law Journal* 26 June 1995, p. A12.
21. Gillian Mezey and Michael King, "The Effects of Sexual Assault on Men: A Survey of 22 Victims," *Psychological Medicine* 19 (1989), p. 208.
22. Joseph Harry, "Conceptualizing Anti-Gay Violence," in Gregory Herek and Kevin Berrill, eds. *Hate Crimes: Confronting Violence*

Against Lesbians and Gay Men (Newbury Park, CA: Sage Publications, 1992), p. 115.

23. Joe Armstrong, "Exploding the Myths About Male Rape," *The Irish Times* 14 October 1996, sec. Well and Good, p. 6.

24. "In Korea, Male to Female Transsexuals Cannot Be Raped . . . Or So Government Says," Seoul, South Korea: Reuters Newswire, 15 June 1996.

25. Ivor Jones, "Cultural and Historical Aspects of Male Sexual Assault," in Gillian Mezey and Michael King, eds., *Male Victims of Sexual Assault* (Oxford: Oxford University Press, 1992), p. 104.

26. Ramon A. Gutierrez, "Must We Deracinate Indians to Find Gay Roots?" *OUT/LOOK* Winter 1989, p. 62.

27. Richard C. Trexler, *Sex and Conquest: Gendered Violence, Political Order, and the European Conquest of the Americas* (Ithaca, NY: Cornell University Press, 1995), p. 6.

28. Ibid., p. 7.

29. Scott Lively, "Gays Weren't Nazi 'Victims,'" *Capital Times* 18 April 1996, p. 15A.

CHAPTER 6

1. *United Press International*, Dateline: Buffalo, NY, 10 January 1985.

2. Abigail Van Buren, "Plea For Help For Male Victims of Rape," *Chicago Tribune* 4 March 1996, p. C4.

3. Anne Minard, "Rape Jury Finds Man Not Guilty," *Morning Star* 27 July 1996, p. 2B.

4. Andrew Alderson, "Speaking Out on the Last Taboo," *Sunday Times*, 6 September 1992, Feature.

5. Scott Sonner, "Gay Leader: 'Rapes Are Bias-Motivated' Violence," United Press International 22 August 1985.

6. Greg Louganis, *Breaking the Surface* (New York: Penguin, 1995), p. 139.

7. Ed Bark, "When a Kiss is No Longer Just a Kiss: Greg Louganis Film Shows Violence but No Tenderness," *The Dallas Morning News* 19 January 1997, p. 41A.

8. Ibid.

9. June Bundy Csida and Joseph Csida, "Buggered at High Noon," *Rape: How to Avoid It and What to Do about It If You Can't* (Chatsworth, CA: Books for Better Living, 1974), pp. 39, 40.

10. James Dickey, *Deliverance* (Boston: Houghton Mifflin Company, 1970), p. 128.

11. Burt Reynolds, "Reynolds Recalls Delivering His Role of a Lifetime," *Austin American Statesman* 18 December 1994, p. G1.

12. Ned Beatty, "Suppose Men Feared Rape," *The New York Times* 16 May 1989, p. A23.
13. Andrea Simakis, "Little Piggies: The Week Q-FM 96 Thought Rape Was Funny," *Columbus Guardian* 15 August 1996, p. 7.
14. Ward W. Triplett, " 'Celtic Pride' misses a shot for a winning sports movie; Audience reaction declares it a 'kind of dumb, OK' comedy," *The Kansas City Star* 19 April 1996, sec: Preview, p. 5.
15. "A Reservoir of Talent or Just Pulp Fiction?" *Evening Standard* 28 December 1995, pp. 32–33.

CHAPTER 8

1. Jordan B. Glaser *et al.*, "Epidemiology of Sexually Transmitted Diseases in Rape Victims," *Review of Infectious Diseases* 2.2 (1989), pp. 246–254.
2. Dave Nimmons and Ilan Meyer, *Research Summary: Oral Sex and HIV Risk Among Gay Men* (New York, Gay Men's Health Crisis, 1995).
3. Kaufman.
4. Burgess.
5. Jenny *et al.*, "Sexually Transmitted Diseases in Victims of Rape," *New England Journal of Medicine* 322.11 (1990), pp. 713–716.
6. Robert Naylor, "Murder Trial Judge's OK of AIDS Defense Stirs Outcry, Debate," *Memphis Commercial Appeal* 10 February 1995, p. 2B.
7. Ibid.
8. Ibid.
9. Jenny Labalme, "Teen Guilty in Shooting Death of Gay Man," *The Indianapolis News*, 6 October 1995, p. A14.
10. Ross Ramsey, "Judge Refuses to Grant New Trial for Condom Rapist," *Houston Chronicle* 2 July 1993, sec. A, p. 26.
11. Cindy Loose, "Condom Doesn't Mean Consent, Jury Says," *Washington Post* 14 July 1993, sec. C, p. 3.
12. Charles Silverstein and Felice Picano, *The New Joy of Gay Sex* (New York: Harper Collins, 1992), p. 153.
13. Charles Silverstein and Edmund White, *The Joy of Gay Sex* (New York: Harper Collins, 1977), pp. 179–180.
14. Ibid., p. 180.
15. "HIV Acts as Trigger: Domestic Violence Prevalent Among Gay and Bisexual Men," *AIDS Alert* 8.10 (1993), p. 151.
16. Ibid.
17. Richard Hillman *et al.*, "Adult Male Victims of Sexual Assault: An Underdiagnosed Condition," *International Journal of STD and AIDS* 2 (1991), p. 24.

18. David Hinckley, "Stations March to the Beat of West Indian Parade," *New York Daily News* 2 September 1995, p. 51.
19. Ibid.
20. Hickson, p. 284.
21. Gayle Young, "Science Today: Violence Against Gays Linked to AIDS," United Press International 25 March 1987.
22. Terry A. Maroney, "Recognizing and Responding to HIV-Related Violence," *Violence Update* May (1994), pp. 5–6.
23. Ibid., p. 5.
24. *Anti-Gay/Lesbian Violence, Victimization, and Defamation in 1991*, National Gay and Lesbian Task Force Policy Institute, p. 8.
25. R. M. Cunningham *et al.*, "The Association of Physical and Sexual Abuse With HIV Risk Behaviors in Adolescence and Young Adulthood: Implications for Public Health," *Child Abuse and Neglect* 18.3 (18 March 1994), pp. 233–245.
26. Stephen Donaldson, "Can We Put an End to Inmate Rape?" *USA Today* May 1995, Feature.

CHAPTER 9

1. Robert R. Hazelwood and Ann Wolbert Burgess, eds., *Practical Aspects of Rape Investigation: A Multidisciplinary Approach* (Boca Raton, FL: CRC Press, 1995), p. xvi.
2. Gordon W. Josephson, "The Male Rape Victim: Evaluation and Treatment," *Journal of the American College of Emergency Physicians* 8, 1979, p. 13.
3. Arthur Schiff, "Examination and Treatment of the Male Rape Victim," *Southern Medical Journal* 73.11 (1980), p. 1500.
4. Ibid.
5. Ibid.
6. Ibid.
7. Calderwood, p. 55.
8. *Strategies for the Treatment and Prevention of Sexual Assault* (Chicago: American Medical Association, 1995).
9. Ellen Yan and Helen Rodriguez, "Patient Attacked; man, 34, Arrested," *Newsday* Nassau and Suffolk edition 10 May 1992, p. 34.

CHAPTER 11

1. Jim Struve, "Dancing With the Patriarchy: The Politics of Sexual Abuse," in Mic Hunter, ed., *The Sexually Abused Male* Vol. 1 (Lexington, MA: Lexington Books/D.C. Heath and Company, 1990), p. 9.

2. Scott Long and Julie Mertus, "What Stonewall Means For the Iron Curtain," *San Francisco Chronicle* 27 June 1994, p. A19.
3. Lucy Jones, "Gay Life in Moscow," *Moscow News* 9 July 1993, sec. Culture, p. 28.
4. Ibid.
5. "The Sex Police Are on the Case," *St. Louis Dispatch* 30 January 1990, p. B2.
6. Ellen Whitford, "Sex Crimes Bill Redefining Rape Is in for a Fight," *Atlanta Constitution* 11 February 1993, p. F1.
7. Sandra McIntosh, "Bill to Redefine Rape Law in Georgia Faces Opposition," *Atlanta Journal and Constitution* 10 October 1993, p. F3.
8. "Toughening the Rape Law," *Atlanta Constitution* 17 February 1993, p. A10
9. *Federal Supplement: Cases Argued and Determined in the United States District Courts, United States Customs Courts, and Rulings of the Judicial Panel on Multidistrict Legislation 363* (St. Paul, MN: West Publishing Company, 1974), p. 606.
10. Ibid., p. 608
11. Ibid.
12. *Southern Reporter, Second Series: Cases Argued and Determined in the Courts of Alabama, Florida, Louisiana, and Mississippi 302* (St. Paul, MN: West Publishing Company, 1975), p. 402.
13. *Southern Reporter, Second Series: Cases Argued and Determined in the Courts of Alabama, Florida, Louisiana, and Mississippi 278* (St. Paul, MN: West Publishing Company, 1973), p. 320.
14. Ibid., p. 322.
15. Steven Lee Myers, "Man's Report of Rape at Barnard is Disputed by Police Investigators," *The New York Times* 24 November 1991, sec. 1, p. 40.
16. John Stevenson, "Defendant Admits Murder, Saying He Was Fending Off Rape Attempt," *Herald-Sun* 24 August 1995, p. C1.
17. "Grafton Man Convicted of Murder," United Press International 8 December 1989.
18. Ron French, "Hate, Not Trash TV, on Trial in Amedure Killing, Gays Say," *The Detroit News* 6 October 1996, p. A1.
19. Gary David Comstock, "Dismantling the Homosexual Panic Defense," *Law and Sexuality* 2 (1992), p. 86.
20. Ibid.
21. Art Pine, "ACLU Arm Slams Navy's Policy on Gays," *Los Angeles Times* 20 August 1994, p. A28.
22. Associated Press 9 July 1993.
23. Ibid.
24. Richie J. McMullen, *Male Rape: Breaking the Silence on the Last Taboo* (London: The Gay Men's Press, 1990), p. 114.

CHAPTER 12

1. John Stoltenberg is an activist and writer. He has been involved in the issues for over 20 years; his books are *Refusing to Be a Man: Essays on Sex and Justice* (1992) and *The End of Manhood* (1994).
2. This is not to say that I am not a threat to perpetrate racism, sexism, homophobia, classism, or any form of violence. It is a continuing struggle. But this struggle is as liberating as the struggle for those to be free of being victimized by these "isms" and the violence they lead to.
3. "White" is a socially constructed term that has no basis in reality. It was first coined during the writing of the U.S. Constitution to distinguish those who could vote from those who could not—European, owning class, Christian, heterosexual, and male. The category has broadened over the years but has always been used to maintain white supremacy.

CHAPTER 13

1. Donaldson, 1995.
2. Senter, p. 21.
3. Fred Pelka, "Raped: A Male Survivor Breaks the Silence," *On the Issues: A Progressive Woman's Quarterly* Spring 1992, p. 40.
4. Ibid.
5. Elisabeth Bumiller, "Gloria Steinem, the Everyday Rebel; Two Decades of Feminism, And the Fire Burns as Bright," *The Washington Post* 12 October 1983, sec. Style, p. B1.
6. K. Bradley Hudson, "Male Rape," *San Francisco Sentinel* 22 September 1993, p. 2.
7. Shere Hite, *Hite Report on Male Sexuality* (New York: Alfred A. Knopf, 1981), p. 735.
8. Ibid.
9. Ibid, p. 736.

CHAPTER 14

1. Rierdan.

APPENDIX ONE

MALE RAPE RESOURCES

Bay Area Women Against Rape/Men Overcoming Sexual Assault
(510) 845-7273—Crisis Line
(510) 465-3890—Business Line

Men Assisting Leading & Educating, Inc. (M.A.L.E.)
P.O. Box 380181
Denver, CO 80238-1181
(800) 949-6253
(303) 320-4365

A national nonprofit organization dedicated to healing male survivors of sexual abuse.

Men's Resource Center
2325 East Burnside St.
Portland, OR 97214
(503) 235-3433

Men Stopping Rape
306 North Brooks St.
Madison, WI 53715
(608) 257-4444

Men Stopping Rape, Inc. has several educational tools for sale, including brochures, licensing for brochures, rape myth posters, a video, and a workshop training reader.

Mothers Against Prison Rape
Box 152
Cary, IL 60013
(815) 931-0881

National Coalition Against Sexual Assault (NCASA)
912 N. 2nd St.
Harrisburg, PA 17102
(717) 232-7460

National Crime Victims Research & Treatment Center
Medical University of South Carolina
171 Ashley Ave.
Charleston, SC 29425
(803) 792-2945

National Domestic Violence/Abuse Hotline
1-800-799-SAFE
1-800-799-7233
1-800-787-3224 (TDD)

National Gay and Lesbian Task Force
1734 14th St., NW
Washington, DC 20009
(202) 332-6483

National HIV/AIDS Hotline
Centers for Disease Control and Prevention
(800) 342-AIDS
(800) 344-SIDA (Spanish)
(800) 243-7889 (TDD)

National Organization on Male Sexual Victimization
P.O. Box 40055
St. Paul, MN 55114

This organization holds national conferences, primarily geared toward psychotherapists. The majority of their work focuses on childhood sexual abuse, but some adult male rape content is included.

National Organization of Victim Assistance (NOVA)
1757 Park Rd., NW
Washington, DC 20010
(800) 879-6682
(202) 232 6682

NOVA is a small, private, nonprofit organization dedicated to improving services to victims and survivors of violent crime and disaster. They offer 24-hour crisis counseling to crime victims and refer callers to supportive services throughout the United States. Technical assistance and training are available by contacting the Training Coordinator. NOVA sponsors conferences and supports legislation to help crime victims and witnesses of crimes and serves as a clearinghouse of information about victim assistance programs and laws in every state.

National Resource Center Against Domestic Violence
(800) 537-2238

National Victim Center
211 Wilson Blvd., Suite 300
Arlington, VA 22201-3001
(800) FYI-CALL
(703) 276-2880

The National Victim Center provides training and technical assistance to victim service providers and criminal justice professionals, and promotes the rights of crime victims through education, information dissemination, and public policy.

Rape, Abuse & Incest National Network (RAIN)
252 10 St., NE
Washington, DC 20002
(202) 544-1034
(800) 656-HOPE (national referral to local service)

Safer Society Foundation, Inc.
P.O. Box 340-I
Brandon, VT 05733-0340
(802) 247-3132

The Safer Society Foundation, Inc., a nonprofit agency, is a national research, advocacy, and referral center on the prevention and treatment of sexual abuse. They provide a variety of services related to the prevention and treatment of sexual abuse, including a computerized resource center, sex offender treatment referrals, a comprehensive resource library, training and consultation, and research assistance. The Safer Society Press publishes a manual and two audiotapes of practical advice for prisoners and staff on avoidance and survival of prison rape.

Stop Prisoner Rape, Inc.
333 North Avenue #4
Los Angeles, CA 90042
(213) 257-6164

Stop Prisoner Rape defines itself as "a small but growing national non-profit organization dedicated to combatting the rape of prisoners and providing such assistance as we can to survivors of jailhouse rape. Soon we hope to start organizing state chapters." Stop Prisoner Rape provides education, information, advocacy, and training.

Survivors
London, England
044-171-0181-986-2721

This London-based organization is dedicated to providing services specifically for male rape survivors, including a hotline, community workshops, media advocacy, and support groups.

Survivors Network of those Abused by Priests
P.O. Box 438679
Chicago, IL 60643-8679
(312) 483-1059

SNAP is a U.S./Canadian self-help organization of men and women who were sexually abused by spiritual elders (e.g., Catholic priests, brothers, nuns, ministers, teachers). Members find healing and empowerment by joining with other survivors. They have numerous local chapters and publish a quarterly newsletter.

The New York City Gay & Lesbian Anti-Violence Project
647 Hudson St.
New York, NY 10014
24-hour hotline: (212) 807-0197
Office: (212) 807-6761
Fax: (212) 807-1044

The NYC AVP, a crime victim assistance agency founded in 1980, is the city's primary resource for lesbian and gay survivors of sexual assault, domestic violence, bias assault, HIV/AIDS-related violence, and other forms of criminal victimization. AVP is the only program in New York City that specifically serves gay men who are survivors of sexual assault. It provides a range of services to assist sexual assault survivors. All services are free and confidential. These include: a 24-hour crisis intervention hotline; short-term in-person counseling; support groups; police accompaniment and advocacy; hospital accompaniment; court accompaniment, monitoring, and advocacy; advocacy with social service agencies; assistance in filing for compensation for medical expenses, loss of work, and the like; information and referrals. This organization publishes an excellent brochure on male rape.

Vancouver Society for Male Survivors of Sexual Abuse
311-1008 Homer St.
Vancouver, BC V6B 2X1
(604) 682-6482

The Vancouver Society for Male Survivors of Sexual Abuse is a nonprofit society, established to provide therapeutic services for males who have been sexually abused at some time in their lives. They provide treatment and support services, acquire and develop education materials, gather statistics, and provide consultation.

APPENDIX TWO

MALE RAPE BIBLIOGRAPHY

*T*his select bibliography primarily includes material on same-sex rape of adult males in noninstitutional environments. Some of these works are outdated or insensitive, and this compilation is intended for research purposes only. It should not be considered a general reading list as a healing tool for survivors.

BOOKS AND ANTHOLOGIZED WORKS

Brownmiller, Susan. *Against Our Will: Men, Women, and Rape*. New York: Simon & Schuster, 1975.

Csida, June Bundy, and Joseph Csida. *Rape: How to Avoid It and What to Do About It If You Can't*. Chatsworth, CA: Books for Better Living, 1974.

Dickey, James. *Deliverance*. Boston: Houghton Mifflin Company, 1970.

Fenwick, R. D. *The Advocate Guide to Gay Health*. New York: Dutton, 1978, pp. 72–75.

Funk, Rus Ervin. *Stopping Rape*. Philadelphia: New Society Publishers, 1994.

Garnets, Linda, et al. "Violence and Victimization of Lesbians and Gay Men: Mental Health Consequences." *Psychological Perspectives on Lesbian and Gay Male Experiences*. Eds. Linda Garnets and Douglas Kimmel. New York: Columbia University Press, 1993: 579–597.

Groth, Nicholas. *Men Who Rape*. New York: Plenum Press, 1979.

Harry, Joseph. "Conceptualizing Anti-Gay Violence." *Hate Crimes: Confronting Violence Against Lesbians and Gay Men*. Eds. Gregory Herek and Kevin Berrill. Newbury Park, CA: Sage Publications, 1992.

Hunter, Mic, ed. *The Sexually Abused Male, Volume 1: Impact, Prevalence, and Treatment*. Lexington, MA: Lexington Books/D.C. Heath and Company, 1990.

———, ed. *The Sexually Abused Male, Volume 2: Application of Treatment Strategies*. Lexington, MA: Lexington Books/D.C. Heath and Company, 1990.

Isely, Paul J. "Adult Male Sexual Assault in the Community: A Literature Review and Group Treatment Model." *Rape and Sexual Assault III—A Research Handbook*. Ed. Ann Wolbert Burgess. New York: Garland Publishing, 1991: 161–178.

Island, David, and Patrick Letellier. *Men Who Beat the Men Who Love Them: Battered Gay Men and Domestic Violence*. Binghamton, NY: Harrington Park Press, 1991.

Kokopeli, Bruce, and George Lakey. "More Power Than We Want: Masculine Sexuality and Violence." *Men and Intimacy*. Ed. Franklin Abbott. Freedom, CA: Crossing Press, 1990: 8–15.

Louganis, Greg. *Breaking the Surface*. New York: Penguin, 1995.

McMullen, Richie J. *Male Rape: Breaking the Silence on the Last Taboo*. London: The Gay Men's Press, 1990.

Mezey, Gillian, and Michael King, eds. *Male Victims of Sexual Assault*. Oxford: Oxford University Press, 1992.

Russell, Diana E. H. *Sexual Exploitation: Rape, Child Sexual Abuse, and Workplace Harassment*. Newbury Park, CA: Sage, 1984, pp. 67–78.

Scacco, Anthony M., ed. *Male Rape: A Casebook of Sexual Aggressions*. New York: AMS, 1982.

Silverstein, Charles, and Felice Picano. "Rape." *The New Joy of Gay Sex*. New York: Harper Collins, 1992: 153–154.

——— and Edmund White. "Rape." *The Joy of Gay Sex*. New York: Crown, 1978: 179–180.

Trexler, Richard C. *Sex and Conquest: Gendered Violence, Political Order, and the European Conquest of the Americas*. Ithaca, NY: Cornell University Press, 1995.

JOURNAL ARTICLES

Adams, Edward A. "Rape Trauma Syndrome is Extended to Men." *New York Law Journal* 3 January (1996): 1.

Anderson, Craig L. "Males as Sexual Assault Victims: Multiple Levels of Trauma." *Journal of Homosexuality* 7 (1982): 145–175.

Berger, Ronald J., *et al.* "The Dimensions of Rape Reform Legislation." *Law and Society Review* 22.2 (1988): 329–357.

Bienen, Leigh. "Rape III—National Developments in Rape Reform Legislation." *Women's Rights Law Reporter* 6.3 (1980): 170–213.

Bush, Robert A., Jr., *et al.* "Trauma and Other Noninfectious Problems in Homosexual Men." *Medical Clinics of North America* 70.3 (1986): 549–566.

Calderwood, Deryck. "The Male Rape Victim." *Medical Aspects of Human Sexuality* 7 (1987): 53–55.

Casey, C. "Dealing With Male Rape." *Police Review* 29 January (1993): 17.

Chen, Y. N., *et al.* "Traumatic Rectal Hematoma Following Anal Rape." *Annals of Emergency Medicine* 15 (1986): 850–852.

Cohen-Addad, Gerard. "Rape and Homosexuality." *Medicine and Law* 9 (1990): 751–754.

Comstock, Gary David. "Dismantling the Homosexual Panic Defense." *Law and Sexuality* 2 (1992): 81–102.

Cox, Gail Diane. "A 'Good Soldier' Stands Accused of Assault." *National Law Journal* 26 June (1995): A12.

Coxon, A. P., *et al.* "Eliciting Sensitive Sexual Information: The Case of Gay Men." *Sociology Review* 41 (1992): 537–555.

Crass, Richard A., *et al.* "Colorectal Bodies and Perforation." *American Journal of Surgery* 142 (1981): 85–88.

Doan, Lynnette A., and Richard C. Levy. "Male Sexual Assault." *Journal of Emergency Medicine* 1 (1983): 45–49.

Donnelly, Denise A., and Stacy Kenyon. "Honey, We Don't Do Men: Gender Stereotypes and the Provision of Services to Sexually Assaulted Males," *Journal of Interpersonal Violence* 11.3 (1996): 441–448.

Duncan, David F. "Prevalence of Sexual Assault Victimization Among Heterosexual and Gay/Lesbian University Students." *Psychological Reports* 66 (1990): 65–66.

Forman, Bruce D. "Reported Male Rape." *Victimology: An International Journal* 7 (1982): 235–236.

Frazier, Patricia A. "A Comparative Study of Male and Female Rape Victims Seen at a Hospital Based Rape Crisis Program." *Journal of Interpersonal Violence* 8.1 (1993): 65–76.

Geist, Richard F. "Sexually Related Trauma." *Emergency Medicine Clinics of North America* 6.3 (1988): 439–466.

Glaser, Jordan B., *et al.* "Epidemiology of Sexually Transmitted Diseases in Rape Victims." *Reviews of Infectious Diseases* 2.2 (1989): 246–254.

Goyer, Peter F., and Henry C. Eddleman. "Same-Sex Rape of Nonincarcerated Men." *American Journal of Psychiatry* 141.4 (1984): 576–579.

Groth, Nicholas A., and Ann Wolbert Burgess. "Male Rape: Offenders and Victims." *American Journal of Psychiatry* 137 (1980): 806–810.

Gutierrez, Ramon A. "Must We Deracinate Indians to Find Gay Roots?" *OUT/LOOK*, Winter (1989): 62.

Hickson, Ford C. I., *et al.* "Gay Men as Victims of Nonconsensual Sex." *Archives of Sexual Behavior* 23.3 (1994): 281–294.

Hillman, Richard, *et al.* "Adult Male Victims of Sexual Assault: An Underdiagnosed Condition." *International Journal of STD and AIDS* 2 (1991): 22–24.

———, *et al.* "Rape and Subsequent Seroconversion to HIV." *British Medical Journal* 299 (1989): 1100.

———, *et al.* "Sexual Assault of Men: A Series." *Genitourinary Medicine* 66 (1990): 247–250.

"HIV Acts as Trigger: Domestic Violence Prevalent Among Gay and Bisexual Men." *AIDS Alert* 8.10 (1993): 151.

Huckle, P. L. "Male Rape Victims Referred to a Forensic Psychiatric Service." *Medicine, Science, and the Law* 35.3 (1995): 187–192.

Josephson, Gordon W. "The Male Rape Victim: Evaluation and Treatment." *Journal of the American College of Emergency Physicians* 8 (1979): 13–15.

Kaszniak, Alfred W., *et al.* "Amnesia as a Consequence of Male Rape: A Case Report." *Journal of Abnormal Psychology* 97.1 (1988): 100–104.

Kaufman, Arthur, *et al.* "Male Rape Victims: Noninstitutionalized Assault." *American Journal of Psychiatry* 137.2 (1980): 221–223.

King, Michael B. "Male Rape: Victims Need Sensitive Management." *British Medical Journal* 201 (1990): 1345–1346.

———. "Sexual Assaults on Men: Assessment and Management." *British Journal of Hospital Medicine* 53.6 (1995): 245–246.

Kobernick, M. E., *et al.* "Emergency Department Management of the Sexual Assault Victim." *Journal of Emergency Medicine* 2.3 (1985): 205–214.

Lacey, H. B., and R. Roberts. "Sexual Assault on Men." *International Journal of STD and AIDS* 2 (1991): 258–260.

Laurent, Claire. "Male Rape." *Nursing Times* 89.6 (1993): 18–19.

Lipscomb, Gary, *et al.* "Male Victims of Sexual Assault." *Journal of the American Medical Association* 267.22 (1992): 3064–3066.

McConaghy, N., and Zamir, R. "Heterosexual and Homosexual Coercion,

Sexual Orientation, and Sexual Roles in Medical Students." *Archives of Sexual Behavior* 24.5 (1995): 489–502.

Maletsky, Barry M. "Effects on Victim of Homosexual Rape." *Medical Aspects of Human Sexuality* 19.1 (1985): 203.

Maroney, Terry A. "Recognizing and Responding to HIV-Related Violence." *Violence Update* (1994): 5–6.

Medical Center for Human Rights. "Characteristics of Sexual Abuse of Men During War in the Republic of Croatia and Bosnia and Herzogovina." Zagreb, Croatia: Medical Center for Human Rights, 1995.

Mezey, Gillian, and Michael King. "Male Victims of Sexual Assault." *Medicine, Science, and the Law* 27.2 (1987): 122–124.

———. "The Effects of Sexual Assault on Men: A Survey of 22 Victims." *Psychological Medicine* 19 (1989): 205–209.

Myers, Michael. "Men Sexually Assaulted as Adults and Sexually Abused as Boys." *Archives of Sexual Behavior* 18.3 (1989): 203–215.

Redmund, D. E., *et al.* "Spontaneous Ejaculation Associated With Anxiety; Psychophysiological Considerations." *American Journal of Psychiatry* 140.9 (1983): 1163–1166.

Riggs, Larry. "Up Against the Looking Glass: Heterosexual Rape as Homosexual Epiphany in *The Accused*." *Literature/Film Quarterly* 17.4 (1989): 214–223.

Rogers, Paul. "Male Rape: The Impact of a Legal Definition on the Clinical Area." *Medicine, Science and the Law* 35.4 (1995): 303–306.

Scarce, Michael. "The Reality of Male Rape." *National Coalition Against Sexual Assault Journal* Winter (1993): 7–8.

———. "Same-Sex Rape of Male College Students." *Journal of American College Health* 45.4 (1997): 171–173.

———. "Harbinger of Plague: A Bad Case of Gay Bowel Syndrome." *Journal of Homosexuality* 34.2 (1997): 1–35.

Schiff, Arthur. "Examination and Treatment of the Male Rape Victim." *Southern Medical Journal* 73.11 (1980): 1498–1502.

Schneider, L. J. "Effects of Victim Gender and Physical vs. Psychological Trauma/Injury on Observers' Perceptions of Sexual Assault and its Aftereffects." *Sex Roles: A Journal of Research* 30.12 (1994): 793–808.

Sorenson, Susan, *et al.*, "The Prevalence of Adult Sexual Assault: The Los Angeles Epidemiologic Catchment Area Project." *American Journal of Epidemiology* 126.6 (1987): 1154–1164.

Stoltenberg, John. "A Coupla Things I've Been Meaning to Say about Really Confronting Male Power." *Empathy: An Interdisciplinary Journal for Persons Working to End Oppression on the Basis of Sexual Identities* 2.3 (1992/1993): 29–32.

Strategies for the Treatment and Prevention of Sexual Assault. Chicago: American Medical Association, 1995.

Struckman-Johnson, Cindy. "Opening the Debate on a Taboo Topic: Male Rape." *Journal of Sex Research* 30.2 (1993): 181–183.

————, and David Struckman-Johnson. "Acceptance of Male Rape Myths Among College Men and Women." *Sex Roles* 27.3–4 (1992): 85–100.

Van Tienhoven, H. "Sexual Torture of Male Victims." *Torture* 3 (1993): 7.

Waterman, Caroline, Lori J. Dawson, and Michael J. Bologna. "Sexual Coercion in Gay Male Relationships: Predictors and Implications for Support Services." *Journal of Sex Research* 26.1 (1989): 118–124.

Whatley, Mark A., and Ronald E. Riggio. "Gender Differences in Attributions of Blame for Male Rape Victims." *Journal of Interpersonal Violence* 8.4 (1993): 502–511.

White, James, and Jonnie L. Wesley. "Male Rape Survivors: Guidelines for Crisis Counselors." *Crime Victims Digest* April (1987): 3–5.

MAGAZINE ARTICLES

"1576 Ad Warns of Male Rape." *Creative Review* 1 March 1996: 18.

Gordon, William. "Male Rape: Tragedy, Fantasy, or Badge of Honor?" *Christopher Street* August 1992: 9–10.

Krueger, Fred. "Violated." *Boston Magazine* May 1985: 138–142.

Malmsten, Erik. "Listening to Men Who Are Survivors of Incest and Sexual Assault." *Changing Men* Winter/Spring 1993: 38–45.

Pelka, Fred. "Raped: A Male Survivor Breaks His Silence." *On The Issues: A Progressive Woman's Quarterly* Spring 1992: 8+.

Rochman, Sue. "Silent Victims: Bringing Male Rape Out of the Closet." *Advocate* 30 July 1991: 38–43.

Senter, Jim. "Male Rape: The Hidden Crime." *Changing Men* Spring/Summer 1988: 20–21.

Shuger, Scott. "American Inquisition: The Military vs. Itself; Unfair Enforcement of the US Military Ban on Homosexuals." *The New Republic* 7 December 1992: 23.

NEWSPAPER ARTICLES

"Academics Appeal for Research into Male Rape." *The Herald* (Glasgow) 3 July 1996: 7.

Armstrong, Joe. "Exploding the Myths about Male Rape." *The Irish Times* 14 October 1996 sec. Well and Good: 6.

Beatty, Ned. "Suppose Men Feared Rape." *The New York Times* 16 May 1989: A23.

Braiden, Olive. Letter. "Male Victims of Rape." *The Irish Times* 13 February 1995: 15.

Bruckheim, Allan. "Men Who Are Raped Can Suffer, Too." *Chicago Tribune* 19 October 1987, sec. Tempo: 2.

Collins, Glenn. "Relationships: Counseling Male Rape Victims." *The New York Times* 18 January 1982: A15.

Cooper, Glenda. "Male Rapists Strike in the Home." *The Independent* 3 July 1996: 3.

Donaldson, Stephen. Letter. "Rape Must Be Viewed as Both a Men's and Women's Issue; A Vicious Cycle." *The New York Times* 24 August 1993: A14.

Edelhart, Courtney. "Male Rape Survivors Also Deal With Myths." *Chicago Tribune* 1 June 1995, sec. Chicagoland: 4.

Garfield, Simon. "Inside Story: When Man Rapes Man." *The Independent* 6 December 1992: 17.

Gorenstein, Nathan. "Rape of Men Often Stays Hidden Crime." *The Houston Chronicle* 13 October 1991, sec. Lifestyle: 3.

Hudson, K. Bradley. "Male Rape." *San Francisco Sentinel* 23 September 1993: 1+.

Jones, Syl. "Trauma of Male Rape Can Echo Through a Life and Ruin Others." *Star Tribune* 11 October 1996: 27A.

Leibovich, Mark. "Help for Forgotten Victims." *Chicago Tribune* 29 August 1995: 7.

———. "Male Sexual Assault Victims Get a New Advocate Soon." *The Times Union* (Albany, NY) 4 September 1995: C3.

Matthews, Cara. "Making a Bit of Difference; Volunteers Dispel Myths, Help Rape Survivors." *Newsday* 25 January 1995: B7.

Medick, Erin Marie. "Males Also Victims of Rape." *The Columbus Dispatch* 13 October 1996: 2A.

Mills, Heather. "Male Rape 'Hidden by Crime Statistics'; Shame and Police Inactivity Could be Conspiring to Understate Attacks." *The Independent* 29 May 1995, sec. Home: 9.

Pokin, Steve. "Tracking Incidence of Male Rape Difficult." *The Press-Enterprise* (Riverside, CA) 10 September 1995, sec. Living: D3.

Powell, Christol. "Male Rape Victims: Help for an Underreported Abuse." *The Washington Post* 12 April 1990, sec. Style: C5.

Powers, Mary. "Men Less Likely to Report Sex Assaults." *The Commercial Appeal* (Memphis) 10 June 1992: B1.

Rierdan, Andi. "How Shame and Fear Take a Toll on Men Who Are Raped." *The New York Times* 4 July 1993, sec. 13CN: 1.

"Rise in Male Rape Victims; Sex Attacks on Men Are on the Increase." *Sunday Mirror* 25 February 1996: 14.

Smith, Michael. "Stigma of Male Rape Hinders Victims' Healing." *Tulsa World* 26 January 1997: A15.

Travis, Alan. "Male Rape Recognised in Law." *The Guardian* 12 July 1994: 1.

Van Buren, Abigail. Letter. "Plea for Help for Male Victims of Rape." *Chicago Tribune* 4 March 1996: C4.

APPENDIX THREE

LEGAL STATUTES IN THE UNITED STATES

*T*he following compilation of state legal statutes reflects the state of rape laws in 1995. They should not be used as a definitive legal guide, as some reform is likely to have already occurred, but they do serve to demonstrate the range of ways that sexual crimes are defined.

ALABAMA

Crime: rape
Gender: specific

Rape is defined as a crime committed against a female. As of 1995, Alabama had a sodomy law, which included same-sex anal rape. In Alabama, sodomy is defined as "deviate" sexual intercourse with another person by forcible compulsion. Both rape and sodomy in the first degree are Class A felonies.

ALASKA

Crime: sexual assault
Gender: neutral
Sexual assault is defined as sexual penetration with another person without the consent of that person.

ARIZONA

Crime: sexual assault
Gender: neutral
Sexual assault is committed by sexual contact or oral sexual contact without the consent of the person.

ARKANSAS

Crime: rape
Gender: neutral
As of 1995, Arkansas still had a sodomy law, defined as "deviate" sexual activity (penetration of the anus or mouth by a penis, other body part, or object). Rape is defined as sexual activity or deviate sexual intercourse with another person by forcible compulsion.

CALIFORNIA

Crime: rape
Gender: neutral
Rape is defined as an act of sexual intercourse without a person's consent. The statute's language of "her" was changed to "person" in 1979.

COLORADO

Crime: sexual assault
Gender: neutral
Sexual assault is defined as either "sexual intrusion" or "sexual penetration" without consent. Sexual intrusion is defined as penetration of the genital or anal opening by an object or any body part other than the mouth, tongue, or penis. Sexual penetration is defined as cunnilingus, fellatio, analingus, or anal intercourse.

CONNECTICUT

Crime: sexual assault
Gender: neutral
Sexual assault is defined as sexual intercourse by the use of force or threat of use of force, including anal penetration.

DELAWARE

Crime: unlawful sexual intercourse
Gender: neutral
Unlawful sexual intercourse is defined as sexual intercourse without consent, including anal penetration.

DISTRICT OF COLUMBIA

Crime: sexual abuse
Gender: neutral
Sexual abuse is defined as forcing a person to engage in a "sexual act," which includes anal penetration.

FLORIDA

Crime: sexual battery
Gender: neutral
    Sexual battery is defined as vaginal, anal, or oral penetration without consent, by a penis or object.

GEORGIA

Crime: rape
Gender: specific
    Rape is defined as carnal knowledge of a female forcibly and against her will. Carnal knowledge is defined as penetration of the female sex organ by the male sex organ. As of 1995, Georgia still had a dual offense of "sodomy; aggravated sodomy." Sodomy is defined as submission to any sexual act involving the sex organs of one person and the mouth or anus of the other. Adult male same-sex rape would be classified as aggravated sodomy, defined as sodomy with force and against the will of the other person.

HAWAII

Crime: rape
Gender: neutral
    Rape in Hawaii is defined as sexual intercourse with a person by forcible compulsion.

IDAHO

Crime: rape
Gender: specific
    Rape in Idaho is defined as forced sexual (vaginal) intercourse with a female. Penetration of the anus or mouth is classified as a "crime against nature."

ILLINOIS

Crime: criminal sexual assault
Gender: neutral
    Criminal sexual assault in Illinois is defined as sexual penetration of another person by the use of force or the threat of use of force.

INDIANA

Crime: rape
Gender: specific
    Rape is defined as forced sexual intercourse with "a member of the opposite sex." Same-sex male rape is classified as "criminal deviate conduct," which includes anal penetration of someone of the same sex.

IOWA

Crime: sexual abuse
Gender: neutral
    Sexual abuse includes forced anal and oral penetration.

KANSAS

Crime: rape
Gender: specific
    Rape is defined as forced sexual intercourse. Sexual intercourse in Kansas is defined as penetration of the female sex organ by a finger, the male sex organ, or object. Anal rape is classified as "aggravated criminal sodomy," distinct from consensual "criminal sodomy."

KENTUCKY

Crime: rape
Gender: neutral
    Rape is defined as sexual intercourse with another person without consent. Sexual intercourse includes anal penetration.

LOUISIANA

Crime: rape
Gender: neutral
    Rape is defined as the act of anal or vaginal sexual intercourse with a male or female person without their consent.

MAINE

Crime: rape
Gender: specific
    In Maine, rape involves the "penetration of the female sex organ by the male sex organ." Nonconsensual anal penetration is classified as "gross sexual misconduct."

MARYLAND

Crime: rape
Gender: specific
    Rape in Maryland involves sexual intercourse without consent. Sexual intercourse is defined as penetration of the female sex organ by the male sex organ. Anal rape would be classified as a "sexual offense."

MASSACHUSETTS

Crime: rape

Gender: neutral

Rape involves sexual intercourse or "unnatural sexual intercourse," which is anything other than penetration of the vagina by the penis.

MICHIGAN

Crime: criminal sexual conduct
Gender: neutral

Criminal sexual conduct involves sexual penetration, which includes anal penetration, without consent.

MINNESOTA

Crime: criminal sexual conduct
Gender: neutral

Criminal sexual conduct involves sexual penetration, which includes anal penetration, without consent.

MISSISSIPPI

Crime: sexual battery
Gender: neutral

Sexual battery involves sexual penetration with another person without "her or his" consent.

MISSOURI

Crime: rape
Gender: specific

Rape in Missouri involves a man committing forced sexual intercourse, where sexual intercourse is defined as penetration of the female sex organ by the male sex organ. Anal rape would constitute "deviate sexual intercourse."

MONTANA

Crime: sexual intercourse without consent
Gender: neutral

Sexual intercourse without consent in Montana involves "sexual intercourse," which is defined as penetration of the vulva, anus, or mouth of one person by the penis, other body part, or object.

NEBRASKA

Crime: sexual assault
Gender: neutral

Sexual assault in Nebraska involves sexual penetration without consent. "Sexual penetration" includes cunnilingus, fellatio, and anal intercourse.

NEVADA

Crime: sexual assault
Gender: neutral

Sexual assault involves sexual penetration without consent. "Sexual penetration" includes cunnilingus, fellatio, or any intrusion of the genital or anal openings of the body of another.

NEW HAMPSHIRE

Crime: aggravated felonious sexual assault
Gender: neutral

Aggravated felonious sexual assault involves sexual penetration without consent. "Sexual penetration" includes sexual (vaginal) intercourse, cunnilingus, fellatio, and anal intercourse.

NEW JERSEY

Crime: sexual assault
Gender: neutral
Sexual assault involves sexual penetration without consent. "Sexual penetration" includes vaginal intercourse, cunnilingus, fellatio, or anal intercourse.

NEW MEXICO

Crime: criminal sexual penetration
Gender: neutral
Criminal sexual penetration involves nonconsensual sexual (vaginal) intercourse, cunnilingus, fellatio, or anal intercourse.

NEW YORK

Crime: sexual misconduct
Gender: specific
Rape involves sexual intercourse without consent, where sexual intercourse is the penetration of the vagina by the penis. Anal rape is classified as "deviate sexual intercourse," defined as sexual conduct between unmarried persons that involves contact between the penis and anus, the mouth and penis, or the mouth and vulva.

NORTH CAROLINA

Crime: rape
Gender: specific
Rape in North Carolina involves vaginal intercourse without consent. Anal rape is classified as a "sexual offense," defined as a sexual act without consent. This "sexual act" includes cunnilingus, fellatio, analingus, and anal intercourse.

NORTH DAKOTA

Crime: sexual assault
Gender: neutral
    Sexual assault in North Dakota involves a sexual act without consent, where a sexual act includes contact between the penis and vulva, penis and anus, mouth and penis, mouth and vulva, or an object and the victim's anus, vulva, or penis.

OHIO

Crime: rape
Gender: neutral
    Rape in Ohio involves sexual penetration without consent, which includes anal and oral rape.

OKLAHOMA

Crime: rape
Gender: neutral
    Rape is defined as nonconsensual sexual intercourse with a male or female, including anal rape.

OREGON

Crime: rape
Gender: specific
    Rape in Oregon is defined as nonconsensual sexual intercourse with a female. The rape of a man is classified as sodomy, also referred to as deviate sexual intercourse.

PENNSYLVANIA

Crime: rape

Gender: specific

Rape in Pennsylvania involves nonconsensual sexual intercourse with a female. The rape of a man is classified as involuntary deviate sexual intercourse.

RHODE ISLAND

Crime: sexual assault
Gender: neutral

Sexual assault is defined as sexual penetration without consent. Sexual penetration includes sexual (vaginal) intercourse, cunnilingus, fellatio, anal intercourse, or penetration of the genital or anal opening by an object.

SOUTH CAROLINA

Crime: criminal sexual conduct
Gender: neutral

Criminal sexual conduct involves sexual battery, which includes sexual (vaginal) intercourse, cunnilingus, fellatio, anal intercourse, and object penetration of a person's genital or anal opening.

SOUTH DAKOTA

Crime: rape
Gender: neutral

Rape in South Dakota involves sexual penetration, which includes sexual (vaginal) intercourse, anal intercourse, fellatio, cunnilingus, and object penetration of a person's genital or anal opening.

TENNESSEE

Crime: *aggravated rape*
Gender: *neutral*

Aggravated rape involves sexual penetration, which includes sexual (vaginal) intercourse, anal intercourse, fellatio, cunnilingus, and object penetration of a person's genital or anal opening.

TEXAS

Crime: *sexual assault*
Gender: *neutral*

Sexual assault involves nonconsensual penetration of the anus or female sexual organ of another person.

UTAH

Crime: *rape*
Gender: *specific*

Rape involves sexual (vaginal) intercourse without consent. The rape of a man is classified as the dual offense of sodomy/forcible sodomy. Consensual sodomy is a Class B misdemeanor. Forcible sodomy and rape are both felonies of the first degree.

VERMONT

Crime: *sexual assault*
Gender: *neutral*

Sexual assault involves a sexual act without consent. A sexual act includes contact between the penis and vulva, penis and anus, mouth and penis, mouth and vulva, or object penetration of a person's genital or anal opening.

VIRGINIA

Crime: rape
Gender: specific
Rape in Virginia involves nonconsensual vaginal intercourse. Forcible sodomy is nonconsensual cunnilingus, fellatio, analingus, or anal intercourse.

WASHINGTON

Crime: rape
Gender: neutral
Rape in Washington involves nonconsensual penetration of the mouth, vagina, or anus by the penis or an object.

WEST VIRGINIA

Crime: sexual assault
Gender: neutral
Sexual assault in West Virginia involves nonconsensual sexual intercourse, including vaginal intercourse, anal intercourse, cunnilingus, and analingus. Also included is the penetration of the vagina or anus by an object.

WISCONSIN

Crime: sexual assault
Gender: neutral
Sexual assault in Wisconsin involves nonconsensual sexual intercourse, including vaginal intercourse, anal intercourse, cunnilingus, and analingus. Also included is the penetration of the vagina or anus by an object.

WYOMING

Crime: sexual assault
Gender: neutral

Sexual assault in Wyoming involves nonconsensual sexual intercourse, including vaginal intercourse, anal intercourse, cunnilingus, and analingus. Also included is the penetration of the vagina or anus by an object.

INDEX